French
in 40 Lessons

by
Sylviane Nouschi
and
Nicole Gandilhon

with the assistance of
Elinor Sigler

PRESSES POCKET

Table of contents

4

Foreword

This book is meant to provide everyone who wants to start learning French or to brush up memories of French with **a simple and handy tool.**

The authors' main concern has been to meet the requirements of those who aim for **good understanding and easy handling** of the language. Their purpose has been to enable everyone to progress step by step and reach an operational level.

In order to achieve this end, they have focused on **the basic elements and structures.** Rather than attempting to describe every mechanism, quote all exceptions or irregular forms, they have tried to give **clear, precise and reliable landmarks.**

Having in mind a concern for **efficiency**, they have deliberately restricted the number of grammatical terms to the sheer minimum and have chosen **accurate but simple explanations.**

The approach is gradual throughout the lessons and throughout the book, so as to deal with the main points one by one, in a constructive manner. The aim is to make sure that the use of every item is mastered before proceeding to the next one.

Every structure studied is illustrated by sentences **in current use in everyday French.** In order to avoid ambiguity, they are **all related to a situation** or context which is briefly indicated in English.

The book consists of:

- Simple and easily assimilated units, dealing with only one difficulty at a time so as to secure mastery of the point studied.

- Explanations and remarks which, in addition to translations into English, make clear the basic structures.

- Exercises in which the structures and vocabulary are repeatedly practised to secure complete understanding.

- Concise explanations of typical expressions and practical information, connected with the points studied, widening the scope to aspects of everyday France.

How to use this book

The following description and explanations will help you organize your time and get the most out of this book.

The book includes:

— 40 lessons of six pages each;
— a short grammar summary.

All of the lessons are organized along the same lines in order to facilitate self-learning. They include three parts, A, B and C, each two pages long. This is to help you work at your own pace. Even if you don't have time to learn an entire lesson, you can start one and study only part of it, without having the impression you're wasting your time.

Lesson outline

| Part A | is subdivided into four sections: A1, A2, A3, A4.

A1: Presentation

The first section introduces the new information (in grammar, vocabulary and pronunciation) you will need to learn and use to make sentences in French.

A2: Examples

This section, based on the material introduced in A1, presents examples which you should then reconstruct by yourself.

A3: Comments

Additional comments regarding the sentences in A2 clarify points of grammar, vocabulary or pronunciation.

A4: Translation

The final section includes the complete translation of part A2.

How to use this book (contd)

Part B is subdivided into four sections: B1, B2, B3, B4, and follows the same outline as Part A, adding further explanation to the points of grammar and some new vocabulary.

Part C The four sections C1, C2, C3 and C4 include exercises, practical information and some comments on life in France.

C1 : Exercises

You should use the exercises to verify that the points of grammar learned in Parts A and B are understood.

C3 : Answers

All the correct answers to the exercises of Part C1 are given, so that you can check your work.

C2 and C4 : Practical information and notes on French life

These sections focus on common expressions as well as on information about life and culture in France and the evolution of the French language.

The **grammar summary** reviews all of the basic grammar points.

■ Some advice
• Study on a regular basis

It is more effective to work at regular intervals, even for a short period of time, than to try to learn several lessons at the same time at widely-separated intervals. Studying for a half hour every day, even if it is only one of the three parts of a lesson, is more effective than skimming over several lessons for three hours every ten days.

• Programme your efforts

Work on each lesson in turn, and don't go on to B without having learned and understood A.
This principle applies equally to the different lessons: don't begin a new lesson without having thoroughly understood the previous one.

• Go back over the lessons

Don't hesitate to review the lessons you have already learned and repeat the exercises. Make sure you have understood and remember them.

■ Suggested work method

● For parts A and B:

1. After studying A1 (or B1), read the series of sentences in A2 (or B2) several times.

2. Read the comments in A3 (or B3).

3. Go back to A2 (or B2) and translate the sentences into English, without looking at A4 (or B4).

4. Check the accuracy of your translation by reading A4 (or B4).

5. Try to reconstruct the sentences in Part A2 (or B2) starting from A4 (or B4) without looking at A2 (or B2). Then verify your accuracy, and so forth.

● For part C:

1. Each time you can, write out the answers to the exercises in C1 before comparing them to the corrected lesson in C3.

2. Study a lesson until you can:
   — translate A4 or B4 into French without looking at A2 or B2;
   — do all of the exercises in C1 without any errors.

● Using the vocabulary list

The vocabulary list (page 277) can be used to find vocabulary in context. As you study each lesson, write the translation of the new words given in parts A and B in the margins. You can thus make your own dictionary.

■■ Recording of the book

A recording is the natural audio-oral companion to the book; it will make it possible for you to practise speaking and comprehension.

A1   PRESENTATION

■ Grammar

● Imperative

The French imperative form is one of the simplest verbal forms.

The second person plural is used to address either a person you don't know well or several persons.

It usually ends with **ez**.

> **Regardez !**   *Look, look at!*
> **Regardez Anne !**   *Look at Anne!*

■ Vocabulary

où ?	*where?*
là	*there*
là-bas	*over there*
oui	*yes*
et	*and*

● **Notre-Dame** is the Paris cathedral.

● **Anne, Louis** are first names.

A2   EXAMPLES *(Visiting Paris)*

1. **Regardez !**
2. **Louis, regardez !**
3. **Regardez Notre-Dame !**
4. **Où ?**
5. **Là !**
6. **Là-bas ?**
7. **Oui, là-bas !**
8. **Regardez là-bas !**
9. **Anne et Louis, regardez !**
10. **Regardez Notre-Dame, là-bas !**

A3 COMMENTS

■ Pronunciation

- The French **r** is produced at the back of the mouth as if gargling.
- The nearest English equivalent to **e** in **regardez** is *e* in *open*, with lips slightly rounded.
- **ez (regardez)** and **et** have the sound of: *A* in *A B C*.
- **a** or **à** is pronounced like *a* in *father*.
- **o** is pronounced like *o* in *not* (**Notre-Dame**).
- **ou** is pronounced like *oo* in *cool*.
- **oui** is pronounced like *we*.
- The final **e** is silent (**Anne, Notre-Dame**).

⟶ Final consonants are not usually pronounced in French: **Pari(s), Loui(s), ba(s)**.

■ Grammar

⟶ Note that the object following **Regardez !** is not introduced by any preposition: **Regardez Notre-Dame !** *Look **at** Notre-Dame!*

A4 TRANSLATION

1. Look!
2. Louis, look!
3. Look at Notre-Dame!
4. Where?
5. There!
6. Over there?
7. Yes, over there!
8. Look over there!
9. Anne and Louis, look!
10. Look at Notre-Dame, over there!

B1   PRESENTATION

■ Grammar

imperative	singular	plural
2nd person	**reste / regarde** *stay / look*	**restez / regardez** *stay / look*

- When speaking to a relative, a friend, or someone you know well, use the second form singular of the imperative:
  Ex.: **regarde !** *look!*   **reste !** *stay!*

■ Vocabulary

reste !	*stay!*
à côté de	*beside*
ici	*here*
s'il te plaît	*please* (to a person you know well)
s'il vous plaît	*please* (to a person you don't know well)
merci	*thank you*

Hélène is a feminine first name.

B2   EXAMPLES *(Taking a photograph)*

1. **Hélène, reste ici !**
2. **Anne, reste là !**
3. **Reste là, s'il te plaît !**
4. **Hélène, reste à côté de Louis !**
5. **Hélène et Anne, restez là !**
6. **Hélène, regarde Louis !**
7. **Regarde Louis, s'il te plaît !**
8. **Anne et Hélène, regardez Louis !**
9. **Regardez Louis, s'il vous plaît !**
10. **Merci.**

B3   COMMENTS

■ Grammar

- Remember: the second person plural is used to address either a person you don't know well or several persons (see lesson 1, A1).
- Remember to say:
  s'il te plaît   to a person you know well.
  s'il vous plaît   to several persons or to a person you don't know well.

■ Pronunciation

- in **reste** or **restez**, the first **e** is pronounced like *e* in *pet*.
- **ai** has the sound of *A* in *A B C*: **plaît**.
- **i** has the sound of *ee* in *see*: **ici**.
- **o** in **côté** is pronounced like **o** in *note*.
- in **merci, er** is pronounced like *air*.
- **c** followed by **e** or **i** is pronounced like *s* in *set*: **merci**.
- **h** is always silent when it is the first letter of a word.

B4   TRANSLATION

1. Hélène, stay here!
2. Anne, stay there!
3. Stay there, please!
4. Hélène, stay beside Louis!
5. Hélène and Anne, stay there!
6. Hélène, look at Louis!
7. Look at Louis, please!
8. Anne and Hélène, look at Louis!
9. Look at Louis, please!
10. Thank you.

C1 EXERCISES

A. Put the verb in the imperative form:

1. Anne, (regarder) ! (You know Anne very well.)
2. Anne et Hélène, (rester) là !
3. Hélène, (regarder) Louis ! (You don't know Hélène well.)
4. Louis, (rester) là ! (Louis is a relative.)

B. ●● You know all of them very well:

1. Tell Anne to stay beside Louis.
2. Tell Louis and Hélène to look at Anne.
3. Tell Anne to look over there.
4. Tell Hélène to look at Anne.

C. Add the equivalent of <u>please</u> to each sentence in B:

C2 VERBS

Imperative	Infinitive	
regarde/regardez	**regarder**	*to look, to look at*
reste/restez	**rester**	*to stay*

- **er** is the ending of the infinitive of a great number of verbs. They all belong to the same group and are conjugated the same way.
- **er** is pronounced like *A* in *A B C.*

C3 ANSWERS

A. 1. Anne, regarde !
  2. Anne et Hélène, restez là !
  3. Hélène, regardez Louis !
  4. Louis, reste là !

B. 1. Anne, reste à côté de Louis !
  2. Louis et Hélène, regardez Anne !
  3. Anne, regarde là-bas !
  4. Hélène, regarde Anne.

C. 1. Anne, reste à côté de Louis, s'il te plaît !
  2. Louis et Hélène, regardez Anne, s'il vous plaît !
  3. Anne, regarde là-bas, s'il te plaît !
  4. Hélène, regarde Anne, s'il te plaît !

C4 WRITTEN ACCENTS

■ ´ ` ^ are written accents which are placed on vowels.

● ´ is the acute accent. It is only used over **e**.
  é has the sound of the English letter *A* in *A B C*.

● ` is the grave accent. It is mainly used over **e**.
  è has the sound of *e* in *pet*.
  — is also used over **a** and **u** without affecting their pronunciation.

● ^
  is the circumflex accent. It is used over any vowel. It generally lengthens the sound.

➡ Look back at A2 and B2 and note the following words:
  plaît, où, Hélène, à côté.

A1 PRESENTATION

■ Grammar

ne reste pas ⎤
ne restez pas ⎦ → *don't stay*

• The negative of the imperative is formed with: ●●

  ne ... pas *do not, don't* ;
  n' ... pas (with verbs starting with a vowel or **h**),
  on either side of the verb.

■ Vocabulary

écouter	*to listen / to listen to*
chanter	*to sing*
ne... pas encore	*don't... yet*
maintenant	*now*

Antoine is a masculine first name.

A2 EXAMPLES *(On the stage, before the show)*

1. **Reste ici !**
2. **Ne reste pas là !**
3. **Restez ici, s'il vous plaît !**
4. **Ne restez pas là !**
5. **Hélène, écoute, s'il te plaît !**
6. **N'écoute pas Antoine !**
7. **Hélène et Anne, écoutez, s'il vous plaît !**
8. **Ne chantez pas !**
9. **Ne chantez pas maintenant !**
10. **Ne chantez pas encore !**

A3   COMMENTS

■ Grammar: negative imperative

singular	**ne reste pas**	*don't stay*
plural	**ne restez pas**	
singular	**n'écoute pas**	*don't listen*
plural	**n'écoutez pas**	

■ Pronunciation

- **an / en** : two spellings for one sound **(chantez, encore).** This nasal vowel doesn't exist in English. The nearest English equivalent is the vowel sound in *swan* (without pronouncing the **n**).

- **ain** : the nearest equivalent is *an* in *bang* (without pronouncing the **ng**). Ex.: **maintenant.**

- **oi** is pronounced like *wo* in *won.* Ex.: **Antoine.**

- **ch** in **chante** is pronounced like *sh* in *shoe.*

- **c + a, o, u** is pronounced like *c* in *car* **(encore, écoutez).**

A4   TRANSLATION

1. Stay here!
2. Don't stay there!
3. Stay here, please!
4. Don't stay there!
5. Hélène, listen, please!
6. Don't listen to Antoine!
7. Hélène and Anne, listen, please!
8. Don't sing!
9. Don't sing now!
10. Don't sing yet!

2 Parlons français ensemble.

B1 PRESENTATION

■ Grammar

- The first person plural of the imperative always ends with: **-ons**.

reste	*stay*
rest<u>ons</u>	*let's stay*
restez	*stay*

■ Vocabulary

parler	*to speak*
français	*French*
ensemble	*together*
ou	*or*
avec	*with*

B2 EXAMPLES *(To speak or not to speak)*

1. **Parlons français.**
2. **Parlons français ensemble.**
3. **Parlons avec Anne ou Louis.**
4. **Parlons français avec Anne ou Louis.**
5. **Restons ensemble.**
6. **Ne restons pas ici.**
7. **Ne parlons pas ici.**
8. **Ne parlons pas maintenant.**
9. **Chantons !**
10. **Chantons ensemble !**

B3 COMMENTS

■ Pronunciation

- **on**, in **restons**, is a nasal vowel. The nearest vowel sound in English is the *o* in *long* (without pronouncing the *ng*).
- **em** is pronounced like **en (ensemble)**.
- **ç** + vowel is pronounced like *s* in *set* **(français)**.
- in **avec**, the final **c** is heard; it is pronounced like *k* in *deck*.
- **s** between a vowel and a consonant is pronounced like *s* in *set* **(dansons, ensemble)**.

■ Remember

où = *where* but ⟶ **ou** = *or*.

B4 TRANSLATION

1. Let's speak French.
2. Let's speak French together.
3. Let's speak with Anne or Louis.
4. Let's speak French with Anne or Louis.
5. Let's stay together.
6. Let's not stay here.
7. Let's not speak here.
8. Let's not speak now.
9. Let's sing!
10. Let's sing together!

19

C1 EXERCISES

A. ●● Giving orders (in French):

1. Tell Anne and Louis to sing together.
2. Tell Antoine not to listen.
3. Tell Hélène and Anne to listen.
4. Tell Hélène not to look yet.
5. Tell Louis and Anne not to sing.

B. ●● Turn into the first person plural:

1. Regardez !
2. Reste !
3. Écoute !
4. Parlez !

C. ●● Translate into French:

1. Let's stay here!
2. Let's not speak!
3. Let's look over there!
4. Let's sing now!

C2 PREPOSITIONS AND EXPRESSIONS TO INDICATE THE PLACE

⟶ remember **où** = *where?*

par ici	*this way*
par là	*that way*
dans	*in*
devant	*in front of*
derrière	*behind*
entre	*between*
sous	*under*
dessous	*below*
près	*near*
près <u>de</u> Louis	*near Louis* (notice the **de** when the preposition is followed by a noun).

C3 ANSWERS

A. 1. Chantez ensemble !
2. N'écoute pas !
3. Écoutez !
4. Ne regarde pas encore !
5. Ne chantez pas !

B. 1. Regardons !
2. Restons !
3. Écoutons !
4. Parlons !

C. 1. Restons ici !
2. Ne parlons pas !
3. Regardons là-bas !
4. Chantons maintenant !

C4 « LIAISON » ●●

- The final consonant of a word is pronounced when the following word starts with a vowel or **h**. The words run together, this is called a **liaison** in French.

  Ex.: **restez ici**   **parlons ensemble**
         z   z

  pas ici   **pas encore**   **avec Anne**
    z   z   k

- When a word ends with an **e**, the **e** being silent, there is a liaison with the following vowel.

  Ex.: **reste à côté**   **reste ici**
          t   t

  Anne et Louis   **Anne ou Louis**
    n   n

21

3 | J'habite Nice.

A1 PRESENTATION

■ Grammar

• Personal pronouns: subject / singular

je, j' (1st person)	**tu** (2nd person, used to address close friends, relatives, children)
I	*you*

• **je** becomes **j'** when preceding a vowel or **h**:
  j'habite..., *I live in...*

• **Present tense**
  In French, the endings of verbs vary according to the person and number of the subject:
  Je parl<u>e</u>. *I speak.*
  Tu parl<u>es</u>. *You speak.*

■ Vocabulary

habiter	*to live in*
allemand	*German*
italien	*Italian*
anglais	*English*
bonjour	*good morning / good afternoon*
non	*no*
en	*in*

Nice is a French town on the Riviera.

A2 EXAMPLES *(Places and languages)*

1. **Bonjour !**
2. **J'habite en France.**
3. **J'habite Nice.**
4. **Je parle français et italien.**
5. **Tu parles allemand ?**
6. **Non.**
7. **Non, je ne parle pas allemand.**
8. **Tu parles anglais ?**
9. **Oui.**
10. **Oui, je parle français et anglais.**

A3 COMMENTS

■ <u>Pronunciation</u>

• **j** is pronounced like *su* in *pleasure* (ex.: **je, bonjour**).

• The sound of **u** in **tu** doesn't exist in English. It is pronounced like the double *ee* of *cheers* said with pursed lips.

■ <u>Grammar</u>

• In spoken French, the simplest way to turn a statement into a question is to modify the intonation into a rising one.
    Ex.: **Tu parles allemand ?** — *Do you speak German?*

• **oui, non** are often used alone.
    Ex.: **Tu parles anglais ? — Oui.**
    Do you speak English? — Yes, I do.

• Remember in the negative, **ne** and **pas** are used on either side of the verb (see lesson A2, 7).

• In French, adjectives referring to nationality are not capitalized.
    Je parle italien. *I speak Italian.*

A4 TRANSLATION

1. Good morning!
2. I live in France.
3. I live in Nice.
4. I speak French and Italian.
5. Do you speak German?
6. No, I don't.
7. No, I don't speak German.
8. Do you speak English?
9. Yes, I do.
10. Yes, I speak French and English.

B1   PRESENTATION

■ Grammar

• Personal pronouns subjects plural.

nous (1st person plural)	**vous**	for both singular and plural
we	*you*	subjects (like *you* in English)

• Present tense :

nous parlons	*we speak*
vous parlez	*you speak*

⟶   In French, the present tense conveys the meanings of both the English simple present and progressive present. In other words:

$$\textbf{je parle} - \begin{bmatrix} I\ speak \\ I\ am\ speaking \end{bmatrix}$$

■ Vocabulary

aimer bien	*to like*
visiter	*to visit*
trouver	*to think, to find*
très	*very*
bien	*well*
aussi	*too*

boulevard Saint-Germain   (a well-known Left-Bank boulevard)
Saint-Germain-des-Prés   (*Saint-Germain-in-the-fields*, part of the
Paris Latin Quarter)

B2   EXAMPLES *(Living in Paris)*

1. **Nous visitons Paris.**
2. **Vous visitez Paris aussi ?**
3. **Non, nous habitons ici.**
4. **Nous habitons boulevard Saint-Germain.**
5. **Vous habitez près de Saint-Germain-des-Prés ?**
6. **Oui, très près.**
7. **Vous parlez très bien français !**
8. **Vous trouvez ? Merci !**
9. **Vous aimez bien Paris ?**
10. **Oui, nous aimons bien Paris.**

B3 COMMENTS

■ Pronunciation

- **o, au** : two spellings for one sound pronounced like *o* in *note* (a<u>u</u>ssi, c<u>ô</u>té).

- **ien** in **bien** is pronounced like *y* in *yes* followed by the sound of *an* in *bang*.

- **g** before **e** and **i** is pronounced like *j* (**Germain**).

- **s** between two vowels is pronounced like *z* in *zoo* (**visiter**).

- **ss** between two vowels is pronounced like *s* in *set* (**aussi**).

■ Grammar

- Rappel : **Vous aimez bien Paris ?** *Do you like Paris?*
  A rising tone turns a statement into a question.

B4 TRANSLATION

1. We are visiting Paris.
2. Are you visiting Paris too?
3. No, we live here.
4. We live on boulevard Saint-Germain.
5. Do you live near Saint-Germain-des-Prés?
6. Yes, very near.
7. You speak French very well!
8. You think so? Thank you!
9. Do you like Paris?
10. Yes, we like Paris.

3 Exercices

C1 EXERCISES

A. Match the pronouns with the verbs:

je, j', tu, nous, vous ;
regarde - visitez - chantons - habite - regardes - écoutons - parlez

B. Put the verb between brackets in the correct form:

1. Nous (habiter) là bas.
2. Je (rester) ici.
3. Vous (danser) ?
4. Tu (regarder) Louis.

C. Turn the sentences into the negative:
(using **ne... pas** or **n'... pas**)

D. ●● **Translate into French:**

1. We are looking at Anne.
2. You are not singing together.
3. I speak Italian and French.
4. I'm visiting Paris too.

C2 NOUS HABITONS EN EUROPE ●●
WE LIVE IN EUROPE

Pays	Country
Allemagne*	*Germany*
Angleterre	*England*
Belgique	*Belgium*
Danemark	*Denmark*
Espagne	*Spain*
France	*France*
Grèce	*Greece*
Italie	*Italy*
Irlande	*Ireland*
Pays-Bas	*the Netherlands*
Portugal**	*Portugal*

* **gn** is pronounced like *ni* in *onion* (**Allemagne**).
** Note that the final **l** in **Portugal** is heard.

C3   ANSWERS

A. Je regarde - J'habite - Tu regardes - Nous chantons
Nous écoutons - Vous visitez - Vous parlez.

B.
1. Nous habitons là-bas.
2. Je reste ici.
3. Vous dansez ?
4. Tu regardes Louis.

C.
1. Nous n'habitons pas là-bas.
2. Je ne reste pas ici.
3. Vous ne dansez pas ?
4. Tu ne regardes pas Louis.

D.
1. Nous regardons Anne.
2. Vous ne chantez pas ensemble.
3. Je parle italien et français.
4. Je visite Paris aussi.

C4   EXPRESSIONS

Bonjour - Bonsoir - Au revoir

- The *day* (**jour**) is divided into:
  matin *(morning)*   **après-midi** *(afternoon)*   **soir** *(evening)*.

- When you meet a person during the day, say: **bonjour** *(good morning* or *good afternoon)*. At the end of the day, use: **bonsoir** *(good evening)*.

- When you leave somebody, say: **au revoir** *(good bye)*. You can also say: **bonsoir** when leaving someone in the evening.

- **Bonne nuit** is used to wish somebody a *good night*.
    Ex.:   **Bonjour Louis.**   *Good morning Louis.*
           Au revoir Anne.   *Good bye Anne.*
           Bonne nuit Antoine.   *Good night Antoine.*

- In **jour, au revoir, soir**, the final **r** is pronounced.

4   Ils visitent Paris aujourd'hui.

A1   PRESENTATION

■ Grammar

● Personal pronouns subject: 3rd person

	masculine	feminine
singular	**il** *(he, it)*	**elle** *(she, it)*
plural	**ils** *(they)*	**elles** *(they)*

Ex.: **il parle,**   *he speaks*   **elle parle,**   *she speaks*
    ils parlent, *they speak*   **elles parlent,** *they speak*

■ Pronunciation

● In **il** and **ils**, the **l** is heard.

● In **elle** and **elles**, the first **e** is pronounced like **è**, the last one is glided over.

● Note that **-e/ -es/ -ent**, verb endings of the present tense, are all considered like a final **e** and are therefore silent.

■ Vocabulary

aimer	*to love*	**souvent**	*often*
voyager	*to travel*	**parfois**	*sometimes*
aujourd'hui	*today*	**mais**	*but*

Agnès and **Philippe** are first names.

A2   EXAMPLES *(Travelling)*

1. **Agnès et Philippe habitent en Angleterre.**
2. **Ils habitent ensemble.**
3. **Elle voyage souvent.**
4. **Il voyage souvent aussi.**
5. **Ils ne restent pas souvent ici.**
6. **Ils voyagent parfois ensemble.**
7. **Il parle très bien français, mais il ne parle pas espagnol.**
8. **Elle parle anglais.**
9. **Ils visitent Paris aujourd'hui.**
10. **Elle aime Paris.**

4 | They are visiting Paris today.

A3 COMMENTS

■ Grammar

- Verbs ending in **er** in the infinitive have the same conjugation:

aimer	*to love*	**rester**	*to stay*	**écouter**	*to listen*
parler	*to speak*	**danser**	*to dance*	**visiter**	*to visit*
habiter	*to live*	**chanter**	*to sing*	**voyager**	*to travel*

They belong to the 1st group. Present tense:

singular			plural		
je parle	*I*	*speak*	**nous parlons**	*we speak*	
tu parles	*you*	*speak*	**vous parlez**	*you speak*	
il, elle, parle	*he, she, it speaks*		**ils, elles, parlent**	*they speak*	

- When there are several subjects and at least one of them is masculine, the pronoun is always: **ils**.

  Ex.: **Anne et Louis parlent français = ils parlent français.**

■ Pronunciation

- Note that **oy** in **voyage** is pronounced like **oi** + the sound of *y* in *yes*.

- Remember: **en** in **souvent** is a nasal sound which does not exist in English. The nearest equivalent is the vowel sound in *swan* (without pronouncing the *n*).

A4 TRANSLATION

1. Agnès and Philippe live in England.
2. They live together.
3. She often travels.
4. He often travels too.
5. They don't often stay here.
6. They sometimes travel together.
7. He speaks French very well, but he doesn't speak Spanish.
8. She speaks English.
9. They are visiting Paris today.
10. She loves Paris.

B1 PRESENTATION

■ Grammar

• **on**
In conjugation, **on** is considered as a 3rd person singular.
In colloquial French, **on** is often used instead of **nous**.
  Ex. : **On habite ici.** *We live here.*

■ Vocabulary

arriver	*to come / to arrive*
déjeuner	*to have lunch*
demain	*tomorrow*
dix heures	*ten o'clock*
du matin (see C4)	*a.m.*
midi	*noon*
après	*after*

B2 EXAMPLES *(Arrival)*

1. **On arrive !**
2. **On arrive demain.**
3. **On arrive demain à dix heures.**
4. **On arrive demain à dix heures du matin.**
5. **On déjeune ensemble.**
6. **On déjeune ensemble à midi.**
7. **On visite Paris demain après-midi.**
8. **On ne visite pas Notre-Dame.**
9. **On ne parle pas très bien français.**
10. **On ne parle pas encore très bien.**

B3 COMMENTS

■ Grammar

• The present can be used to express a future action when a word in the sentence indicates the future.
  Ex.: **On arrive demain.** *We are coming tomorrow.*

■ Expressions

• **À dix heures du matin** : see C4, p. 33.

■ Pronunciation

• **jeu** in **déjeune** is pronounced like **je**.

• Note the liaisons:

  on arrive **dix heures**
    n   **z**

• Remember: the sound in **on** is the sound of a nasal vowel. The nearest vowel sound in English is the *o* in *long* (without pronouncing the *ng*).

• Remember: the nearest English equivalent of **ain** in **demain** is the sound of *an* in *bang* (without pronouncing the *ng*).

B4 TRANSLATION

1. We are coming!
2. We are coming tomorrow.
3. We are coming tomorrow at ten o'clock.
4. We are coming tomorrow at ten a.m.
5. We are having lunch together.
6. We are having lunch together at twelve.
7. We are visiting Paris tomorrow afternoon.
8. We are not visiting Notre-Dame.
9. We don't speak French very well.
10. We don't speak very well yet.

4 | Exercices

C1 EXERCISES

A. Choose the correct form:

1. Il (parlons, parles, parle) français.
2. Elles (visitent, visitez, visites) Nice.
3. Elle ne (voyages, voyagent, voyage) pas souvent.
4. Ils (aimons, aimes, aiment) Paris?
5. On (chante, chantez, chantes) bien!

B. ●● Use _ils_ or _elles_ to replace the names:

1. Antoine et Louis habitent Paris.
2. Agnès et Philippe ne parlent pas espagnol.
3. Hélène et Agnès arrivent demain.
4. Hélène, Agnès et Antoine déjeunent ensemble.

C. What we know about Marc: What about you?

1. Il habite en France.
2. Il habite Paris.
3. Il ne parle pas anglais.
4. Il aime voyager.
5. Il va souvent à Nice.

C2 NOMBRES / *NUMBERS* (see also lesson 6, C4) ●●

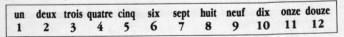

un	deux	trois	quatre	cinq	six	sept	huit	neuf	dix	onze	douze
1	2	3	4	5	6	7	8	9	10	11	12

➡ Note that:

- **sept** is pronounced like *set*.
- **ui** has nearly the sound of *we* with tightened lips **(huit)**.
- The sound **eu** in **neuf, heure,** is pronounced like *ur* in *hurt*.
- In **cinq, huit, neuf,** the final consonant is pronounced.
- In **six, dix** the final **x** is pronounced like *s* in *set*.

C3 ANSWERS

A. 1. Il parle français.
2. Elles visitent Nice.
3. Elle ne voyage pas souvent.
4. Ils aiment Paris ?
5. On chante bien !

B. 1. Ils habitent Paris.
2. Ils ne parlent pas espagnol.
3. Elles arrivent demain.
4. Ils déjeunent ensemble.

C. 1. J'habite en...
2. J'habite...
3. Je parle (*or:* je ne parle pas) anglais.
4. J'aime voyager (*or:* je n'aime pas voyager).
5. Je vais (*or:* je ne vais pas) souvent à Nice.

C4 DIRE L'HEURE / *TELLING TIME*

midi/minuit

onze heures
dix heures
neuf heures
huit heures
sept heures

une heure
deux heures
trois heures
quatre heures
cinq heures

six heures

- **heure** is used both for *o'clock* and *hour*.

- The expressions: **du matin** (*a.m.*), **de l'après-midi** (*p.m. up to six o'clock*), **du soir** (*p.m.*) are used to tell the time more precisely.
  Ex.: **six heures du matin**
  quatre heures de l'après-midi
  dix heures du soir

- **qu** in **quatre** is pronounced like *ck* in *back*.

- Note the unusual liaison: **neuf heures.**
  v

33

A1 PRESENTATION

■ Grammar

● **aller** *(to go)* is an irregular verb. Present tense:

		simple present		progressive present
je	**vais**	*I*	*go*	*am going*
tu	**vas**	*you*	*go*	*are going*
il, elle	**va**	*he, she, it*	*goes*	*is going*
nous	**allons**	*we*	*go*	*are going*
vous	**allez**	*you*	*go*	*are going*
ils, elles	**vont**	*they*	*go*	*are going*

■ Vocabulary

monsieur (M.)	*Mr.*
madame (Mme)	*Mrs.*
trop	*too*
vite	*fast*
loin	*far*
à	*to*
toujours	*always*

Tours is a town on the **Loire** river.

A2 EXAMPLES *(Going places)*

1. Je vais à Tours.
2. Je vais souvent à Tours.
3. Tu vas trop vite !
4. Il ne va pas à Paris.
5. Ils vont souvent à Paris.
6. On ne va pas souvent à Rome.
7. Nous allons parfois à Paris.
8. Vous allez à Rome ?
9. Vous allez loin ?
10. M. et Mme Martin ne vont pas loin.
11. Ils vont à Nice.
12. Ils vont toujours à Nice.

A3   COMMENTS

■ Grammar

- Adverbs indicating frequency like **parfois, souvent, toujours** are usually placed after the verb in the affirmative or after **pas** in the negative. Ex.:

  Je vais souvent en Allemagne.   *I often go to Germany.*
  On ne va pas souvent à Rome.   *We don't often go to Rome.*
  On va parfois à Paris.   *We sometimes go to Paris.*

- Remember: in French, the present tense conveys the meanings of both the English simple present and progressive present.

■ Pronunciation

- **oin** is pronounced like *w* (in *west*) followed by the French nasal vowel **in (loin).**

- **ain, in**: two spellings for one sound **(maintenant, Martin).** (See lesson 2, A3.)

A4   TRANSLATION

1. I'm going to Tours.
2. I often go to Tours.
3. You are going too fast!
4. He isn't going to Paris.
5. They often go to Paris.
6. We don't often go to Rome.
7. We sometimes go to Paris.
8. Are you going to Rome?
9. Are you going far?
10. Mr. and Mrs. Martin are not going far.
11. They are going to Nice.
12. They always go to Nice.

35

5 | Mlle Smith va travailler en France.

B1 PRESENTATION

■ Grammar

• **Aller,** followed by a verb in the infinitive, expresses either an intention or the immediate future. It is the French equivalent of *to be going to.*

je	**vais**	**rester**	*I*	*am*	*going to stay*
tu	**vas**	**travailler**	*you*	*are*	*going to work*
nous	**allons**	**parler**	*we*	*are*	*going to speak*

Ex.:

■ Vocabulary

travailler	*to work*
mademoiselle (Mlle)	*Miss*
octobre	*October*
décembre	*December*
juillet	*July*
bientôt	*soon*
puis	*then*

B2 EXAMPLES *(Plans)*

1. Mlle Smith va travailler en France.
2. Elle va bientôt travailler à Paris.
3. Elle va travailler avec Mme Lenoir.
4. Elles vont travailler ensemble.
5. Vous allez habiter Paris ?
6. Oui, je vais habiter Paris.
7. Je vais habiter boulevard Saint-Germain, avec Hélène.
8. Nous allons parler ensemble.
9. Nous allons parler français ensemble.
10. Je vais rester à Paris en octobre.
11. Puis je vais aller en Italie.
12. Je vais rester en Italie en décembre.

36

B3 COMMENTS

■ Grammar

• à / en

— Generally **à**, meaning *in* or *to*, is used with the name of a town:

à Paris	*in* or *to Paris*
à Nice	*in* or *to Nice*
à Rome	*in* or *to Rome*

— **en**, meaning *in* or *to*, is used with the name of a country:

en Italie	*in* or *to Italy*
en Allemagne	*in* or *to Germany*
en France	*in* or *to France*

■ Pronunciation

• Note that in spoken French the **e** in the middle of a word is often glided over.

Ex.: **mademoiselle, boulevard.**

B4 TRANSLATION

1. Miss Smith is going to work in France.
2. She is going to work in Paris soon.
3. She is going to work with Mrs. Lenoir.
4. They are going to work together.
5. Are you going to live in Paris?
6. Yes, I am going to live in Paris.
7. I am going to live on Boulevard Saint-Germain, with Hélène.
8. We are going to speak together.
9. We are going to speak French together.
10. I am going to stay in Paris in October.
11. Then I am going to go to Italy.
12. I am going to stay in Italy in December.

C1 EXERCISES

A. Use the correct form of the verb <u>aller</u>:

1. Vous (aller) loin.
2. Tu (aller) vite.
3. Je (aller) là-bas.
4. Nous (aller) à Paris.
5. Il (aller) parler.
6. Elles (aller) écouter Louis.
7. Agnès et Philippe (aller) habiter près de Nice.

B. Use <u>a</u> or <u>en</u>:

1. Je vais ... Tours.
2. Il voyage ... Espagne.
3. Ils vont souvent ... Allemagne.
4. Nous travaillons ... Nice.
5. Elle va rester ... Italie ... septembre.

C. Put the adverb in the right place:

1. Nous allons à Rome (parfois).
2. On ne travaille pas ensemble (souvent).
3. Je parle anglais (souvent).
4. Elle reste à côté de Louis (toujours).

C2 MOIS / MONTHS ●●

janvier	*January*
février	*February*
mars	*March*
avril	*April*
mai	*May*
juin *	*June*
juillet	*July*
août **	*August*
septembre	*September*
octobre	*October*
novembre	*November*
décembre	*December*

* **uin** in **juin** is pronounced **u** + the nasal vowel **in**.
** In **août**, **a** is not pronounced.

C3   ANSWERS

A.
1. Vous allez loin.
2. Tu vas vite.
3. Je vais là-bas.
4. Nous allons à Paris.
5. Il va parler.
6. Elles vont écouter Louis.
7. Agnès et Philippe vont habiter près de Nice.

B.
1. Je vais à Tours.
2. Il voyage en Espagne.
3. Ils vont souvent en Allemagne.
4. Nous travaillons à Nice.
5. Elle va rester en Italie en septembre.

C.
1. Nous allons parfois à Rome.
2. On ne travaille pas souvent ensemble.
3. Je parle souvent anglais.
4. Elle reste toujours à côté de Louis.

C4   monsieur (M.), madame (Mme), mademoiselle (Mlle)

- They can be used with a name.
    Ex.: **monsieur Lenoir**
    madame Lenoir
    mademoiselle Lemercier

- They can also be used alone as equivalent of: *Sir, Madam, Miss*.

- **on** in **monsieur** is pronounced like *ur* in *hurt*.

- In the plural: **messieurs, mesdames, mesdemoiselles, mes** is pronounced like **mé**.

■ To introduce oneself or somebody else, the commonly used expression is:

je m'appelle*...	*my name**** is...*
	(literally: I call myself...)
tu t'appelles*...	*your name is...*
il, elle s'appelle*...	*his, her, its name is...*
nous nous appelons...	*our names are...*
vous vous appelez...	*your names are...*
ils, elles s'appellent*...	*their names are...*

* Notice the double **l**, in that case, the first **e** is pronounced like *e* in *pet*. In **appelons** and **appelez**, there is only one **l** and the **e** is glided over.

** **Nom, prénom** / *Name, first name*.

A1   PRESENTATION

■ Grammar

Être		To be	
je	**suis**	*I*	*am*
tu	**es**	*you*	*are*
il, elle	**est**	*he, she, it*	*is*

- In French, an adjective generally has both masculine and feminine forms. It agrees in gender with the noun or the pronoun it refers to.

    Ex.: **Il est français.**   *He is French.*
           Elle est française.   *She is French.*

■ Vocabulary

français(e)	*French*
anglais(e)	*English*
irlandais(e)	*Irish*
grand(e)	*tall*
joli(e)	*pretty*
blond(e)	*fair, blond*
intelligent(e)	*intelligent*
sympathique (masc. and fem.)	*nice*

A2   EXAMPLES *(People)*

1. **Je suis français.**
2. **Je suis française.**
3. **Tu es sympathique.**
4. **Tu es intelligent.**
5. **Tu es intelligente.**
6. **Nicolas n'est pas anglais.**
7. **Il est irlandais.**
8. **Il est grand et blond.**
9. **Il est très sympathique.**
10. **Anne est anglaise.**
11. **Elle est très jolie.**
12. **Elle n'est pas très grande.**

A3 COMMENTS

■ Grammar

• The usual way to form a feminine adjective in the singular is to add an **e** to the masculine adjective:

	masculine	feminine
pretty	**joli**	**jolie**
fair	**blond**	**blonde**

• When the masculine adjective ends with a silent **e**, it isn't modified in the feminine form:

	masculine	feminine
nice	**sympathique**	**sympathique**

• When a masculine adjective ends with a consonant, the consonant is not pronounced. But when the feminine adjective ends with an **e**, the final consonant is pronounced:

	masculine	feminine
tall	**grand**	**grande**
intelligent	**intelligent**	**intelligente**

A4 TRANSLATION

1. I am French (masc.).
2. I am French (fem.).
3. You are nice.
4. You are intelligent (masc.).
5. You are intelligent (fem.).
6. Nicolas is not English.
7. He is Irish.
8. He is tall and fair.
9. He is very nice.
10. Anne is English.
11. She is very pretty.
12. She isn't very tall.

B1 PRESENTATION

■ Grammar

Être		To be	
nous	**sommes**	*we*	*are*
vous	**êtes**	*you*	*are*
ils, elles	**sont**	*they*	*are*

- Adjectives also agree in number with the noun or pronoun they refer to.
- The plural of adjectives is usually formed by adding an **s** to the singular form:

		singular	plural
intelligent	masc.	**intelligent**	**intelligents**
	fem.	**intelligente**	**intelligentes**

■ Vocabulary

allemand(e)	*German*
jeune	*young*
content(e)	*glad, happy*
triste	*sad*
gentil/gentille	*kind*

B2 EXAMPLES *(People)*

1. **Nous sommes allemands.**
2. **Nous sommes allemandes.**
3. **Vous êtes trop jeunes.**
4. **Vous êtes contentes ?**
5. **Elles ne sont pas contentes.**
6. **Elles sont tristes.**
7. **Ils sont tristes.**
8. **Philippe est gentil.**
9. **Anne aussi est gentille.**
10. **Anne et Philippe sont gentils.**
11. **Ils ne sont pas contents.**
12. **Elles ne sont pas gentilles.**

B3 COMMENTS

■ Grammar

- When an adjective refers to several nouns, and at least one of them is masculine, the form of the adjective is masculine plural:

    Pierre et Marie sont gentils.
    Peter and Mary are kind.

- In French, adjectives referring to nationality are not capitalized (see lesson 3, A3), but nouns referring to nationality are.

    Adj.: **Nous sommes allemands.** *We are German.*
    Noun: **Un Allemand.** *A German.*

■ Pronunciation

- **g** + **e** or **i** is pronounced like **j** (ex.: **gentil**); otherwise it is pronounced like *g* in *good* (ex.: **anglais**).

- **ill** + vowel is pronounced like *y* in *yes* (ex.: **gentille**).

B4 TRANSLATION

1. We are German (masc.).
2. We are German (fem.).
3. You are too young.
4. Are you happy?
5. They are not happy (fem.).
6. They are sad (fem.).
7. They are sad (masc.).
8. Philippe is kind.
9. Anne is kind too.
10. Anne and Philippe are kind.
11. They are not happy (masc.).
12. They are not nice (fem.).

C1 EXERCISES

A. Fill in the blanks:

1. ... sont blondes.
2. Je ... près de Frédéric.
3. Elle ... petite.
4. Vous ... très sympathique.
5. ... sommes à Paris.
6. Ils ... devant Notre-Dame.

B. Make 8 sentences with one element of each column:

je	sommes	sympathique
tu	sont	tristes
il	es	jeune
elle	suis	jolies
nous	êtes	contents
vous	est	contents
ils		
elles		

C. ●● Translate into French:

1. You are nice (3 possibilities).
2. Anne and Sophie aren't very pretty.
3. Anne and Nicolas are tall.

C2 NOUS SOMMES EUROPÉENS ●●
WE ARE EUROPEAN

Adjectives (nationality)

Masc.	Fem.	
allemand	allemande	*German*
anglais	anglaise	*English*
belge	belge	*Belgian*
danois	danoise	*Danish*
espagnol	espagnole	*Spanish*
français	française	*French*
grec	grecque	*Greek*
italien	italienne	*Italian*
irlandais	irlandaise	*Irish*
portugais	portugaise	*Portuguese*

C3 ANSWERS

A.
1. Elles sont blondes.
2. Je suis près de Frédéric.
3. Elle est petite.
4. Vous êtes très sympathique.
5. Nous sommes à Paris.
6. Ils sont devant Notre-Dame.

B. Here are some possibilities:
1. Je suis sympathique.
2. Tu es sympathique.
3. Il est jeune.
4. Elle est jeune.
5. Nous sommes contents.
6. Vous êtes tristes.
7. Ils sont contents.
8. Elles sont jolies.

C.
1. Tu es sympathique. / Vous êtes sympathique. / Vous êtes sympathiques.
2. Anne et Sophie ne sont pas très jolies.
3. Anne et Nicolas sont grands.

C4 NOMBRES / *NUMBERS* (see lesson 4, C2) ●●

20	**vingt**	60	**soixante**
30	**trente**	70	**soixante-dix** *(sixty ten)*
40	**quarante**	80	**quatre-vingts** *(four twenty)*
50	**cinquante**	90	**quatre-vingt-dix** *(four twenty ten)*

➡ Notice the odd way of saying **70, 80, 90**.

100	**cent**
1000	**mille***

* Here **ill** is pronounced **il**.

A1 PRESENTATION

■ Grammar

- All French nouns are masculine (masc.) or feminine (fem.).
    - Ex.: **restaurant** (masc.) *restaurant*
      salade (fem.) *salad*

- The singular indefinite article has a masculine and a feminine form:

	singular	
	masculine	feminine
	un	**une**
	a, an	*a, an*

■ Vocabulary

manger	*to eat*	**chaud(e)**	*warm, hot*
préparer	*to prepare*	**froid(e)**	*cold*
acheter	*to buy*	**baguette** (fem.)	*long French*
demander	*to ask for*		*loaf*
repas (masc.)	*meal*	**croissant** (masc.)	*croissant*
bouteille (fem.)	*bottle*	(You can buy a **croissant** and	
vin (masc.)	*wine*	a **baguette** at the baker's.)	
samedi (masc.)	*Saturday*	**de**	*of*

A2 EXAMPLES *(Bread and wine)*

1. **Elle mange un croissant.**
2. **Il mange un croissant chaud.**
3. **Il mange souvent un croissant chaud à neuf heures.**
4. **Vous préparez un repas froid ?**
5. **Oui, nous préparons un repas froid.**
6. **Ils vont acheter une baguette.**
7. **Achète une salade et une bouteille de vin pour demain !**
8. **Nous allons dans un restaurant grec samedi ?**
9. **Non, nous allons dans un restaurant italien.**
10. **Un croissant s'il vous plaît !**
11. **Elle demande un croissant.**
12. **Elle demande un croissant et une baguette.**

7 | We are preparing a cold meal.

A3 COMMENTS

■ Grammar

- The articles and adjectives agree in gender with the noun they accompany.

  Ex.: **un restaurant** (masc.)   *a restaurant*
        une salade (fem.)   *a salad*

- In French, most adjectives come after the noun they accompany.

  Ex.: **un croissant chaud**   *a hot 'croissant'*
        un repas froid   *a cold meal*
        un restaurant grec   *a Greek restaurant*

■ Pronunciation

- **un**: this nasal vowel is pronounced like the vowel sound in *earn*.
- **eille** in **bouteille** is pronounced like *ay* in *gay* + *y* in *yes*.

A4 TRANSLATION

1. She is eating a 'croissant'.
2. He is eating a warm 'croissant'.
3. He often eats a warm 'croissant' at nine.
4. Are you preparing a cold meal?
5. Yes, we are preparing a cold meal.
6. They are going to buy a 'baguette'.
7. Buy a salad and a bottle of wine for tomorrow!
8. Are we going to a Greek restaurant on Saturday?
9. No, we are going to an Italian restaurant.
10. A 'croissant' please!
11. She is asking for a 'croissant'.
12. She is asking for a 'croissant' and a 'baguette'.

B1 PRESENTATION

■ Grammar

- In French the indefinite article has a plural form:

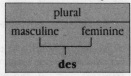

plural	
masculine	feminine
des	

- The plural of nouns is usually formed by adding an **s** to the singular form.

  Ex.: **des étudiants / des étudiantes** *students.*

■ Vocabulary

rencontrer	*to meet*	**livre** (masc.)	*book*
voici	*here is,*	**magazine** (masc.)	*magazine*
	here are	**journaliste** (masc.,	
photo (fem.)	*photo*	fem.)	*journalist*
étudiant (masc.)	*student*	**artiste** (masc., fem.)	*artist*
ami (masc.)	*friend*	**écrivain** (masc.)	*writer*
examen (masc.)	*exam*	**étranger**	*foreign*
		célèbre	*famous*

B2 EXAMPLES *(Studying abroad)*

1. Voici des photos d'Anne, une étudiante anglaise.
2. Ici, elle parle avec des étudiants étrangers.
3. Là, elle visite une cathédrale avec des amis français.
4. Elle habite avec des amis.
5. Elle prépare des examens.
6. Elle va acheter des livres et des magazines français.
7. Peter et John sont des journalistes anglais.
8. Ils parlent avec des artistes.
9. Ils rencontrent des journalistes français.
10. Ils rencontrent aussi des écrivains célèbres.
11. Nous rencontrons souvent des amis ici.
12. Nous allons souvent dans des restaurants étrangers.

B3 COMMENTS

■ Grammar

• In the plural, don't forget to use the indefinite article **des**, even if there is no such article in English.
  In French, it is practically impossible to use a noun alone. An article is almost always necessary.

> Ex.: **des photos** _photos_
> **des examens** _exams_

• The nouns which end with an **s** in the singular do not change in the plural.

> Ex.: **un repas - des repas** _meals_
> **un pays - des pays** _countries_

■ Pronunciation

• **es** in **des** is pronounced like _A_ in _A B C._

• Note that in **cathédrale : th** is pronounced **t.**

• Don't forget the liaison :
  des amis, des artistes, des étudiants, des écrivains.
  z   z   z   z

B4 TRANSLATION

1. Here are photos of Anne, an English student.
2. Here, she is speaking with foreign students.
3. There, she is visiting a cathedral with French friends.
4. She lives with friends.
5. She is preparing exams.
6. She is going to buy French books and magazines.
7. Peter and John are English journalists.
8. They speak with artists.
9. They meet French journalists.
10. They meet famous writers too.
11. We often meet friends here.
12. We often go to foreign restaurants.

C1 EXERCISES

A. Match the articles and nouns:

un - une - des :

restaurants - amie - portrait - amis - photo - amies - photos - ami - bouteilles de vin - repas - baguette - étudiant - livre - artiste - journaliste.

B. Match the articles, nouns and adjectives:

pays	un	française
amie	une	intelligents
photo	des	français
portrait		sympathiques
étudiants		étranger
livres		célèbre
écrivain		étrangers
restaurants		chaud
repas		froids
amis		italienne
journaliste		

C2 UN AMI / UNE AMIE ●●
A FRIEND

- Nouns denoting masculine persons are masculine and nouns denoting feminine persons are feminine.
  The usual way to form a feminine noun is by adding an **e** to the masculine.

  Ex.: **ami   amie**
  étudiant   étudiante

- However, some nouns can be used either for the masculine or for the feminine.

  Ex.: **journaliste**
  artiste

- In a word with a final **e**, the **e** is not pronounced as such but the preceding consonant is: **un étudiant - une étudiante**.

C3 ANSWERS

A. Des restaurants - Une amie - Un portrait - Des amis - Une photo -
Des amies - Des photos - Un ami - Des bouteilles de vin - Un repas -
Des repas - Une baguette - Un étudiant - Un livre - Un artiste -
Une artiste - Un journaliste - Une journaliste.

B. Some possibilities:
Un pays étranger.
Une amie française.
Une amie italienne.
Une photo célèbre.
Un portrait célèbre.
Des étudiants intelligents.
Des livres français.
Des écrivains étrangers.
Des restaurants sympathiques.
Des repas froids.
Un ami français.
Une journaliste italienne.
Un journaliste étranger.

C4 AUJOURD'HUI... DEMAIN
TODAY   TOMORROW

lundi	*Monday*
mardi	*Tuesday*
mercredi	*Wednesday*
jeudi	*Thursday*
vendredi	*Friday*
samedi	*Saturday*
dimanche	*Sunday*

- The days of the week are all masculine.
- Note that in French, the name of the day is used without any
preposition.

  Ex.: **lundi**   = *on Monday.*
       dimanche = *on Sunday.*

51

8   C'est une maison confortable.

A1   PRESENTATION

■ Grammar

- **c'est** can be the equivalent of: *he is, she is, it is* or *this is*, when followed by a noun in the singular.

  Ex. : **C'est un ami.**   *He is a friend.*
         C'est une amie.   *She is a friend.*
         C'est un studio.   *It is a studio.*

- **c'est** can be followed by an adjective or adverb alone. It is then the equivalent of: *it is* or *that is.*

  Ex.: **C'est gentil.**   *It is nice.*

- The negative form is: **ce n'est pas,** *it is not* ; (in colloquial French: **c'est pas**).

■ Vocabulary

à louer	*to let* (US: *to rent, for rent*)
voisin (masc.)	*neighbour*
appartement (masc.)	*flat* (US: *apartment*)
immeuble (masc.)	*building*
maison (fem.)	*house*
petit(e)	*small*
grand(e)	*big, large*
confortable	*comfortable*
moderne	*modern*
pas cher	*not expensive, cheap*
vraiment	*really*

A2   EXAMPLES *(Looking for a flat)*

1. **C'est Anne.**
2. **C'est une amie.**
3. **C'est Pierre.**
4. **C'est un voisin.**
5. **C'est un appartement à louer.**
6. **C'est un petit appartement dans un grand immeuble.**
7. **C'est une maison confortable.**
8. **Ce n'est pas une maison très moderne.**
9. **C'est loin ?**
10. **Non, ce n'est pas loin.**
11. **Ce n'est pas cher.**
12. **Ce n'est vraiment pas cher !**

A3 COMMENTS

■ Grammar

- As we have seen, in French most adjectives come after the noun they accompany (see lesson 7, A3).
  However, some short, commonly used adjectives are placed before the noun (see list in C2).
  Ex.: **C'est un petit appartement.** *It is a small flat.*

- Note that in colloquial French, you may hear **c'est pas** instead of **ce n'est pas.**
  Ex.: **C'est pas grand (ce n'est pas grand).**
  It's not big.

■ Pronunciation

- **c'est** is pronounced like *set* without the *t*.
- **ce** is pronounced like *ce* in *certain*.
- **im** in **immeuble** is pronounced like *im* in *important*.

A4 TRANSLATION

1. This is Anne.
2. She is a friend.
3. This is Pierre.
4. He is a neighbour.
5. It is a flat for rent.
6. It is a small flat in a big building.
7. It is a comfortable house.
8. It isn't a very modern house.
9. Is it far?
10. No, it isn't far.
11. It isn't expensive.
12. It's really cheap!

B1   PRESENTATION

■ Grammar

- When followed by a noun in the plural, **c'est** becomes **ce sont**.
    Ex.:   **Ce sont des appartements très chers.**
        They are very expensive flats.

- The negative form is : **ce ne sont pas**.

- Note that : **ce sont**, contrary to **c'est**, is never used with an adjective alone.

■ Vocabulary

pièce (fem.)	*room*
chambre (fem.)	*bedroom*
chaise (fem.)	*chair*
lampe (fem.)	*lamp*
fenêtre (fem.)	*window*
rideau (masc.)	*curtain*
tapis (masc.)	*carpet (US: rug)*
cher	*expensive*
sombre	*dark*
beau (masc.) / **belle** (fem.)	*beautiful*
bon marché	*cheap*

B2   EXAMPLES *(Furnishing a flat)*

1. **Ce sont des immeubles chers.**
2. **Ce sont des appartements très confortables.**
3. **Ce sont des pièces sombres.**
4. **Ce ne sont pas de grandes pièces.**
5. **Ce sont de petites chambres.**
6. **Ce ne sont pas des chaises confortables.**
7. **Ce sont de jolies lampes.**
8. **Ce sont de grandes fenêtres.**
9. **Ce sont de beaux rideaux.**
10. **Ce ne sont pas des tapis bon marché !**
11. **Ce ne sont pas de beaux tapis.**
12. **Ce sont des immeubles modernes.**

B3 COMMENTS

■ Grammar

- Note that **des** becomes **de** when there is an adjective before the noun.

> **Ce sont des lampes.**
> *They are lamps.*
> **Ce sont de jolies lampes.**
> *They are pretty lamps.*

- Words ending in **eau** add an **x**, instead of an **s**, to make the plural.
  Ex.: **De beaux rideaux.** *Beautiful curtains.*

- Remember: adjectives agree in gender and number with the noun (or the nouns) they refer to (see lesson 6, A1, B1).

> **Un appartement confortable.**
> *A comfortable flat.*
> **Des appartements confortables.**
> *Comfortable flats.*
>
> **Un petit appartement.**
> *A small flat.*
> **De petits appartements.**
> *Small flats.*

■ Pronunciation

- **o, au, eau**: three spellings for the sound of *o* in *note*.
  Ex.: **Sophie, restaurant, beau, rideau.**

B4 TRANSLATION

1. They are expensive buildings.
2. They are very comfortable flats.
3. They are dark rooms.
4. They are not big rooms.
5. They are small bedrooms.
6. They are not comfortable chairs.
7. They are pretty lamps.
8. They are big windows.
9. They are beautiful curtains.
10. They are not cheap carpets!
11. They are not beautiful carpets.
12. They are modern buildings.

C1 EXERCISES

A. ●● **Use c'est or ce sont with the following expressions:**

1. ... un ami.
2. ... une voisine.
3. ... des immeubles modernes.
4. ... Michel.
5. ... de belles maisons.
6. ... un écrivain célèbre.
7. ... un étudiant étranger.
8. ... des croissants chauds.

B. **Put the adjectives in the right place, and mind the gender and number:**

1. moderne : c'est une lampe.
2. joli : c'est une chambre.
3. mauvais : c'est un restaurant.
4. froid : c'est un repas.
5. petit : c'est une maison.
6. bon : ce sont des bouteilles.
7. confortable : ce sont des appartements.
8. jeune : ce sont des étudiants.

C. ●● **Read these sentences and pay attention to the liaisons:**

1. C'est Anna, c'est une amie.
2. Ce n'est pas une journaliste, c'est une étudiante.
3. Elle habite un petit appartement dans un petit immeuble.

C2 COMMONLY USED ADJECTIVES GENERALLY PLACED BEFORE THE NOUN

Masculine	Feminine	
bon	**bonne**	*good*
cher	**chère**	*dear, expensive*
grand	**grande**	*tall, big, great*
jeune	**jeune**	*young*
joli	**jolie**	*pretty*
long	**longue**	*long*
mauvais	**mauvaise**	*bad*
petit	**petite**	*little, small*
beau *	**belle**	*beautiful*
vieux *	**vieille**	*old*
nouveau *	**nouvelle**	*new*

* Note some adjectives whose feminine form is not made the usual way.

C3   ANSWERS

A. 1. C'est un ami.
2. C'est une voisine.
3. Ce sont des immeubles modernes.
4. C'est Michel.
5. Ce sont de belles maisons.
6. C'est un écrivain célèbre.
7. C'est un étudiant étranger.
8. Ce sont des croissants chauds.

B. 1. C'est une lampe moderne.
2. C'est une jolie chambre.
3. C'est un mauvais restaurant.
4. C'est un repas froid.
5. C'est une petite maison.
6. Ce sont de bonnes bouteilles.
7. Ce sont des appartements confortables.
8. Ce sont de jeunes étudiants.

C. Shows where the liaison is:

1. C'est—Anna, c'est—une—amie.
2. Ce n'est pas—une journaliste, c'est—une—étudiante.
3. Elle habite—un petit—appartement dans—un petit—immeuble.

C4   **LOGEMENT** / *HOUSING*

séjour (masc.)	*living room*
salon (masc.)	*drawing room* (US : *living room*)
salle à manger (fem.)	*dining room*
cuisine (fem.)	*kitchen*
salle de bains (fem.)	*bathroom*
jardin (masc.)	*garden*
garage (masc.)	*garage*

9 | Tu as des enfants aussi ?

A1 PRESENTATION

■ Grammar

Avoir	To have
j'ai	I have
tu as	you have
il, elle a	he, she, it has

➡ Note that **avoir** is the French equivalent of: *to have got.*
Ex.: *I have got a car.* **J'ai une voiture.**
He's got two children. **Il a deux enfants.**
You've got a nice house. **Tu as une belle maison.**

■ Vocabulary

rue (fem.)	street
enfant (masc. fem.)	child
fils (masc.)	son
fille (fem.)	daughter, girl
docteur (masc.)	doctor
métier (masc.)	job
chat (masc.)	cat
en (avion)	by (plane)
intéressant	interesting

Évry is a town near **Paris.**
Nantes is a town on the **Loire** river.

A2 EXAMPLES *(Talking about the family)*

1. J'ai un appartement rue Monge à Paris.
2. J'ai une maison près de Nantes.
3. Il a une maison à Nice, il y va en avion.
4. J'ai deux enfants.
5. Tu as des enfants aussi ?
6. Oui, un fils et une fille.
7. Agnès a un métier intéressant.
8. Elle travaille à Évry, elle y va en train.
9. Guy est docteur, il a une grande maison.
10. Il a des enfants.
11. Il a un chat.
12. Il a une petite voiture.

A3   COMMENTS

■ Grammar

• Remember:
  — **à** is a preposition: **à Nice, à Évry** (The accent doesn't affect the pronunciation);
  — **a** is the 3rd person singular of the verb **avoir.**

• **rue Monge:** note that most of the time, no preposition is used before the expression: **rue...**

• **y,** there refers to a place which has already been mentionned. It is placed just before the verb.

> Ex.:   **Il y va en avion** (**y** refers to Nice).
> *He goes there by plane.*
> **Elle y va en train** (**y** refers to Évry).
> *She goes there by train.*

■ Pronunciation

• **gu + i**
  gu + e → is pronounced like *g* in *good* (ex.: **Guy).**
  gu + y

• **ion** in **avion** is pronounced like *y* in *yes* followed by the nasal vowel **on.**

• In **fils**, the **s** is pronounced like *s* in *set*, but the **l** is not heard.

• **y** (there) is pronounced like *ee* in *see*.

A4   TRANSLATION

1. I have got a flat on rue Monge, in Paris.
2. I have got a house near Nantes.
3. He has got a house in Nice, he goes there by plane.
4. I have got two children.
5. Have you got children too?
6. Yes, a son and a daughter.
7. Agnès has an interesting job.
8. She works in Évry, she goes there by train.
9. Guy is a doctor, he has got a big house.
10. He has got children.
11. He has got a cat.
12. He has got a small car.

B1 PRESENTATION

■ Grammar

Avoir		To have	
nous	avons	*we*	*have*
vous	avez	*you*	*have*
ils, elles	ont	*they*	*have*

• In French, **avoir** is used in a series of expressions where *to be* is used in English (see C2).

  Ex. : **avoir faim**   *to be hungry*
  　　　 avoir soif   *to be thirsty*

■ Vocabulary

semaine (fem.)	*week*
vacances (fem. plural)	*holidays*
valise (fem.)	*suitcase*
sac (masc.)	*bag*
parent (masc.)	*relative*
hôtel (masc.)	*hotel*
avenue (fem.)	*avenue*
neuf/neuve	*new*

B2 EXAMPLES *(To have and have not)*

1. **Nous avons une vieille voiture.**
2. **Ils ont une voiture neuve.**
3. **Ils ont de longues vacances.**
4. **Nous avons trois semaines de vacances.**
5. **Vous avez des valises ?**
6. **Oui, nous avons deux valises et un sac.**
7. **Elles ont des sacs neufs.**
8. **Agnès et Guy ont des parents à Nice.**
9. **Nous avons des voisins sympathiques.**
10. **Ils ont un hôtel avenue Masséna.**
11. **Vous avez faim ?**
12. **Non, mais nous avons soif.**

B3 COMMENTS

■ Vocabulary

• Note that:
  — **neuf, neuve** means: which has not yet been used.

  — **nouveau** or **nouvelle** is closer to the meaning of *recent*.
  Ex.: **un nouveau livre**   *a new book*
         une voiture neuve   *a new car*

• Remember that **parents** in French means both *parents* and *relatives*.

■ Grammar

• *three weeks' holidays,* **trois semaines de vacances** (= literally *three weeks of holidays*).

→ Note that there is no equivalent of **'** or **'s** in French.

■ Pronunciation

• **aim** in **faim** is pronounced like **ain** in **maintenant** (see lesson 4, B3).

• Final consonants are silent except **c, f, l, q, r** which are usually sounded.
  Ex.: **neuf, soif, sac, hôtel, cinq, Marc.**

B4 TRANSLATION

1. We have an old car.
2. They have a new car.
3. They have long holidays.
4. We have three weeks' holidays.
5. Have you got suitcases?
6. Yes, we have two suitcases and a bag.
7. They have new bags.
8. Agnès and Guy have relatives in Nice.
9. We have nice neighbours.
10. They have a hotel on avenue Masséna.
11. Are you hungry?
12. No, but we are thirsty.

C1 EXERCISES

A. Put the verb <u>avoir</u> in the correct form:

1. Je ... trois photos de Guy.
2. Tu ... des voisins sympathiques.
3. Il ... deux fils et une fille.
4. Elle ... un sac neuf.
5. Ils ... une vieille voiture.
6. Tu ... une voiture neuve ?
7. Nous ... des amis en Espagne.
8. Ils ... des métiers intéressants.
9. Vous ... des enfants ?

B. Fill in the blanks with <u>à</u> or <u>a</u>:

1. Il ... un restaurant rue Monge, ... Paris.
2. Elle habite ... côté de Notre-Dame.
3. Je vais travailler ... Évry.
4. Elle ... une valise, il ... un sac.
5. Nous arrivons ... Nantes ... midi.

C. ●● Translate into French:

1. I have got two cases.
2. He has got foreign friends.
3. We have got two young cats.
4. Have you got a case? (2 possibilities)

C2 EXPRESSIONS ●●

- **avoir** is used in the following expressions:

avoir chaud	*to be warm*
avoir froid	*to be cold*
avoir soif	*to be thirsty*
avoir faim	*to be hungry*
avoir peur*	*to be afraid*
avoir raison	*to be right*
avoir tort	*to be wrong*
avoir de la chance	*to be lucky*
avoir l'habitude de	*to be used to*

* In **peur**, **eur** is pronounced like *er* in *her*.

C3   ANSWERS

A.
1. J'ai trois photos de Guy.
2. Tu as des voisins sympathiques.
3. Il a deux fils et une fille.
4. Elle a un sac neuf.
5. Ils ont une vieille voiture.
6. Tu as une voiture neuve ?
7. Nous avons des amis en Espagne.
8. Ils ont des métiers intéressants.
9. Vous avez des enfants ?

B.
1. Il a un restaurant rue Monge, à Paris.
2. Elle habite à côté de Notre-Dame.
3. Je vais travailler à Évry.
4. Elle a une valise, il a un sac.
5. Nous arrivons à Nantes à midi.

C.
1. J'ai deux valises.
2. Il a des amis étrangers.
3. Nous avons deux jeunes chats.
4. Avez-vous une valise ? / As-tu une valise ?

C4   J'AI TRENTE ANS ●●
I'M THIRTY

- You also use **avoir** to express age in French.
  The equivalent of *How old are you?* is **Quel âge as-tu ? Quel âge avez-vous ?** (literally: *what age have you?*).

  Ex.: **J'ai vingt ans.**   *I am twenty.*
  Elle a cinquante ans.   *She is fifty.*
  Quel âge a-t-il ?   *How old is he?*
  Il a trente ans.   *He is thirty.*

- Remember: **ans** *(years)* can't be omitted (as it is in English).

10   Est-ce que c'est facile ?

A1   PRESENTATION

■ Grammar

● **Est-ce que... ?**
  The most commonly used way of turning a statement into a question is to start with: **est-ce que... ?**

Tu chantes	→ **Est-ce que tu chantes ?**
You sing	*Do you sing?*
Il est jeune	→ **Est-ce qu'il est jeune ?**
He is young	*Is he young?*
C'est une voiture neuve	→ **Est-ce que c'est une voiture neuve ?**
It's a new car	*Is it a new car?*

⟶ The intonation is a rising one.

■ Vocabulary

utiliser	*to use*
commencer	*to start*
bureau (masc.)	*office*
secrétaire (masc., fem.)	*secretary* (for a person)
ordinateur (masc.)	*computer*
directeur (masc.)	*manager*
facile	*easy*
tard	*late*
tôt	*early*
en panne	*out of order*

A2   EXAMPLES *(Jobs)*

1. **Est-ce que Bruno a un bon métier ?**
2. **Est-ce qu'il travaille dans un bureau ?**
3. **Est-ce que tu commences à huit heures ?**
4. **Est-ce que vous commencez tôt ?**
5. **Est-ce que vous avez des secrétaires ?**
6. **Est-ce qu'elles utilisent des ordinateurs ?**
7. **Est-ce que c'est facile ?**
8. **Est-ce qu'ils sont souvent en panne ?**
9. **Est-ce que c'est un nouveau directeur ?**
10. **Est-ce qu'il est sympathique ?**
11. **Est-ce que c'est trop tard ?**
12. **Est-ce que nous travaillons aujourd'hui ?**

A3 COMMENTS

■ Pronunciation

- **est-ce** is pronounced like *S* in *R,S,T.*
- **que** becomes **qu'** before a vowel.
  Ex.: **Est-ce qu'il travaille ?**
  Est-ce qu'elles utilisent des ordinateurs ?
- **Bruno, bureau, restaurant, beaucoup : o, eau, au,** three spellings for one sound: **o** like *o* in *go.*
- In **eur (ordinateur, directeur)** the final **r** is heard.
- **anne** in **panne** is pronounced like *ann* in *anniversary.*

■ Grammar

- Note that there is no change in the order of the words in the statement after **est-ce que... ?**
- Remember that **est-ce que** is invariable.

Est-ce que tu chantes ?	*Do you*		*Are you*	
Est-ce que vous chantez ?	*Do you*	*sing?*	*Are you*	*singing?*
Est-ce qu'elles chantent ?	*Do they*		*Are they*	

A4 TRANSLATION

1. Does Bruno have a good job? / *or* Has Bruno got...
2. Does he work in an office?
3. Do you start at eight?
4. Do you start early?
5. Do you have secretaries? / *or* Have you got...
6. Do they use computers?
7. Is it easy?
8. Are they often out of order?
9. Is he a new manager?
10. Is he nice?
11. Is it too late?
12. Do we work today?

10 Avez-vous de longues vacances ?

B1 PRESENTATION

■ Grammar

● **Voyages-tu seul ?**   *Do you travel alone?*

So far we have seen two ways of turning a statement into a question (see B3). There is also a 3rd way when the subject is a pronoun. Subject and verb can be inverted (mostly with **vous, il, elle, ils, elles**):

   Aimez-vous Brahms ?   *Do you like Brahms?*

■ Vocabulary

inviter	*to invite*
jouer	*to play*
comprendre	*to understand*
concert (masc.)	*concert*
musée (masc.)	*museum*
théâtre (masc.)	*theatre*
pièce (fem.)	*play*
libre	*free*
récent(e)	*recent*
seul(e)	*alone*
quelquefois	*sometimes*

B2 EXAMPLES *(Entertainment)*

1. Avez-vous de longues vacances ?
2. Voyages-tu seul ?
3. Sont-ils libres le samedi ?
4. Invitent-elles des amis mercredi ?
5. Vont-ils écouter un concert ?
6. Aimez-vous Brahms ?
7. Rencontrez-vous souvent des artistes ?
8. Est-ce qu'il visite quelquefois des musées ?
9. Joue-t-elle dans un nouveau théâtre ?
10. Est-ce une pièce récente ?
11. Est-elle facile à comprendre ?
12. Parlez-vous français ?

B3   COMMENTS

■ Grammar

- Remember: two ways of turning a statement into a question:
  1. The speaker may simply use rising intonation at the end of the sentence (see lesson 3, A3).
     Ex.: **Tu chantes ?**   *Do you sing? / Are you singing?*
  2. **est-ce que** can be used at the beginning of the sentence.
     Ex.: **Est-ce que tu chantes ?**

- When the verb is inverted:
  — it is joined to the pronoun by a hyphen.
     Ex.: **Parlez-vous ?**   *Do you speak? / Are you speaking?*
  — if the verb ends with a vowel, **t** is introduced between the verb and **il** or **elle.**
     Ex.: **A-t-il... ?**   *Has he got...?*
            Commence-t-elle... ?   *Is she beginning...?*
            Visite-t-il...?   *Is he visiting...?*

■ Pronunciation

- Note that in **théâtre**, **th** is pronounced **t**.

B4   TRANSLATION

1. Do you have long holidays?
2. Do you travel alone?
3. Are they free on Saturdays?
4. Are they inviting friends on Wednesday?
5. Are they going to listen to a concert?
6. Do you like Brahms?
7. Do you often meet artists?
8. Does he sometimes visit museums?
9. Is she playing in a new theatre?
10. Is it a recent play?
11. Is it easy to understand?
12. Do you speak French?

C1 EXERCISES

A. Turn these statements into questions (three ways):

1. Elles voyagent souvent.
2. Ils ont une voiture neuve.
3. Vous commencez tôt.
4. Elle a un bon métier.
5. Vous allez très vite.
6. C'est un nouveau théâtre.

B. Put the words in order:

1. Paris / elles / visitent ?
2. Faim / tu / as ?
3. Travaille / est-ce / qu'elle / aujourd'hui ?
4. Vous / un / ordinateur / avez ?
5. Est-ce / que / cher / c'est ?
6. Habite / est-ce / qu'il / loin ?

C. ●● Practise the liaison:

1. Est-ce que c'est_un sac neuf ?
2. J'habite dans_un nouvel_appartement près de Grigny.
3. Est-ce qu'elle_a une maison avec_un jardin ?
4. Travaillent_-ils ?
5. Est-ce que ce sont des_amis ?
6. Cet_ami est_intelligent, il_est très_intéressant.

C2 COMMENT ALLEZ-VOUS ? ●●
HOW ARE YOU?

- **aller**, in questions where the verb is inverted, is commonly used in French to ask people how they are when you meet them:

Comment allez-vous ? / Comment vas-tu ?	*How are you?*
Comment va-t-elle ?	*How is she?*
Comment va-t-il ?	*How is he?*
Comment vont-ils ?	*How are they?*
Je vais bien.	*I'm fine.*
Je vais très bien.	*I'm very well.*
Je ne vais pas très bien.	*I'm not very well.*

- In colloquial French, **ça va ?** *(is everything all right?)* and **ça va** *(everything is all right)* are very much used.

C3 ANSWERS

A. 1. Elles voyagent souvent ? / Est-ce qu'elles voyagent souvent ? / Voyagent-elles souvent ?

2. Ils ont une voiture neuve ? / Est-ce qu'ils ont une voiture neuve ? / Ont-ils une voiture neuve ?

3. Vous commencez tôt ? / Est-ce que vous commencez tôt ? / Commencez-vous tôt ?

4. Elle a un bon métier ? / Est-ce qu'elle a un bon métier ? / A-t-elle un bon métier ?'

5. Vous allez très vite ? / Est-ce que vous allez très vite ? / Allez-vous très vite ?

6. C'est un nouveau théâtre ? / Est-ce que c'est un nouveau théâtre ? / Est-ce un nouveau théâtre ?

B. 1. Elles visitent Paris ? / Visitent-elles Paris ?

2. Tu as faim ? / As-tu faim ?

3. Est-ce qu'elle travaille aujourd'hui ?

4. Vous avez un ordinateur ? / Avez-vous un ordinateur ?

5. Est-ce que c'est cher ?

6. Est-ce qu'il habite loin ?

C4 A VERY USEFUL EXPRESSION : **IL Y A...**

- **il y a** is the French equivalent of both *there is* and *there are*.

  Ex.: **Il y a un appartement à louer.**
  There is a flat to let.

  Il y a une jolie maison ici.
  There is a nice house here.

  Il y a des restaurants rue Monge.
  There are restaurants on Monge Street.

- Notice the pronunciation ''eeleeya'' (the three words run together).

- In spoken French, you very often hear **y a (ya)**, instead of **il y a**.

- In the interrogative :

Il y a un concert aujourd'hui ?
Est-ce qu'il y a un concert aujourd'hui ? ⟶ *Is there a concert today ?*
Y a-t-il un concert aujourd'hui ?

A1   PRESENTATION

■ Grammar

● Definite articles

masculine	← singular →	feminine
le	← *the* →	**la**

● The article agrees in gender with the noun it accompanies:
Le bureau. *The desk.*   **Le train.** *The train.*
La secrétaire. *The secretary.*   **La valise.** *The suitcase.*

● **le, la** become **l'** before a vowel or **h**:
L'étudiant. *The student.* **L'avion.** *The plane.* **L'heure.** *The hour.*

■ Vocabulary

partir	*to leave*
oublier	*to forget*
porter	*to carry*
métro (masc.)	*tube (*US: *subway)*
taxi (masc.)	*taxi*
autobus/bus (masc.)	*bus*
gare (fem.)	*station*
quai (masc.)	*platform*
rouge	*red*
beaucoup de monde	*a lot of people*
en grève	*on strike*
à l'heure	*on time*
sur	*on*

A2   EXAMPLES *(Means of transport)*

1. Le métro est en grève mais il y a des taxis.
2. Il y a des bus près de la maison.
3. Le bus va partir dans cinq minutes.
4. Ce n'est pas le 20 (vingt), c'est le 30 (trente).
5. Est-ce que l'avion est à l'heure ?
6. La gare est loin ?
7. Non, la gare n'est pas loin.
8. Le train n'est pas à l'heure.
9. N'oublie pas la petite valise !
10. Il porte le sac rouge.
11. Il y a des gens sur le quai.
12. C'est l'heure ! Au revoir !

A3 COMMENTS

■ Grammar

• Remember: to make a sentence negative use **ne... pas**, or **n'... pas** on either side of the verb (see lesson 2, A1).
  Le train n'est pas à l'heure. *The train isn't on time.*

• Note two ways of translating *people* in French:
  — **monde (monde** (masc.) = *world*) which is singular and practically never used as a subject.
    Ex.: **Il y a du monde.** *There are (a lot of) people.*
  — **gens (gens** (masc.) = *people*) which is plural.
    Ex.: **Il y a des gens.** *There are (a lot of) people.*

• Note that for bus numbers, the definite article is used in French.
    Ex. : **le 20, le 30.**

■ Pronunciation

• In **bus**, the final **s** is heard.

A4 TRANSLATION

1. The tube is on strike, but there are taxis.
2. There are buses near the house.
3. The bus is leaving in five minutes.
4. It isn't a 20, it's a 30.
5. Is the plane on time?
6. Is the station far?
7. No, the station isn't far.
8. The train isn't on time.
9. Don't forget the little case!
10. He is carrying the red bag.
11. There are people on the platform.
12. It's time! Good bye!

11 Nous allons inviter les voisins.

B1 PRESENTATION

■ Grammar

● Definite articles.
There is only one plural article:

les	*the*

The article agrees in number with the noun it accompanies.
Ex.: **les trains, les gares, les avions, les heures.**

● **es** in **les** is pronounced like *A* in *A, B, C.*

■ Vocabulary

apporter	*to bring*
chercher	*to fetch / to look for*
verre (masc.)	*glass*
assiette (fem.)	*plate*
table (fem.)	*table*
serviette (fem.)	*napkin*
invité (masc.)	*guest*
pain (masc.)	*bread*
boisson (fem.)	*drink*
blanc/blanche	*white*

B2 EXAMPLES *(Getting ready for a party)*

1. **Nous allons inviter les voisins.**
2. **Où sont les grands verres ?**
3. **Est-ce que les verres sont sur la table ?**
4. **Les verres sont dans la salle à manger.**
5. **Est-ce que Pierre apporte les vins ?**
6. **Allez chercher les bouteilles, s'il vous plaît.**
7. **Où sont les assiettes ?**
8. **Demande à Antoine.**
9. **Où sont les serviettes blanches ?**
10. **Les voisins vont apporter les boissons.**
11. **Va acheter le pain, s'il te plaît.**
12. **Les invités sont là, apportez les chaises !**

B3 COMMENTS

■ Grammar

- We have seen that **aller** + infinitive may be equivalent of *to be going to*.

    Ex.: **Nous allons inviter.** *We are going to invite.*

    The French equivalent of *go and* + verb is also: **aller** + infinitive.

    Ex.: **Allez chercher.** *Go and fetch, go and get.*
    Va acheter. *Go and buy.*

- Note that the equivalent of *to ask somebody* is **demander à quelqu'un**.

    Ex.: **Demande à Antoine.** *Ask Antoine.*

■ Pronunciation

- Don't forget the liaison when **les** is followed by a vowel or **h**.

    Ex.: **les assiettes, les amis.**
    z   z

B4 TRANSLATION

1. We are going to invite the neighbours.
2. Where are the big glasses?
3. Are the glasses on the table?
4. The glasses are in the dining-room.
5. Is Pierre bringing the wines?
6. Go and fetch the bottles, please.
7. Where are the plates?
8. Ask Antoine.
9. Where are the white napkins?
10. The neighbours are going to bring the drinks.
11. Go and buy the bread, please.
12. The guests are here, bring the chairs!

C1 EXERCISES

A. Match the articles and nouns:

le — la — les — l'

voiture — valises — enfant — gare — studio
ordinateur — enfants — cinéma.

B. Fill in the gaps with: le, la, les, l':

1. Elle regarde ... photos.
2. ... métro est devant ... restaurant.
3. ... enfant cherche ... petite voiture.
4. ... invités apportent ... vins.
5. Allez-vous à ... gare ?
6. ... immeuble est derrière ... théâtre.

C. ●● Translate into French:

1. Go and fetch the red case.
2. He is going to bring the photos.
3. They are going to visit the museum.
4. Go and speak with the guests.

C2 COULEURS / *COLOURS*

Remain the same in the masculine or feminine	Add an **e** in the feminine	Are different in the feminine
rouge *red* **jaune** *yellow* **rose** *pink*	**vert(e)** *green* **bleu(e)** *blue* **noir(e)** *black* **gris(e)** *grey* **brun(e)** *brown*	**blanc/blanche** *white* **violet/violette** *purple*

- Some more colours: **rouge cerise**   *cherry-red*
  bleu marine   *navy-blue*
  vert émeraude   *emerald-green*

C3 ANSWERS

A. le studio — le cinéma — la voiture — la gare — les valises — les enfants — l'enfant — l'ordinateur.

B. 1. Elle regarde les photos.
2. Le métro est devant le restaurant.
3. L'enfant cherche la petite voiture.
4. Les invités apportent les vins.
5. Allez-vous à la gare ?
6. L'immeuble est derrière le théâtre.

C. 1. Va chercher la valise rouge. / Allez chercher la valise rouge.
2. Il va apporter les photos.
3. Ils vont visiter le musée.
4. Va parler avec les invités. / Allez parler avec les invités.

C4 MOYENS DE TRANSPORT
MEANS OF TRANSPORT

- **RER (Réseau Express Régional)** :
rapid transit to the suburbs from the centre of Paris.

- **SNCF (Société Nationale des Chemins de Fer Français)** :
French Railways.

- **TGV (Train à Grande Vitesse)** :
the fastest and one of the most comfortable trains in the world, runs at speeds of up to 500 **km/h (kilomètres à l'heure)**.

Mesures	*Measures*
un centimètre	*a centimetre*
un mètre	*a metre*
un kilomètre	*a kilometre* (= 0.62 mile)

A1 PRESENTATION

■ Grammar

● **quel,** *what.*
The exclamative **quel** *(= what)* agrees in gender and number with the noun it refers to:

quel (masc. sg.)	**quels** (masc. pl.)
quelle (fem. sg.)	**quelles** (fem. pl.)

The exclamation can be formed with: **quel** + noun

Quel homme !	*What a man!*	**Quels artistes !**	*What artists!*
Quelle femme !	*What a woman!*	**Quelles photos !**	*What photos!*

or: **quel** + adjective + noun

Quel grand bateau !	*What a big boat!*
Quels bons vins !	*What good wines!*
Quelle jolie fille !	*What a pretty girl!*
Quelles belles robes !	*What beautiful dresses!*

■ Vocabulary

temps (masc.)	*weather*	**journée** (fem.)	*day*
orage (masc.),		**année** (fem.)	*year*
tempête (fem.)	} → *storm*	**terrible**	*terrible*
pluie (fem.)	*rain*	**splendide**	*splendid*
nuage (masc.)	*cloud*	**magnifique**	*magnificent*
coucher		**drôle**	*funny*
de soleil (masc.)	*sunset*		

A2 EXAMPLES *(Weather)*

1. **Quel temps !**
2. **Quel orage !**
3. **Quelle pluie !**
4. **Quelles tempêtes !**
5. **Quel froid terrible !**
6. **Quelle mauvaise année !**
7. **Quelle belle journée !**
8. **Quel temps splendide !**
9. **Quel magnifique coucher de soleil !**
10. **Quels drôles de nuages !**
11. **Quelles terribles tempêtes !**
12. **Quels vents violents !**

A3 COMMENTS

■ Grammar

- Note that there is no article before the noun in the exclamative.

  Quelle journée !   **Quel orage !**
  What a day!   *What a storm!*

- **drôle** when placed before the noun it refers to is always followed by **de** and conveys the meaning of *strange*.

  Ex.: **C'est une drôle de fille.**
  She is a funny girl (meaning an *odd girl*).

  But **cette fille est drôle** can mean either *that girl is amusing* or *that girl is odd*.

- **journée** and **année** are generally used to insist on the length of time of a day or a year, otherwise **jour** and **an** are used.

■ Pronunciation

- Note that **el** in **quel** is pronounced **èl** like *e* in *pet*.

- Remember that **qu** in the final **que** (ex.: **magnifique**) is pronounced like *ck* in *back*.

- Note that in **temps**, neither **p** nor **s** are heard.

- Note that **er** in **coucher**, **ée** in **journée**, have the sound of *A* (in *A, B, C*).

A4 TRANSLATION

1. What weather!
2. What a storm!
3. What rain!
4. What storms!
5. What terrible cold!
6. What a bad year!
7. What a beautiful day!
8. What splendid weather!
9. What a magnificent sunset!
10. What funny clouds!
11. What terrible storms!
12. What violent winds!

12 | Regardez les singes ! Comme ils sont drôles !

B1 PRESENTATION

■ Grammar

- **Que, comme,** *how.*
  Another exclamatory form is obtained by putting **que** or **comme** before a statement:

  1 | **que** or **comme** + subject + **être** + adjective

  Que le ciel est bleu !
  Comme le ciel est bleu ! ⎤→ *How blue the sky is!*
  Qu'elle est belle ! → *How beautiful she is!*
  Comme c'est beau !
  Que c'est beau ! ⎤→ *How beautiful it is!*

  2 | **que** or **comme** + subject + verb

  Que cette voiture va vite ! *How fast this car is going!*
  Comme il parle bien ! *How well he speaks!*

■ Vocabulary

avoir l'air	*to look,*	**yeux** (masc. pl.)	*eyes*
	to sound	**lion** (masc.)	*lion*
détester	*to hate*	**éléphant** (masc.)	*elephant*
chien (masc.)	*dog*	**serpent** (masc.)	*snake*
oiseau (masc.)	*bird*	**joyeux**	*merry*
singe (masc.)	*monkey*	**fort**	*strong*

B2 EXAMPLES *(Animals)*

1. **Comme j'aime ce chat !**
2. **Que j'aime ce chat gris !**
3. **Que ce chien a l'air intelligent !**
4. **Comme les oiseaux chantent fort ce matin !**
5. **Qu'ils ont l'air joyeux !**
6. **Regardez les singes ! Comme ils sont drôles !**
7. **Qu'ils sont drôles !**
8. **Comme ce lion a l'air triste !**
9. **Qu'il a les yeux tristes !**
10. **Que l'éléphant est drôle !**
11. **Comme il est fort !**
12. **Que je déteste les serpents !**

B3 COMMENTS

■ Grammar

- Note that **fort** can be either an adjective meaning *strong*, or an adverb meaning *loud*.

  Ex.: **C'est un garçon très fort.** *He is a very strong boy.*
  Ne parle pas trop fort. *Don't speak too loud.*

- Note that when parts of the body are not the subject of the sentence, the definite article is used.

  Ex.: **Il a les yeux bleus.** *He has blue eyes.*
  Elle a les yeux tristes. *Her eyes are sad.*

- Note that with the exclamative **comme** *(how)* the construction remains the same as in a simple statement.

  Ils ont l'air joyeux. *They look merry.*

  Comme ⎤
  Qu' ⎦ ils ont l'air joyeux ! *How merry they look!*

■ Pronunciation

- Remember that **j** (in **je, bonjour, joli, jeune,** etc.) is pronounced like *su* in *pleasure*.

- Remember that **oy** in **joyeux** is pronounced like **oi** followed by the sound of *y* in *yes*.

B4 TRANSLATION

1. How I love this cat!
2. How I love this grey cat!
3. How intelligent this dog looks!
4. How loud the birds are singing this morning!
5. How merry they sound!
6. Look at the monkeys! How funny they are!
7. How funny they are!
8. How sad this lion looks!
9. How sad his eyes are!
10. How funny the elephant is!
11. How strong he is!
12. How I hate snakes!

C1 EXERCISES

A. Match the words:

quelle	hôtel	bel	!
quelles	yeux	belles	!
quels	voiture	jolie	!
quel	vacances	splendides	!

B. ●● Turn into the exclamative:
Ex.: Les enfants ont l'air contents / Comme ils ont l'air contents ! / Qu'ils ont l'air contents !

1. Ce nouveau livre est drôle.
2. Ces photos sont superbes.
3. Les lions ont l'air terribles.
4. Cet appartement a l'air confortable.
5. Cette chemise est chère.
6. C'est loin.
7. Vous parlez fort.

C. ●● Translate into French:

1. What a beautiful autumn!
2. How nice you are!
3. How slowly this bus is going!
4. How thirsty I am!
5. How funny this little dog is!
6. How well they work!
7. What an interesting film!

C2 EMOTIONS ●●

Quel bonheur !	*What a blessing!*
Quelle tristesse !	*How sad!*
Quelle horreur !	*How horrible!*
Quel dommage !	*What a shame!*
Quel malheur !	*What a pity!*

C3 ANSWERS

A.
1. Quelle jolie voiture !
2. Quelles belles vacances !
3. Quels yeux splendides !
4. Quel bel hôtel !

B.
1. Que ce nouveau livre est drôle ! / Comme ce nouveau livre est drôle !
2. Que ces photos sont superbes ! / Comme ces photos sont superbes !
3. Que les lions ont l'air terribles ! / Comme les lions ont l'air terribles !
4. Que cet appartement a l'air confortable ! / Comme cet appartement a l'air confortable !
5. Que cette chemise est chère ! / Comme cette chemise est chère !
6. Que c'est loin ! / Comme c'est loin !
7. Que vous parlez fort ! / Comme vous parlez fort !

C.
1. Quel bel automne !
2. Que vous êtes (tu es) gentil !
3. Que cet autobus avance lentement !
4. Que j'ai soif !
5. Comme ce petit chien est drôle !
6. Comme ils (elles) travaillent bien !
7. Quel film intéressant !

C4 LE CORPS HUMAIN / *THE HUMAN BODY*

tête (fem.)	*head*	**joue** (fem.)	*cheek*
cheveux (masc., usually pl.)	*hair*	**menton** (masc.)	*chin*
visage (masc.)	*face*	**cou** (masc.)	*neck*
front (masc.)	*forehead*	**bras** (masc.)	*arm*
œil (masc. sg.)	*eye*	**main** (fem.)	*hand*
yeux (masc. pl.)	*eyes*	**doigt** (masc.)	*finger*
nez (masc.)	*nose*	**pouce** (masc.)	*thumb*
bouche (fem.)	*mouth*	**jambe** (fem.)	*leg*
oreille (fem.)	*ear*	**pied** (masc.)	*foot*

13   Cette chemise coûte deux cents francs.

A1   PRESENTATION

■ Grammar

● **ce / cette + noun**

are the French equivalents of: *this/that* + noun.
— **ce** + a masculine singular.
    Ex.: **Ce journaliste.**   *This (that) journalist.*
— **cette** + a feminine singular.
    Ex.: **Cette amie.**   *This (that) friend.*

● **ces + a noun in the plural**

is the French equivalent of: *these/those* + noun.
    Ex.: **Ces livres.**   *These (those) books.*
        Ces maisons.   *These (those) houses.*

■ Vocabulary

coûter	*to cost*
poser	*to put*
manteau (masc.)	*coat*
robe (fem.)	*dress*
pantalon or **pantalons** (masc.)	*trousers*
chemise (fem.)	*shirt*
chaussure (fem.)	*shoe*
imperméable (masc.)	*raincoat*
vêtements (masc. pl.)	*clothes*
court	*short*

The **franc** is the French currency.

A2   EXAMPLES *(Buying clothes)*

1. **Tu aimes ce manteau ?**
2. **Cet imperméable est trop long.**
3. **Je vais acheter cette robe.**
4. **Cette robe est trop courte !**
5. **J'aime cette chemise.**
6. **Est-ce que cette chemise est chère ?**
7. **Cette chemise coûte deux cents francs (200 F).**
8. **Je n'aime pas ces chaussures avec ce pantalon.**
9. **Est-ce que ces chaussures sont chères ?**
10. **Ces chaussures coûtent quatre cents francs (400 F).**
11. **N'achète pas ces pantalons, ils sont trop courts.**
12. **Pose ces vêtements sur cette chaise, s'il te plaît.**

A3 COMMENTS

■ Pronunciation

- **cet / cette** are pronounced like *set*.

- **ces** is pronounced like **cé** (**é**, sound of *A* in *A, B, C*).

- When the noun which follows starts with a vowel or h, **ce** becomes **cet**.

  Ex.: **Cet ami.**   *This (that) friend.*
       Cet imperméable.   *This (that) raincoat.*

- Don't forget the liaison:

  Ex.: **Cet enfant.**   **Ces enfants.**
         t   z

- Note that in **franc**, the c is not heard.

■ Grammar

- Remember that in French the endings of the verbs vary according to the person and number of the subject:

  J'aime cette chemise.   *I like this shirt.*
  Tu aimes cette chemise.   *You like this shirt.*
  Ils aiment cette chemise. *They like this shirt.*

A4 TRANSLATION

1. Do you like this coat?
2. That raincoat is too long.
3. I'm going to buy that dress.
4. That dress is too short!
5. I like this shirt.
6. Is this shirt expensive?
7. This shirt costs two hundred francs.
8. I don't like these (those) shoes with those (these) trousers.
9. Are these shoes expensive?
10. These shoes cost four hundred francs.
11. Don't buy those trousers, they are too short.
12. Put these clothes on that chair, please.

B1   PRESENTATION

■ Grammar

- *this*, when used alone is translated by **ceci** ;
  that, when used alone is translated by **cela**.
  But, in colloquial French, **cela** is frequently contracted to **ça**.

  Ex.:   **Je n'aime pas cela.** ⎤
          Je n'aime pas ça.   ⎦→   *I don't like that (it).*

  ça is very commonly used and can mean *this/that* or *it*, according to the context.

- **ceci, cela, ça** usually refer to an object or concept which has already been mentioned or can be clearly identified in the situation or context.

- **ne... plus, n'... plus,**   *not... any more, no longer.*

■ Vocabulary

goûter	*to taste*
disque (masc.)	*record*
album (masc.)	*album*
mille (1 000)	*thousand (1,000)*
superbe	*superb*
délicieux	*delicious*
malade	*sick, ill*
armagnac (masc.)	*is a kind of brandy.*

B2   EXAMPLES *(Likes and dislikes)*

1. Voici un nouveau disque ; écoute ça, c'est superbe.
2. Tu trouves ? Je n'aime pas ça.
3. Regarde ça, c'est un nouvel album.
4. Je vais acheter ça pour Pierre.
5. Ça coûte cher ?
6. Ça coûte trois mille francs (3 000 F).
7. Ne parlons plus de ça.
8. Voilà un vieil armagnac, tu aimes ça ?
9. Goûte ça, c'est délicieux.
10. Ne fume pas comme ça, tu vas être malade !
11. Ne parle pas comme ça, ce n'est pas gentil.
12. Je déteste ça.

B3 COMMENTS

■ Grammar

- Notice that **ça** is used either as a subject or an object.
    Ex.: **Ça coûte cher.**   *It costs a lot.*
          Je n'aime pas ça.   *I don't like that.*
- **ne... plus, n'... plus**, like **ne... pas**, is placed on either side of the verb.
    Ex.: **Elle n'habite plus ici.** *She doesn't live here any more.*

■ Vocabulary

- In the singular:
    — **vieux**   when preceding a vowel or **h** become   **vieil**
    — **nouveau**   **nouvel**
    Ex.: **Un vieil armagnac.**
          Un nouvel album.

- Remember:
    g + e or **i** is pronounced **j** (ex.: **gentil**) (see lesson 12, B3).
    g + other vowels is pronounced **g** like in *good* (ex.: **goûte**).

B4 TRANSLATION

1. Here is a new record; listen to this, it's superb.
2. You think so? I don't like it.
3. Look at that, it's a new album.
4. I'm going to buy it for Pierre.
5. Does it cost a lot?
6. It costs three thousand francs.
7. Let's not speak about that any more.
8. Here is an old brandy, do you like it?
9. Taste that, it's delicious.
10. Don't smoke like that, you are going to be sick.
11. Don't speak like that, it's not nice.
12. I hate that.

C1 EXERCISES

A. Match:

ce — cet — cette — ces

disque — manteau — livres — bouteille — examen — robes — amie — vins — ami.

B. ●● Transform as in the example:
Un portrait célèbre. Ce portrait est célèbre.

1. Une pièce sombre.
2. Un mauvais restaurant.
3. Une jupe courte.
4. Des étudiants étrangers.
5. Des maisons modernes.

C. ●● Translate into French:

1. They don't like that.
2. I hate that book.
3. She is going to buy these shoes.
4. Don't look at that.

C2 EXPRESSIONS ●●

Ça va ?	*Is everything all right?*
Ça va / ça va bien !	*Everything's fine!*
Ça va mal	*Things are going badly.*
Ça va aller	*It is going to be all right.*
Ça dépend	*It depends.*
C'est ça	*That's right / that's correct.*
Ça suffit !	*That's enough!*

C3 ANSWERS

A. ce disque — ce manteau.
cet examen — cet ami.
cette amie — cette bouteille.
ces livres — ces robes — ces vins.

B. 1. Cette pièce est sombre.
2. Ce restaurant est mauvais.
3. Cette jupe est courte.
4. Ces étudiants sont étrangers.
5. Ces maisons sont modernes.

C. 1. Ils n'aiment pas ça. / Elles n'aiment pas ça.
2. Je déteste ce livre.
3. Elle va acheter ces chaussures.
4. Ne regarde pas ça. / Ne regardez pas ça.

C4 ADJECTIVES USED BOTH IN THE MASCULINE AND FEMININE

Superbe and **malade** like **jeune, sympathique, triste,** and **célèbre** are used both for the masculine and feminine. Here are some more adjectives of the same kind:

large	*broad, wide*
pauvre	*poor*
riche	*rich*
simple	*simple*
utile	*useful*
vide	*empty*

A1   PRESENTATION

■ Grammar

- In French, the relative pronouns which are most often used are:

qui	*who, that, which*	used as <u>subject</u>
que	*whom, that, which*	used as <u>direct object</u>

Both may refer to persons or things.

Ex.:   **Écoute l'homme qui parle à la radio.**
Listen to the man who is speaking on the radio.

L'homme que vous allez rencontrer est américain.
The man you're going to meet is American.

Apporte le livre qui est sur la table, s'il te plaît.
Bring the book which is on the table, please.

Où est le livre que tu utilises ?
Where is the book you use?

■ Vocabulary

montre (fem.)	*watch*
homme (masc.)	*man*
femme (fem.)	*woman*
chanson (fem.)	*song*
liberté (fem.)	*freedom*
en vitrine	*in the shopwindow*
à côté	*next door*

A2   EXAMPLES *(Specifying which one)*

1. **J'aime bien la montre qui est en vitrine.**
2. **J'aime bien la montre que tu as aujourd'hui.**
3. **Regarde l'homme qui est sur la photo.**
4. **Voici l'homme que j'aime !**
5. **La femme qui habite à côté est une journaliste danoise.**
6. **La femme que tu regardes est une artiste.**
7. **Les gens qui sont sur cette photo habitent en Espagne.**
8. **J'invite des gens que tu aimes bien.**
9. **Ils écoutent des chansons qui parlent de liberté.**
10. **Écoute la chanson qu'ils chantent.**
11. **Nous allons visiter l'appartement qui est à louer.**
12. **Nous allons visiter l'appartement que nous allons acheter.**

A3   COMMENTS

■ Grammar

- **qui** and **que** may refer to a masculine or feminine, singular or plural noun.

- **que** becomes **qu'** before a vowel or **h**, but **qui** does not change.
  Ex.: **L'ordinateur qu'elle utilise.**
  The computer she uses.

  L'ordinateur qui est sur le bureau.
  The computer that is on the desk.

- **que** as a relative pronoun used as direct object can never be omitted in French.
  Ex.: **L'homme que j'aime.**   *The man I love.*
  Le repas que je prépare.   *The meal I'm preparing.*

- Remember: **nous allons,** *we are going to.*
  Aller, *to go,* is an irregular verb (see lesson 5, A1). Followed by a verb in the infinitive, **aller** expresses either an intention or the immediate future. It is the French equivalent of *to be going to* (see lesson 5, B1).

■ Pronunciation

- **qu** is pronounced like *ck* in *back.*

- The first **e** in **femme** is pronounced like *a* in *Pat* (the second is mute).

A4   TRANSLATION

1. I like the watch that is in the shopwindow.
2. I like the watch you have on today.
3. Look at the man who is in the photograph.
4. Here is the man I love!
5. The woman who lives next door is a Danish journalist.
6. The woman you are looking at is an artist.
7. The people who are in this photograph live in Spain.
8. I am inviting some people that you like.
9. They are listening to songs that speak of freedom.
10. Listen to the song they are singing.
11. We are going to visit the flat that is to let.
12. We are going to visit the flat we are going to buy.

B1 PRESENTATION

■ Grammar

* **qui** and **que** are often used in the expressions: **c'est... qui, c'est... que.**

  Ex.: **Louis est ici.** **_C'est Louis qui est ici._**
  It is Louis who is here.
  Anne chante. **_C'est Anne qui chante._**
  It is Anne who is singing.
  J'utilise ce livre. **_C'est ce livre que j'utilise._**
  It is this book I use.

  In the sentences in italics, **_Louis, Anne, ce livre_** are emphasized.

* **ce qui, ce que** are compound relative pronouns which are equivalent to _what._

  > **ce qui** is used as <u>subject</u>
  > **ce que** is used as <u>object</u>

  Ex.: **Regarde ce qui est ici.** _Look what is here._
  Regarde ce que j'ai. _Look what I've got._

■ Vocabulary

préférer	_to prefer_	**étage** (masc.)	_floor_
expliquer	_to explain_	**tableau** (masc.)	_painting_
guide (masc.)	_guide_	**premier**	_first_
salle (fem.)	_room_	**en ce moment**	_at the moment_

B2 EXAMPLES _(Visiting a museum)_

1. **C'est le musée que je préfère.**
2. **C'est un musée qui est à Amsterdam.**
3. **C'est un jeune guide qui parle.**
4. **Écoute ce que le guide explique.**
5. **Écoute ce qu'explique le guide.**
6. **Ce qu'il explique est intéressant.**
7. **Regarde ce qu'il y a dans cette salle.**
8. **C'est une salle qui est vide en ce moment.**
9. **Allons visiter ce qu'il y a au premier étage.**
10. **Ce sont des tableaux qui sont très modernes.**
11. **Je n'aime pas ce qui est dans la première salle.**
12. **Mais j'aime bien ce qui est dans la salle à côté.**

B3 COMMENTS

■ Grammar

- Remember that in the plural, **c'est... qui, c'est... que** become **ce sont... qui, ce sont... que**.

  Ex.: **Ce sont des amis qui sont drôles.**
  They are friends who are funny.
  Ce sont les amis que je préfère.
  They are the friends I prefer.

- Note that after **ce que**, the verb may be inverted if the subject is not a pronoun:

  Écoute ce que les enfants chantent. } *Listen to what the*
  Écoute ce que chantent les enfants. *children are singing.*

  Écoute ce que le guide explique. } *Listen to what the*
  Écoute ce qu'explique le guide. *guide is explaining.*

  → But:

  Écoute ce qu'ils chantent. *Listen to what they are singing.*
  Écoute ce qu'il explique. *Listen to what he is explaining.*

- **premier** in the feminine becomes **première**. Note the grave accent. Also note the grave accent in **préfère**.

B4 TRANSLATION

1. It is the museum I prefer.
2. It is a museum that is in Amsterdam.
3. It is a young guide who is speaking.
4. Listen to what the guide is explaining.
5. Listen to what the guide is explaining.
6. What he is explaining is interesting.
7. Look what there is in that room.
8. It is a room which is empty at the moment.
9. Let's go and visit what there is on the first floor.
10. They are paintings which are very modern.
11. I don't like what there is in the first room.
12. But I like what is in the room next door.

C1 EXERCISES

A. Choose between <u>qui</u> and <u>que</u>:

1. J'ai une fille ... travaille à Évry.
2. C'est un nouveau directeur ... je n'aime pas.
3. Allez chercher les verres ... sont sur la table.
4. Nous avons des amis ... habitent Paris.
5. Voici un restaurant ... est très sympathique.
6. Pluie, nuages : c'est le temps ... je déteste !
7. C'est un repas froid ... vous préparez ?

B. Choose between <u>ce qui</u>, <u>ce que</u>, <u>ce qu'</u>:

1. ... est dans ce musée est très moderne.
2. Elle prépare ... nous allons manger.
3. Nous écoutons ... explique le journaliste.
4. Apporte ... il y a sur la table, s'il te plaît.

C. Translate into French:

1. It is a wine I often buy.
2. Anne and Pierre are neighbours we sometimes meet.
3. They are friends Antoine does not like.
4. Listen to what this woman is explaining.
5. They are looking at the children who are playing in front of the building.

C2 LES NOMBRES / *NUMBERS*

13 treize	**20 vingt***
14 quatorze	**21 vingt et un****
15 quinze	**31 trente et un****
16 seize	**41 quarante et un****
17 dix-sept	**51 cinquante et un****
18 dix-huit	**61 soixante et un****
19 dix-neuf	

* Note that in **vingt**, neither the **g** nor the **t** is pronounced.
** Note that the **et** (literally *twenty and one*) is necessary only with **un**.

22 vingt-deux	**23 vingt-trois**	**24 vingt-quatre**	**25 vingt-cinq**, etc.
32 trente-deux	**33 trente-trois**	**34 trente-quatre**	**35 trente-cinq**, etc.

C3 ANSWERS

A. 1. J'ai une fille qui travaille à Évry.
2. C'est un nouveau directeur que je n'aime pas.
3. Allez chercher les verres qui sont sur la table.
4. Nous avons des amis qui habitent Paris.
5. Voici un restaurant qui est très sympathique.
6. Pluie, nuages : c'est le temps que je déteste !
7. C'est un repas froid que vous préparez ?

B. 1. Ce qui est dans ce musée est très moderne.
2. Elle prépare ce que nous allons manger.
3. Nous écoutons ce qu'explique le journaliste.
4. Apporte ce qu'il y a sur la table, s'il te plaît.

C. 1. C'est un vin que j'achète souvent.
2. Anne et Pierre sont des voisins que nous rencontrons parfois.
3. Ce sont des amis qu'Antoine n'aime pas.
4. Écoutez ce qu'explique cette femme.
5. Ils/Elles regardent les enfants qui jouent devant l'immeuble.

C4 **LES NOMBRES ORDINAUX** ●●
ORDINAL NUMBERS

premier (masc.), **première** (fem.)	1er	*first*
deuxième / second(e)	2^e	*second*
troisième	3^e	*third*
quatrième	4^e	*fourth*
cinquième	5^e	*fifth*
sixième	6^e	*sixth*
septième	7^e	*seventh*
huitième	8^e	*eighth*
neuvième	9^e	*ninth*
dixième	10^e	*tenth*

and so on... But for *21st, 31st, 41st,* etc., the French equivalents are :
vingt et unième, trente et unième, quarante et unième...

● Note that **x** in **sixième, dixième** is pronounced *z*.

93

A1 PRESENTATION

■ Grammar

- The demonstrative pronoun agrees in gender with the noun it refers to:
  masc. sg.: **celui**   fem. sg.: **celle**

  With **ci** added to the pronoun, it is the equivalent of: *this one.*
  masc. sg.: **celui-ci**   fem. sg.: **celle-ci**   *this one.*

  With **là** added to the pronoun it is the equivalent of: *that one.*
  masc. sg.: **celui-là**   fem. sg.: **celle-là**   *that one.*

  Ex.: **Est-ce que tu utilises un ordinateur ? — Oui, celui-ci.**
  Are you using a computer? — Yes, this one.

  Est-ce que vous avez une voiture ? — Oui, c'est celle-ci.
  Have you got a car? — Yes, it is this one.

■ Vocabulary

traverser	*to cross*
tourner	*to turn*
bureau de poste (masc.), **poste** (fem.)	→ *post office*
aéroport (masc.)	*airport*
rapide	*fast*
juste	*just*
en face	*opposite*

A2 EXAMPLES *(This one or that one?)*

1. **Où est la rue de la Gare ? Est-ce que c'est celle-ci ?**
2. **Non, ce n'est pas celle-ci.**
3. **C'est celle qui traverse le boulevard.**
4. **C'est celle qui est juste après la poste.**
5. **Celle-là ?**
6. **Oui, celle-là. Tournez là.**
7. **Est-ce qu'il y a des bus qui vont à la gare ?**
   Est-ce que celui-ci y va ?
8. **Celui-ci, non. Celui-ci va à l'aéroport.**
9. **Celui qui est en face va à la gare.**
10. **Celui-là ?**
11. **Oui, celui-là.**
12. **Celui-là est très rapide.**

94

A3   COMMENTS

■ Grammar

- The demonstrative pronoun can be followed by a relative (see lesson 14); in that case **ci** and **là** are omitted. Ex.:

Utilises-tu un ordinateur ? — Oui, celui qui est dans le bureau.
Are you using a computer? — Yes, the one that is in the office.

Avez-vous une voiture ? — Oui, celle qui est en face.
Have you got a car? — Yes, the one which is opposite.

- Note that in **celui-ci, non** *(this one doesn't)*, **non** is used to avoid repeating the complete negative form, here **n'y va pas**.

  In **celui-ci, oui** *(this one does)*, **oui** is used to avoid repeating the complete statement, here **y va**.

- Pay attention to the order of the words in:
  bureau de poste = *post office.*

  In French the noun which is determined by another noun comes first; they are linked by the preposition **de**:
  une station de métro = *a tube station.*
  une pièce de théâtre = *a theatre play.*

→ Don't forget the preposition **de**.

A4   TRANSLATION

1. Where is Station Road? Is it this one?
2. No, it isn't this one.
3. It is the one that crosses the boulevard.
4. It is the one that is just after the post office.
5. That one?
6. Yes, that one. Turn there.
7. Are there buses that go to the station?
   Does this one go there?
8. This one doesn't. This one goes to the airport.
9. The one opposite goes to the station.
10. That one?
11. Yes, that one.
12. That one is very fast.

B1 PRESENTATION

■ Grammar

- The demonstrative pronoun agrees in number with the noun it refers to :
  masc. pl. : **ceux**   fem. pl. : **celles**
— With **ci** added to the pronoun, it is the equivalent of : *these (ones)*.
  masc. pl. : **ceux-ci**   fem. pl. : **celles-ci**   *these (ones)*.
— With **là** added to the pronoun it is the equivalent of : *those (ones)*.
  masc. pl. : **ceux-là**   fem. pl. : **celles-là**   *those (ones)*.

Ex. : **Est-ce que tu utilises des ordinateurs ? — Oui, ceux-ci.**
  Are you using computers ? — Yes, these (ones).
  Est-ce que vous avez des cartes postales ? — Oui, celles-ci.
  Have you got postcards ? — Yes, these (ones).

■ Vocabulary

essayer	*to try /*	**champion** (masc.)	*champion*
	to try on	**short** (masc.)	*a pair of*
jeter un ⎤	*to have*		*shorts*
coup d'œil à ⟶	*a look at*	**tee-shirt** (masc.)	*tee-shirt*
lunettes (fem. pl.)	*glasses*	**léger**	*light*
sport (masc.)	*sport*	**autre**	*other*
rayure (fem.)	*stripe*	**pas mal**	*nice*
		comme	*like*

B2 EXAMPLES *(Sportswear)*

1. **Avez-vous des lunettes de soleil comme celles-ci ?**
2. **Non, mais essayez celles-là, elles sont très légères.**
3. **Elles sont trop petites, je vais essayer celles que vous avez en vitrine.**
4. **Avez-vous d'autres chaussures de sport ? Celles-là ne sont pas confortables.**
5. **Jetez un coup d'œil à celles qui sont là.**
6. **Celles-là ?**
7. **Oui, celles qui ont des rayures bleues.**
8. **Ce sont celles que les champions utilisent !**
9. **Ce short est trop court, je vais essayer un de ceux-là.**
10. **Je vais aussi essayer des tee-shirts ; ceux-ci ne sont pas mal.**
11. **Celui-là est trop cher !**
12. **Jetez un coup d'œil à ceux-là.**

B3   COMMENTS

■ Pronunciation

• The pronunciation of **ayer** in **essayer** : is **é** followed by the sound of *y* in *yes* followed by **é**.

• Note the grave accent in the feminine form of the adjectives :
> **léger   légère**
>
> **cher   chère**

■ Vocabulary

• Note that :
> **sport**
>
> **champion**
>
> **tee-shirt**

are the same in French and English.

• *Shorts* is used in the singular in French : **un short**.

More is said about this in C4.

B4   TRANSLATION

1. Have you got sunglasses like these?
2. No, but try those on, they are very light.
3. They are too small, I am going to try on those you have in the window.
4. Have you got any other sports shoes? Those aren't comfortable.
5. Have a look at those there.
6. Those?
7. Yes, those that have got blue stripes.
8. They are the ones the champions use!
9. These shorts are too short, I am going to try on a pair of those.
10. I am going to try on tee-shirts too; these are nice.
11. That one is too expensive!
12. Have a look at those.

C1 EXERCISES

A. ●● **Replace the words in italics by** <u>celui</u>, <u>celle</u>, <u>ceux</u> or <u>celles</u>:

1. J'aime bien *la montre* qui est en vitrine.
2. Il emporte *le sac* qui est sur la chaise.
3. Allons regarder *les tableaux* qui sont au premier étage.
3. Combien coûte *l'ordinateur* que vous utilisez ?
4. C'est *l'appartement* qui est à louer ?
5. Écoute *les chansons* qu'elle chante.

B. Write the adjective in the correct form:

1. Une valise (léger).
2. Des étudiantes (étranger).
3. Des pays (étranger).
4. La (premier) chanson.
5. Des chaussures (cher).

C. ●● Translate into French:

1. This book isn't very interesting. That one is.
2. That exercise is easy, this one isn't.
3. Have you got any other sunglasses? These are too expensive.

C2 COUP DE FOUDRE / *LOVE AT FIRST SIGHT*

- The word **coup** is used in many expressions in French; here are some:

coup de soleil	*sunburn*
coup de pied	*kick*
coup de poing	*blow (with the fist)*
coup de feu	*shot*
coup de vent	*gust of wind*
coup de fil (téléphone)	*telephone call*
tout à coup	*all of a sudden*
du premier coup	*on the first try*

- **Un dicton : « Faire d'une pierre deux coups. »** (literally : *"Hit twice with one stone."*)
  A saying: "To kill two birds with one stone."

C3 ANSWERS

A. 1. J'aime bien celle qui est en vitrine.
2. Il emporte celui qui est sur la chaise.
3. Allons regarder ceux qui sont au premier étage.
4. Combien coûte celui que vous utilisez ?
5. C'est celui qui est à louer ?
6. Écoute celles qu'elle chante.

B. 1. Une valise légère.
2. Des étudiantes étrangères.
3. Des pays étrangers.
4. La première chanson.
5. Des chaussures chères.

C. 1. Ce livre n'est pas très intéressant. Celui-là, oui.
2. Cet exercice est facile. Celui-ci, non.
3. Est-ce que vous avez d'autres lunettes de soleil ? Celles-ci sont trop chères.

C4 IN FRENCH MANY WORDS CONNECTED WITH SPORTS ARE BORROWED FROM ENGLISH

basketball
football
hockey
rugby
tennis
volleyball

16   Quelle valise emportons-nous ?

A1   PRESENTATION

▪ Grammar

- The French interrogative adjective is **quel** *(which, what)*.
  Its form depends on the gender and number of the noun concerned:

masc. sg.	**quel**	fem. sg.	**quelle**
masc. pl.	**quels**	fem. pl.	**quelles**

Quel livre regardes-tu ?	*Which book are you looking at?*
Quels livres regardes-tu ?	*Which books are you looking at?*
Quelle photo préfères-tu ?	*Which photo do you prefer?*
Quelles photos préfères-tu ?	*Which photos do you prefer?*

▪ Vocabulary

emporter	*to take (away)*
porter	*to wear*
manteau (masc.)	*coat*
voyage (masc.)	*journey, trip*
or (masc.)	*gold*
livre de poche (masc.)	*paperback*
étagère (fem.)	*shelf*
quart (masc.)	*quarter*
marron	*brown*

A2   EXAMPLES *(Packing)*

1. **Quelle valise emportons-nous ?**
2. **La grande valise noire.**
3. **Quel manteau est-ce que tu vas emporter ?**
4. **Le neuf.**
5. **Quelle montre ?**
6. **La montre en or.**
7. **Quelles chaussures vas-tu porter pour le voyage ?**
8. **Les marron ; elles sont très confortables.**
9. **Quels livres préfères-tu emporter ?**
10. **Les livres de poche qui sont sur l'étagère.**
11. **À quelle heure va-t-on arriver ?**
12. **À neuf heures moins le quart.**

A3 COMMENTS

■ Grammar

- One of the most frequent ways of answering a question with **quel** is to use the definite article **le, la** or **les** plus a noun and adjective(s); note that, very often, the noun is understood.

  Ex.: **Le neuf.**   *The new one.*
        Les marron.   *The brown ones.*

- Remember that **marron** (literally: *chestnut*), though it is used as an adjective, is invariable.

- Remember the two meanings of **porter**:

                        to carry:
  Il porte les valises.   *He is carrying the suitcases.*

                        to wear:
  Il porte un manteau gris.   *He is wearing a grey coat.*

- Note that in a question where the verb is inverted, **t** is introduced between the verb and the pronouns: **il, elle** or **on**, if the verb ends with a vowel.

  → À quelle heure
  | **va-t-on arriver ?**
  | **va-t-il arriver ?**
  | **va-t-elle arriver ?**

A4 TRANSLATION

1. Which suitcase shall we take?
2. The big black suitcase.
3. Which coat are you going to take?
4. The new one.
5. Which watch?
6. The gold watch.
7. Which shoes are you going to wear for the journey?
8. The brown ones; they are very comfortable.
9. Which books do you prefer to take?
10. The paperbacks that are on the shelf.
11. What time will we arrive?
12. At quarter to nine.

B1   PRESENTATION

■ Grammar

● The interrogative pronoun corresponding to **quel** is **lequel**, it also agrees in gender and number with the noun it refers to:

masc. sg.	**lequel**	fem. sg.	**laquelle**	*which one*
masc. pl.	**lesquels**	fem. pl.	**lesquelles**	*which ones*

(Note the resemblance with the definite articles. See lesson 11.)

Regarde ces livres ! Lequel/lesquels préfères-tu ?
Look at these books! Which one/ones do you prefer?

Voici les photos ! Laquelle/lesquelles préfères-tu ?
Here are the photos! Which one/ones do you prefer?

■ Vocabulary

désirer	*to want, to desire*
représenter	*to represent*
dictionnaire (masc.)	*dictionary*
couverture (fem.)	*cover*
carte de vœux (fem.)	*greeting card*
à gauche	*on the left*
à gauche de	*to the left of*
à droite	*on the right*
à droite de	*to the right of*

B2   EXAMPLES *(At the bookshop)*

1. **Avez-vous de nouveaux livres ? Lesquels ?**
2. **Ceux qui sont dans la vitrine.**
3. **Lequel désirez-vous regarder ?**
4. **Celui qui est à gauche sur l'étagère.**
5. **Lequel ? Celui-ci ou celui-là ?**
6. **Celui qui est à droite des dictionnaires.**
7. **Celui qui a une couverture rouge.**
8. **Laquelle ? Celle qui représente un coucher de soleil ?**
9. **Oui, celle-là.**
10. **J'ai de nouvelles cartes de vœux. Lesquelles préférez-vous ?**
11. **Celles que vous avez dans la main.**
12. **Ce sont celles que je préfère.**

B3 COMMENTS

■ Pronunciation

● The nearest equivalent to **œu** in **vœux** is *e* in *open* with lips slightly rounded. The same sound is found in:

nœud (masc.)	*knot*
œufs (masc. pl.)	*eggs*

But in

œuf (masc. sg.)	*egg*
bœuf (masc.)	*beef*
sœur (fem.)	*sister*

it is pronounced like *ur* in *hurt*.

■ Grammar

● **la main**: note that in French, nouns referring to parts of the body or clothes are generally preceded by a definite article and <u>not</u> a possessive adjective.

Ex.: **Il a un livre à la main.**
He's got a book in his hand.
Il a une baguette sous le bras.
He's got a 'baguette' under his arm.
Il a les mains dans les poches.
He's got his hands in his pockets.

B4 TRANSLATION

1. Have you got any new books? Which ones?
2. Those that are in the shopwindow.
3. Which one do you want to look at?
4. The one that is on the left, on the shelf.
5. Which one? This one or that one?
6. The one that is to the right of the dictionaries.
7. The one that has got a red cover.
8. Which one? The one with a sunset on it?
9. Yes, that one.
10. I have got new greeting cards. Which ones do you prefer?
11. Those you have in your hand.
12. They are the ones I prefer.

C1   EXERCISES

A. Choose between quel, quelle, quels, quelles:

1. ... magazine est-ce que tu emportes ?
2. ... écrivains français préférez-vous ?
3. ... amies allons-nous inviter lundi ?
4. ... examen prépares-tu ?
5. ... carte allez-vous utiliser ?
6. ... chaussures aime-t-elle ?
7. ... disques est-ce que tu vas acheter ?
8. ... chanson préfère-t-il ?

B. In the preceding exercise replace the interrogative adjective and noun by the corresponding pronoun.

> Ex.: Quel magazine... ? Lequel ... ?

C. ●● Translate into French:

1. The children are wearing yellow raincoats.
2. Anne is carrying a child in her arms.
3. Which car are you going to buy?
4. The red one.
5. Which one?
6. That one.

C2   EN... / MADE OF...

en or	*gold*
en argent	*silver*
en fer	*iron*
en bois	*wood*
en plastique	*plastic*
en verre	*glass*
en laine	*wool*
en coton	*cotton*
en cuir	*leather*

→ Remember that **en** can sometimes be replaced by **de**.

Ex.: **une robe en coton / une robe de coton,** *a cotton dress.*

But the preposition <u>cannot</u> be omitted.

C3 ANSWERS

A. 1. Quel magazine est-ce que tu emportes ?
2. Quels écrivains français préférez-vous ?
3. Quelles amies allons-nous inviter lundi ?
4. Quel examen prépares-tu ?
5. Quelle carte allez-vous utiliser ?
6. Quelles chaussures aime-t-elle ?
7. Quels disques est-ce que tu vas acheter ?
8. Quelle chanson préfère-t-il ?

B. 1. Lequel est-ce que tu emportes ?
2. Lesquels préférez-vous ?
3. Lesquelles allons-nous inviter lundi ?
4. Lequel prépares-tu ?
5. Laquelle allez-vous utiliser ?
6. Lesquelles aime-t-elle ?
7. Lesquels est-ce que tu vas acheter ?
8. Laquelle préfère-t-il ?

C. 1. Les enfants portent des imperméables jaunes.
2. Anne porte un enfant dans les bras.
3. Quelle voiture vas-tu (allez-vous) acheter ?
4. La rouge.
5. Laquelle ?
6. Celle-là.

C4 QUELLE HEURE EST-IL ? ●●
WHAT TIME IS IT?

7 o'clock *It's seven (o'clock).* **Il est sept heures.** (Note : **heures** can't be omitted.)	7.15 *It is (a) quarter past seven.* **Il est sept heures et quart.** (Literally : *it is seven hours and quarter.*)
7.30 *It's half past seven.* **Il est sept heures et demie.** (Literally : *it is seven hours and half.*)	7.45 *It's (a) quarter to eight.* **Il est huit heures moins le quart.** (Literally : *it is eight hours less the quarter.*)
8.10 *It's ten past eight.* **Il est huit heures dix.** (Literally : *it is eight hours ten.*)	8.40 *It's twenty to nine.* **Il est neuf heures moins vingt.** (Literally : *it is nine hours less twenty.*)

Note : hours first, then minutes.

A1 PRESENTATION

■ Grammar

- The partitive construction.
  It requires **de** + the appropriate singular definite article:
  — before a feminine noun: **de la, de l'**
  — before a masculine noun: **du** (which is a contracted form of: **de le**); **de l'** (if the noun starts with a vowel or **h**)

  — In the plural, there is only one possibility for both masculine and feminine nouns: **des**

■ Vocabulary

faire	*to make, to do*
beurre (masc.)	*butter*
légume (masc.)	*vegetable*
viande (fem.)	*meat*
fromage (masc.)	*cheese*
cigarette (fem.)	*cigarette*
argent (masc.)	*money*
fruit (masc.)	*fruit*
lait (masc.)	*milk*
crème (fem.)	*custard*
sucre (masc.)	*sugar*
eau (fem.) **(minérale)**	*(mineral) water*

A2 EXAMPLES *(Making a shopping list)*

1. Il y a du beurre ?
2. Est-ce qu'il y a de la salade ?
3. Y a-t-il des légumes ?
4. Je vais acheter de la viande.
5. Achète du pain et du fromage.
6. Achète des cigarettes aussi.
7. N'oublie pas d'acheter des cigarettes.
8. Est-ce que tu as de l'argent ?
9. Est-ce que nous avons des fruits ?
10. Achète du lait, je vais faire de la crème anglaise.
11. Je vais aussi acheter du sucre.
12. Est-ce qu'on a de l'eau minérale ?

A3 COMMENTS

■ Grammar

- Whether as the equivalents of *some* or *any*, or without any English equivalent, **du, de la, des** can't be omitted in a French partitive construction.

    Ex.: **Est-ce que j'achète aussi du sucre ?** *Do I buy sugar too ?*

- In French, **fruit** can be singular or plural: **un fruit, des fruits**.

■ Pronunciation

- **acheter / achète,** *to buy / buy*
    Notice the **è** in: **j'achète**
    tu achètes
    il/elle achète
    ils/elles achètent
    achète !

    Remember: **è** is pronounced like *e* in *pet*.

    But in: **(nous) achetons**
    (vous) achetez

    the **e** is glided over.

A4 TRANSLATION

1. Is there any butter?
2. Is there any salad?
3. Are there any vegetables?
4. I'm going to buy some meat.
5. Buy some bread and some cheese.
6. Buy some cigarettes too.
7. Don't forget to buy cigarettes.
8. Have you got some money?
9. Do we have any fruit?
10. Buy some milk, I'm going to make custard.
11. I'm going to buy sugar too.
12. Have we got any mineral water?

B1 PRESENTATION

■ Grammar

- In the negative, the partitive construction changes:

  — **du, de la, des** become **de**.
    Ex.: **Il n'y a pas de salade / il n'y a pas de lait / il n'y a pas de légumes.**
    There is no salad / there is no milk / there are no vegetables.

  — **de l', des** (when followed by a vowel or **h**) become **d'**.
    Ex.: **Il n'y a pas d'eau minérale / ils n'ont pas d'enfants.**
    There is no mineral water / they have no children.

■ Vocabulary

changer	*to change*
faire beau	*to be fine*
autoroute (fem.)	*motorway* (US: *freeway*)
neige (fem.)	*snow*
brouillard (masc.)	*fog*
soleil (masc.)	*sun*
parapluie (masc.)	*umbrella*
ciel (masc.)	*sky*
vent (masc.)	*wind*
étoile (fem.)	*star*
ruisseau (masc.)	*brook*

B2 EXAMPLES *(The weather)*

1. **Il y a de la neige sur l'autoroute.**
2. **Il n'y a pas de neige en ville.**
3. **Elle est sous la pluie et elle n'a pas d'imperméable !**
4. **Il n'y a pas de brouillard en ville.**
5. **On a de la chance, il n'y a pas de brouillard aujourd'hui.**
6. **Est-ce qu'on va avoir du soleil ou de la pluie dimanche ?**
7. **Il n'y a pas de nuages, il va faire beau.**
8. **On n'a pas de chance : le temps va changer.**
9. **Il n'y a pas d'étoiles.**
10. **Nous n'avons pas de parapluie.**
11. **Il n'y a pas d'eau dans le ruisseau ; il est sec.**
12. **Le ciel est rouge ; il n'y a pas de vent ; il va faire beau demain.**

B3 COMMENTS

■ Grammar

• **faire,** *to do, to make,* is an irregular verb.

Present tense:

je	**fais**	*I*		*do*	*make*
tu	**fais**	*you*		*do*	*make*
il, elle, on	**fait**	*he, she, it*		*does*	*makes*
nous	**faisons***	*we*		*do*	*make*
vous	**faites**	*you*		*do*	*make*
ils, elles	**font**	*they*		*do*	*make*

■ Pronunciation

• * Note that **faisons** is pronounced **fesons**.

• Remember:
  — **ei (neige)** has the sound of **è**.
  — **ui (fruit, pluie, ruisseau, parapluie)** is the sound of **u** quickly followed by the sound of **i**.

→ Note that **faire** conveys both the meaning of *to do* and *to make*.

B4 TRANSLATION

1. There is snow on the motorway.
2. There isn't any snow in town.
3. She is out in the rain and she hasn't got a raincoat!
4. There is no fog in town.
5. We are lucky, there is no fog today.
6. Are we going to have sun or rain on Sunday?
7. There aren't any clouds, it's going to be fine.
8. We are unlucky: the weather is going to change.
9. There aren't any stars.
10. We haven't got an umbrella.
11. There is no water in the brook; it is dry.
12. The sky is red; there's no wind; it will be fine tomorrow.

C1 EXERCISES

A. Swap the word in brackets with the word given at the end. Make the necessary changes:

1. Nous n'avons pas d'(ordinateur) — secrétaire.
2. Vous mangez de la (salade) — fruits.
3. Il n'y a pas de (vent) — neige.
4. Ils achètent du (vin) — viande.
5. On n'a pas de (chance) — argent.
6. Est-ce que tu as du (sucre) — lait ?

B. ●● Turn into the negative:

1. J'ai du sucre.
2. Nous avons des enfants.
3. Ils achètent des livres.
4. Il y a de l'eau sur la table.
5. Il a de la chance.

C. ●● Translate into French:

1. Have you got any money?
2. They haven't got a car.
3. I'm going to buy some bread.
4. Do you eat fruit?

C2 LE TEMPS / THE WEATHER ●●

- **faire** is used in many impersonal expressions to speak of the weather: **il fait**, here, is the equivalent of *it is*:

il fait froid	*it is cold*
il fait chaud	*it is hot*
il fait bon	*it is warm*
il fait beau	*it is fine*
il fait mauvais	*the weather is bad*
il fait soleil	*it is sunny*
il fait sec	*it is dry*
il fait jour	*it is daylight*
il fait nuit	*it is dark*

- Some common expressions about the weather refer to animals.
    Ex.: **Un temps de chien** *(dog)*, **un froid de canard** *(duck)*.
    But: *it's raining cats and dogs*, **il tombe des cordes** (literally: *ropes are falling*).

C3 ANSWERS

A. 1. Nous n'avons pas de secrétaire.
2. Vous mangez des fruits.
3. Il n'y a pas de neige.
4. Ils achètent de la viande.
5. On n'a pas d'argent.
6. Est-ce que tu as du lait ?

B. 1. Je n'ai pas de sucre.
2. Nous n'avons pas d'enfants.
3. Ils n'achètent pas de livres.
4. Il n'y a pas d'eau sur la table.
5. Il n'a pas de chance.

C. 1. Avez-vous de l'argent ?
2. Ils n'ont pas de voiture.
3. Je vais acheter du pain.
4. Mangez-vous des fruits ?

C4 SAISONS ET FÊTES ●●
SEASONS AND FEAST DAYS

printemps (masc.)	*spring*	
été (masc.)	*summer*	
automne (masc.)	*autumn*	
hiver (masc.)	*winter*	
Pâques	*Easter*	
Noël	*Christmas*	
Jour de l'An	*New Year's Day*	

- Note : **en été** *in summer*
  en automne *in autumn*
  en hiver *in winter*
  But : **au printemps** *in spring*

- Remember that when the names of the seasons are used as·subject or direct object the article cannot be omitted.

  Ex.: **L'automne est parfois sec.** *Autumn is sometimes dry.*
  J'aime l'été. *I like summer.*

A1   PRESENTATION

■ Grammar

* To ask a question about either a number or a quantity, the interrogative word is the same in French : **Combien de/d'**, *How many/How much.*

  Ex.:   **Combien de chats avez-vous ?**
  How many cats have you got?
  Combien d'argent avez-vous ?
  How much money have you got?

— For a large number **beaucoup de/d'** followed by a plural is the equivalent of *a lot of, many.*

— For a small number **peu de/d'** followed by a plural is the equivalent of *few.*

— For a small number **quelques** followed by a plural is the equivalent of *a few.*

■ Vocabulary

entrer	*to go in, to enter*	**billet** (masc.)	*ticket*
crier	*to shout*	**millier** (masc.)	*thousand*
joueur (masc.)	*player*	**quelqu'un**	*somebody/*
équipe (fem.)	*team*		*anybody*
stade (masc.)	*stadium*	**personne**	*nobody*
personne (fem.)	*person*	**plusieurs**	*several*
match (masc.)	*match (*US: *game)*	**déjà**	*already*

A2   EXAMPLES *(Before a football match)*

1. **Combien y a-t-il de joueurs dans une équipe de football ?**
2. **Combien de joueurs y a-t-il dans une équipe de football ?**
   Onze.
3. **Y a-t-il quelqu'un dans le stade ?**
4. **Non, il n'y a personne.**
5. **Combien de personnes vont regarder le match ?**
6. **Beaucoup de gens vont regarder le match.**
7. **Combien de personnes vont aller à ce match ?**
8. **Plusieurs milliers de personnes vont aller à ce match.**
9. **Peu de gens ont déjà des billets.**
10. **Il y a pas mal de personnes qui chantent.**
11. **Quelques personnes crient.**
12. **Il y a beaucoup de voitures près du stade.**

A3 COMMENTS

■ Grammar

- **Combien y a-t-il de joueurs ? / Combien de joueurs y a-t-il ?**
  How many players are there?
  Note that the question can be asked in two different ways.

- Remember that **personne** is a feminine noun but can also be an invariable indefinite word meaning *nobody*.

  Ex.: **Quelques personnes regardent le match.**
  A few people are watching the match.

  Personne ne regarde le match.
  Nobody is watching the match.

→ Note that **personne** *(nobody)* is always used with **ne**.

- Note that **déjà** is placed after the verb.
  Ex.: **Ils préparent déjà le repas.**
  They are already preparing the meal.

  Nous avons déjà un chat, un chien et des oiseaux, ça suffit !
  We already have a cat, a dog and birds, that's enough!

A4 TRANSLATION

1. How many players are there on a football team?
2. How many players are there on a football team? Eleven.
3. Is there anybody in the stadium?
4. No, there's nobody.
5. How many people are going to watch the match?
6. A lot of people are going to watch the match.
7. How many people are going to go to this match?
8. Several thousand people are going to go to this match.
9. Few people already have tickets.
10. There are quite a lot of people who are singing.
11. A few people are shouting.
12. There are many cars near the stadium.

B1 PRESENTATION

■ Grammar

- To express the notion of quantity with non-countable nouns:
- For a large quantity: **beaucoup de/d'** followed by a singular is the equivalent of *a lot of, much*.
- For a small quantity: **peu de/d', un peu de/d'** followed by a singular are the equivalents of *little, a little*.
- For a small quantity: **quelque** followed by a singular is the equivalent of *some*.
- A subjective judgment about a number or a quantity will be expressed by:

trop de/d'	*too many, too much*
assez de/d'	*enough*
pas assez de/d'	*not enough*

■ Vocabulary

sembler	*to seem*	**bizarre**	*odd*
imagination (fem.)	*imagination*	**assez**	*enough*
humour (masc.)	*humour*	**pas mal**	*quite a lot*
talent (masc.)	*talent*		
travail (masc.)	*work*		
patience (fem.)	*patience*		

B2 EXAMPLES *(At the fortune-teller's)*

1. Vous semblez avoir assez d'imagination.
2. Vous avez beaucoup d'humour.
3. Mais vous semblez un peu triste.
4. Dans peu de temps vous allez rencontrer quelqu'un.
5. Cette personne a beaucoup de talent.
6. Elle a peu d'argent.
7. Elle semble être un peu bizarre.
8. Vous allez rester quelque temps ensemble.
9. Combien de temps ? Peu de temps.
10. Vous allez avoir pas mal de travail et beaucoup d'argent.
11. Vous allez avoir beaucoup de chance.
12. Ayez un peu de patience !

B3 COMMENTS

Grammar

- Note that **sembler** can be followed by:
  - an infinitive
    - Ex.: **Cet étudiant semble avoir beaucoup de travail.**
      This student seems to have a lot of work.
  - an adjective
    - Ex.: **Cet étudiant semble très sympathique.**
      This student seems very nice.

- **pas mal** is a colloquial expression meaning *quite a lot, quite enough.*
  - Ex.: **Il y a pas mal de gens ce soir.**
    There are quite a lot of people tonight.

    J'ai pas mal de travail à faire aujourd'hui.
    I have quite a lot of work to do today.

- Remember that **combien de temps ?** is the equivalent of *how long?*
  - Ex.: **Combien de temps est-ce que le match va durer* ?**
    How long is the match going to last?

* **durer** : *to last.*

B4 TRANSLATION

1. You seem to have enough imagination.
2. You have a good sense of humour.
3. But you seem a little sad.
4. In a short while you are going to meet someone.
5. This person has a lot of talent.
6. He/she has little money.
7. He/she seems a bit odd.
8. You are going to stay together for a while.
9. How long? A short while.
10. You are going to have quite a lot of work and a lot of money.
11. You are going to be very lucky.
12. Have a little patience!

115

C1 EXERCISES

A. Ask the question in another way:

1. Combien y a-t-il d'appartements dans cet immeuble ?
2. Combien y a-t-il d'ordinateurs dans ce bureau ?
3. Combien d'aéroports y a-t-il à Paris ?
4. Combien y a-t-il de livres sur l'étagère ?

B. ●● Find the questions using __combien de__ :

1. J'ai trois enfants.
2. Ils vont emporter deux valises.
3. Nous invitons six personnes.
4. Il y a des milliers d'étoiles dans le ciel !
5. Elle va chanter plusieurs chansons.
6. Il y a pas mal de personnes dans le stade.

C. ●● Translate into French:

1. How long is he going to stay here? He is going to stay here a few days.
2. A lot of children play here on Wednesdays.
3. Many people are on strike today.
4. How long is the film going to last?
5. This person seems to have little work.

C2   ●● 10, 12, 15, 20... 1 000 000 000

dizaine (fem.)	*ten*
douzaine (fem.)	*dozen*
quinzaine (fem.)	*fifteen*
vingtaine (fem.)	*a score*
cinquantaine (fem.)	*fifty*
centaine (fem.)	*hundred*
millier (masc.)	*thousand*
million (masc.)	*million*
milliard (masc.)	*milliard* (US: *billion*)

C3 ANSWERS

A. 1. Combien d'appartements y a-t-il dans cet immeuble ?
2. Combien d'ordinateurs y a-t-il dans ce bureau ?
3. Combien y a-t-il d'aéroports à Paris ?
4. Combien de livres y a-t-il sur l'étagère ?

B. 1. Combien d'enfants avez-vous ?
Combien avez-vous d'enfants ?
2. Combien de valises vont-ils emporter ?
Combien vont-ils emporter de valises ?
3. Combien de personnes invitons-nous ?
Combien invitons-nous de personnes ?
4. Combien y a-t-il d'étoiles dans le ciel ?
Combien d'étoiles y a-t-il dans le ciel ?
5. Combien de chansons va-t-elle chanter ?
Combien va-t-elle chanter de chansons ?
6. Combien y a-t-il de personnes dans le stade ?
Combien de personnes y a-t-il dans le stade ?

C. 1. Combien de temps va-t-il rester ici ? Il va rester ici quelques jours.
2. Beaucoup d'enfants jouent ici le mercredi.
3. Beaucoup de gens sont en grève aujourd'hui.
4. Combien de temps va durer le film ?
5. Cette personne semble avoir peu de travail.

C4 MESURES / *MEASURES*

- Here are some commonly used measures of weight:
    gramme (g) (masc.)
    kilogramme (kg) (masc.)
    tonne (t) (fem.)

➡️ Note that for half a kilo, the word **livre** (fem.) is used. Ex.:

Combien pèse ce paquet ? *How much does this parcel weigh?*
Ce paquet pèse trois kilos. *This parcel weighs three kilos.*
Achète une livre de cerises. *Buy a pound of cherries.*

- For liquids, **litre (l)** (masc.) and **demi-litre** (masc.) are the most commonly used expressions:
    Ex.: **Il y a deux litres de lait sur l'étagère.**
    There are two litres of milk on the shelf.

117

A1 PRESENTATION

■ Grammar

- The comparative is formed by adding:
    + **plus... que** *-er... than, more... than*
    = **aussi... que** *as... as*
    − **moins... que** *less... than*

  on either side of the adjective (whatever the length of the adjective).

  Ex.: **Pierre est plus jeune que Louis.**
  Pierre is younger than Louis.
  Louis est plus sympathique que Pierre.
  Louis is nicer than Pierre.

- The superlative is formed by placing:
    le, la, les plus... *the most*
    le, la, les moins... *the least*

  before the adjective.

  The article agrees in gender and number with the noun:

  Ex.: **Ces voitures sont les moins chères.**
  These cars are the least expensive.

■ Vocabulary

groupe (masc.)	*group*	**journal** (masc.)	*newspaper*
train (masc.)	*train*	**monde** (masc.)	*world*
moto (fem.)	*motorcycle*	**ville** (fem.)	*town*
église (fem.)	*church*		

A2 EXAMPLES *(Comparing)*

1. **Je suis plus jeune que Mme Lenoir.**
2. **Tu es le plus sympathique du groupe.**
3. **Un avion est plus rapide qu'un train.**
4. **Un livre est plus cher qu'un journal.**
5. **Il est aussi grand qu'Antoine.**
6. **Une grosse moto est aussi chère qu'une voiture.**
7. **M. Martin n'est pas aussi intelligent que Mme Martin.**
8. **Une église est plus petite qu'une cathédrale.**
9. **Une rue est moins large qu'un boulevard.**
10. **C'est la rue la plus large de la ville.**
11. **Paris n'est pas aussi grand que Londres.**
12. **Paris n'est pas la plus grande ville du monde.**

A3   COMMENTS

■ Grammar

- Note that **que** becomes **qu'** before a vowel or **h**.
  - Ex.: **Anne est plus jolie qu'Hélène.**
    - *Anne is prettier than Hélène.*
    - **Hélène est plus grande qu'Anne.**
    - *Hélène is taller than Anne.*

- Note that after a superlative, the complement is introduced by **de** or the contracted form **du**.
  - Ex.: **Le plus grand immeuble de la ville.**
    - *The tallest building in town.*
    - **La plus belle fille du monde.**
    - *The most beautiful girl in the world.*

- The names of towns and cities are either masculine or feminine. Here are some feminine ones:
  - **Athènes** *(Athens)*, **Marseille, Rome, Venise** *(Venice).*

- Remember that adjectives agree in gender and number with the noun they refer to.
  - Ex.: **La plus belle maison. Les plus belles maisons.**
    - *The most beautiful house. The most beautiful houses.*

■ Pronunciation

- Note the **è** in **chère**, feminine of **cher**.

- Note that in **ville**, **-ille** is pronounced **il**.

A4   TRANSLATION

1. I'm younger than Mrs. Lenoir.
2. You are the nicest of the group.
3. A plane is faster than a train.
4. A book is more expensive than a newspaper.
5. He is as tall as Antoine.
6. A big motorcycle is as expensive as a car.
7. Mr. Martin isn't as intelligent as Mrs. Martin.
8. A church is smaller than a cathedral.
9. A street is less broad than a boulevard.
10. It is the widest street in town.
11. Paris is not as large as London.
12. Paris is not the largest city in the world.

B1 PRESENTATION

■ Grammar

- Most adverbs are also used in comparisons.
  Most adverbs are formed by adding **ment** to the feminine adjective. They are invariable. Ex.:

masculine singular	feminine singular	adverb
lent *(slow)*	**lente**	**lentement** *(slowly)*
rapide *(quick)*	**rapide**	**rapidement** *(quickly)*

- They are usually placed after the verb they modify.

  Ex.: **Elle parle bizarrement.**
  She speaks strangely.
  Vous ne marchez pas rapidement.
  You don't walk quickly.

■ Vocabulary

vélo (masc.)	*bike*
bateau (masc.)	*boat*
doucement	*softly*
rapidement	*quickly*
rarement	*rarely*
lentement	*slowly*

B2 EXAMPLES *(More comparisons)*

1. **Elle parle doucement.**
2. **Parle plus lentement, s'il te plaît.**
3. **Il marche rapidement.**
4. **Tu marches plus rapidement qu'Anne.**
5. **Vous voyagez plus rarement que Pierre.**
6. **Vous n'habitez pas aussi loin que Pierre.**
7. **Un bateau ne va pas aussi vite qu'un avion.**
8. **Il danse aussi bien que Philippe.**
9. **Un vélo ne va pas aussi vite qu'une moto.**
10. **Tu vas en Angleterre moins souvent qu'en Italie.**
11. **Nous allons au théâtre aussi souvent que possible.**
12. **Nous allons au théâtre le plus souvent possible.**

B3 COMMENTS

■ Grammar

• Not all adverbs end in **ment**, especially adverbs of:

— time:	**souvent**	*often*
	maintenant	*now*
	parfois	*sometimes*
— place:	**ici**	*here*
	loin	*far*
and of course:	**bien**	*well*

■ Vocabulary

• **doucement / lentement:** when referring to motion, you can often use one or the other without changing the meaning. In that case, **doucement** means *slowly*.

Ex.: **Elle avance doucement** (or **lentement**).
She's walking slowly.

• In colloquial French, words of three syllables or more which are often used in everyday life are shortened to their first two syllables.

Ex.: **photo(graphie), moto(cyclette),
vélo(cipède), auto(mobile).**

■ Pronunciation

• Note that in **rapid(e)ment, rar(e)ment, lent(e)ment, douc(e)ment**, the **e** is glided over.

B4 TRANSLATION

1. She speaks softly.
2. Speak more slowly, please.
3. He walks quickly.
4. You walk more quickly than Anne.
5. You travel more rarely than Pierre.
6. You don't live as far away as Pierre.
7. A boat doesn't go as fast as a plane.
8. He dances as well as Philippe.
9. A bike doesn't go as fast as a motorcycle.
10. You go to England less often than to Italy.
11. We go to the theatre as often as possible.
12. We go to the theatre as often as possible.

C1   EXERCISES

A. Compare using the adjective in brackets:

1. un avion	(rapide)	un vélo
2. Pierre	(intelligent)	Louis
3. Anne	(gentille)	Hélène
4. M. Martin	(célèbre)	Picasso
5. Des magazines	(chers)	des livres
6. Paris	(grand)	Londres

B. Put the adverb in the comparative (mind the sign in brackets):

1. Il voyage (souvent) Pierre. (–)
2. Tu danses (bien) Louis ! (–)
3. Vous habitez (loin) Mme Martin. (=)
4. Une voiture va (lentement) un avion. (+)
5. Nous n'allons pas (vite) Anne. (=)

C. Answer by <u>vrai</u> *(right)* or <u>faux</u> *(wrong)*:

1. Un boulevard est plus large qu'une rue.
2. Un bateau est aussi rapide qu'un avion.
3. Une cathédrale est moins grande qu'une église.
6. Rome est la plus grande ville d'Europe.

C2   IRREGULAR COMPARATIVES AND SUPERLATIVES

- **bon** *(good):*
  meilleur (masc. sg.) ⎤ **que**   **meilleure** (fem. sg.) ⎤ **que**
  meilleurs (masc. pl.) ⎦   **meilleures** (fem. pl.) ⎦
  = *better than...*
  le, la, les meilleur(e)(s) = *the best...*

- **bien** *(well):*
  mieux que = *better... than*
  le mieux = *the best*

- **mauvais** *(bad):*
  pire que = *worse than* (both masc. and fem.)
  le pire = *the worst...*

- **mal** *(badly):*
  pire que = *worse than...*
  le pire = *the worst*

C3   ANSWERS

A. 1. Un avion est plus rapide qu'un vélo.
    2. Pierre est plus intelligent que Louis.
    3. Anne est aussi gentille qu'Hélène.
    4. M. Martin est moins célèbre que Picasso.
    5. Des magazines sont moins chers que des livres.
    6. Paris est moins grand que Londres.

B. 1. Il voyage moins souvent que Pierre.
    2. Tu danses moins bien que Louis !
    3. Vous habitez aussi loin que Mme Martin.
    4. Une voiture va plus lentement qu'un avion.
    5. Nous n'allons pas aussi vite qu'Anne.

C. 1. **vrai** / *right.*
    2. **faux** / *wrong.*
    3. **faux** / *wrong.*
    4. **faux** / *wrong.*

C4   USEFUL ADVERBS

certainement	*certainly*
bien sûr	*of course*
heureusement	*fortunately*
justement	*precisely*
malheureusement	*unfortunately*
sûrement	*surely*
vraiment*	*really*

* Notice the absence of **e**. When the masculine adjective ends with a vowel, **ment** is added directly to the adjective.

A1 PRESENTATION

■ Grammar

- Remember the two interrogative forms:
  — Manges-tu ?
  — Est-ce que tu manges ?

- To ask a question about the object, use **que** or **qu'** placed just before the interrogative form.

  Ex.: **Que manges-tu ? / Qu'est-ce que tu manges ?**
  What are your eating?
  Qu'apportez-vous ? / Qu'est-ce que vous apportez ?
  What are you bringing?

■ Vocabulary

regarder	*to watch*
penser	*to think*
télévision (fem.)	*television*
feuilleton (masc.)	*serial, series*
chaîne (fem.)	*channel*
émission (fem.)	*broadcast (*US: *show)*

A2 EXAMPLES *(Television)*

1. Qu'est-ce qu'il y a à la télévision aujourd'hui ?
2. Qu'est-ce que tu regardes d'habitude ?
3. Que préférez-vous ?
4. Que regardez-vous l'après-midi ?
5. Qu'est-ce que vous pensez des feuilletons américains ?
6. Que pensez-vous de l'émission ?
7. Qu'est-ce qu'il y a sur la première chaîne ?
8. Qu'allons-nous regarder maintenant ?
9. Qu'est-ce que nous allons regarder ?
10. Qu'est-ce que vous aimez ?
11. Qu'est-ce que vous aimez le mieux ?
12. Que vont-ils faire après l'émission ?

A3 COMMENTS

■ Grammar

- Though both forms are equivalent, **qu'est-ce que** is more often used in colloquial French.
  Notice that the words run together: **qu'est-ce que tu manges ?**

- Note that **la première chaîne** *(channel 1)* literally means *the first channel* (it is the same for channel 2, 3, 4...).

  premier agrees with the noun it accompanies.
  - Ex.: **Le premier jour ; les premiers jours.**
    The first day ; the first days.
    La première heure ; les premières heures.
    The first hour ; the first hours.

→   Don't forget the grave accent in the feminine.

■ Pronunciation

- **ion** (in **télévision, émission**) is pronounced like *ee* + *y* + the nasal vowel **on**.

- Remember the liaison between the final consonant of a word and the initial vowel of the following word:

  Qu'est-ce que nous allons regarder ?
           z

  Qu'est-ce que vous aimez ?   **Que vont-ils faire ?**
         z   **t**

A4 TRANSLATION

1. What's on television today?
2. What do you usually watch?
3. What do you prefer?
4. What do you watch in the afternoon?
5. What do you think of American serials?
6. What do you think of the broadcast?
7. What's on channel 1?
8. What are we going to watch now?
9. What are we going to watch?
10. What do you like?
11. What do you like most?
12. What are they going to do after the show?

B1 PRESENTATION

■ Grammar

- When used with a preposition, **que** becomes **quoi**.
  The preposition always precedes **quoi**.
  Ex.: **Avec quoi travailles-tu ?** *What are you working with?*
  À quoi penses-tu ? *What are you thinking about?*
  Pour quoi faire ? *What for?*

- **quoi** is also found in **pourquoi**, the French equivalent of *why*. The answer to a question with **pourquoi** usually starts with **parce que**.
  Ex.: **Pourquoi manges-tu ?** **— Parce que j'ai faim.**
  Why do you eat? *Because I am hungry.*

■ Vocabulary

rêver	*to dream*
marcher	*to walk*
faire une promenade	*to go for a walk, a ride*
campagne (fem.)	*country, countryside*
nature (fem.)	*nature*
animal (masc.), pl.: **animaux**	*animal*
promenade (fem.)	*walk, ride*
marche (fem.)	*walking*
politique (fem.)	*politics*
musique (fem.)	*music*
n'importe quoi	*anything*
par exemple	*for instance*

B2 EXAMPLES *(Why and why not...)*

1. À quoi pensez-vous ?
2. De quoi rêvez-vous ?
3. De quoi ? D'une maison à la campagne.
4. Pourquoi préférez-vous la campagne ?
5. Parce que j'aime la nature.
6. Pourquoi a-t-elle un chien ?
7. Parce qu'elle aime les animaux.
8. Pourquoi n'allez-vous pas faire une promenade après manger ?
9. Pourquoi n'allez-vous pas faire une promenade à vélo ?
10. Parce que nous aimons la marche.
11. De quoi parlez-vous quand vous marchez ?
12. De n'importe quoi, de sport, de politique, de musique par exemple.

B3 COMMENTS

■ Grammar

- In a negative question with the verb inverted, **ne... pas** is placed on either side of the group verb-pronoun.

  Ex.: **N'allez-vous pas faire une promenade ?**
  Aren't you going for a walk?

  In a negative question with **est-ce que, ne... pas** is on either side of the verb.

  Ex.: **Est-ce que vous n'allez pas faire une promenade ?**
  Aren't you going for a walk?

- Note that the French equivalent of a gerund is often either a substantive:

  Ex.: **la marche**   *walking*
      la peinture   *painting*

  or an infinitive (after a preposition).

  Ex.: **après manger**   *after eating*
      sans parler   *without speaking*

- With **parler de**, when the complement is a general concept, the article is omitted. Ex.:

  parler de musique, parler de cinéma, parler de théâtre, parler de sport : *to talk about music, ... films, ... theatre, ... sports.*

■ Pronunciation

- Note that the nearest English equivalent sound to **quoi** is *qua* in *quality*.

B4 TRANSLATION

1. What are you thinking about?
2. What are you dreaming of?
3. Of what? Of a house in the country.
4. Why do you prefer the country?
5. Because I love nature.
6. Why has she got a dog?
7. Because she loves animals.
8. Why don't you go for a walk after eating?
9. Why don't you go for a bike ride?
10. Because we like walking.
11. What do you talk about while walking?
12. Anything, sports, politics, music for instance.

C1 EXERCISES

A. Choose between: que / qu'est-ce que / qu'est-ce qu':

1. ... chantes-tu ?
2. ... vous regardez ?
3. ... visitons-nous aujourd'hui ?
4. ... préparent-elles ?

5. ... elle a ?
6. ... c'est ?
7. ... il aime ?

B. ●● Use que and qu'est-ce que to form questions as in the example:
Il mange une tarte : Qu'est-ce qu'il mange ? / Que mange-t-il ?

1. Elles achètent des livres.
2. Il utilise un ordinateur.
3. Elle regarde un film.
4. Elle porte une grosse valise.
5. Ils vont apporter le vin.
6. Il va faire une photo.

C. Match the questions and answers:

Q.
1. Pourquoi invites-tu les voisins ?
2. Pourquoi habitez-vous ici ?
3. Pourquoi est-ce que tu achètes un croissant ?
4. Pourquoi va-t-elle souvent à Nice ?
5. Pourquoi a-t-il beaucoup de travail ?
6. Pourquoi est-ce qu'il y a beaucoup de monde sur le quai ?

A.
7. Parce qu'il est médecin.
8. Parce qu'ils sont sympathiques.
9. Parce que c'est près de la gare.
10. Parce que le train va partir.
11. Parce que j'ai faim.
12. Parce qu'elle a des parents à Nice.

C2 THESE VERBS ARE TRANSITIVE IN FRENCH

regarder	*to look at*
chercher	*to look for*
attendre	*to wait for*
écouter	*to listen to*
demander	*to ask for*

C3 ANSWERS

A.
1. Que chantes-tu ?
2. Qu'est-ce que vous regardez ?
3. Que visitons-nous aujourd'hui ?
4. Que préparent-elles ?
5. Qu'est-ce qu'elle a ?
6. Qu'est-ce que c'est ?
7. Qu'est-ce qu'il aime ?

B.
1. Qu'est-ce qu'elles achètent ? / Qu'achètent-elles ?
2. Qu'est-ce qu'il utilise ? / Qu'utilise-t-il ?
3. Qu'est-ce qu'elle regarde ? / Que regarde-t-elle ?
4. Qu'est-ce qu'elle porte ? / Que porte-t-elle ?
5. Qu'est-ce qu'ils vont apporter ? / Que vont-ils apporter ?
6. Qu'est-ce qu'il va faire ? / Que va-t-il faire ?

C.
1. Pourquoi invites-tu les voisins ? → 8. Parce qu'ils sont sympathiques.
2. Pourquoi habitez-vous ici ? → 9. Parce que c'est près de la gare.
3. Pourquoi est-ce que tu achètes un croissant ? → 11. Parce que j'ai faim.
4. Pourquoi va-t-elle souvent à Nice ? → 12. Parce qu'elle a des parents à Nice.
5. Pourquoi a-t-il beaucoup de travail ? → 7. Parce qu'il est médecin.
6. Pourquoi est-ce qu'il y a beaucoup de monde sur le quai ? → 10. Parce que le train va partir.

C4 N'IMPORTE QUOI ●●
ANYTHING

The meaning of *any* can be conveyed by the expression **n'importe...**

n'importe où	*anywhere*
n'importe comment*	*anyhow*
n'importe qui	*anybody/anyone*
n'importe quoi	*anything*
n'importe quand	*any time*

* Note that **n'importe comment** often means *carelessly*.

A1   PRESENTATION

■ Grammar

- To ask a question about a person, **qui** is the word to use. It may be used as subject.

  Ex.: **Qui est là ?**   *Who is there?*

  Qui est-ce ?   *Who is it?*

  Qui est-ce qui commence ?   *Who starts?*

- Here note **qui est-ce qui...** when the question is asked with **est-ce**.

■ Vocabulary

gouverner	*to govern*
nommer	*to name*
faire un discours	*to make a speech*
voter	*to vote*
président (masc.)	*president*
république (fem.)	*republic*
ministre (masc.)	*minister*
candidat (masc.)	*candidate*
élection (fem.)	*election*
affiche (fem.)	*poster*
prochain	*next*

A2   EXAMPLES *(Government)*

1. **Qui gouverne ce pays ?**
2. **Qui est le président de la République ?**
3. **Qui va nommer les ministres ?**
4. **Qui est-ce qui va nommer les ministres ?**
5. **Qui va être Premier ministre ?**
6. **Qui est-ce qui va voter pour le président ?**
7. **Qui est-ce qui est candidat ?**
8. **Qui est candidat aux prochaines élections ?**
9. **Qui parle aux journalistes ?**
10. **Qui va faire un discours ce soir ?**
11. **Qui est sur l'affiche ?**
12. **Qui vote pour ce candidat ?**

A3 COMMENTS

■ Grammar

- Note that **qui** remains the same even when preceding a vowel or **h**.
  Ex.: **Qui est là ?**
  Qui apporte les affiches ?

- **élection** is generally used in the plural **(les élections)** unless it is followed by a complement.
  Ex.: **L'élection de l'Assemblée.**
  The election of the Assembly.

- Remember that **aller** followed by a verb in the infinitive conveys either an intention or the immediate future.
  Ex.: **Qui va nommer les ministres ?**
  Who is going to name the ministers?
  Qui va être le Premier ministre ?
  Who is going to be Prime Minister?

■ Pronunciation

- **tion** (ex.: **élection**) is pronounced **sion** unless it is preceded by **s** as in **question** *(question)*, in which case the **t** is pronounced **t**.

A4 TRANSLATION

1. Who governs this country?
2. Who is the President of the Republic?
3. Who is going to name the ministers?
4. Who is going to name the ministers?
5. Who is going to be Prime Minister?
6. Who is going to vote for the President?
7. Who is a candidate?
8. Who is a candidate for the next election?
9. Who is speaking to the journalists?
10. Who is going to make a speech tonight?
11. Who is on the poster?
12. Who votes for this candidate?

B1   PRESENTATION

■ Grammar

- **qui** may also be used as a direct object. Ex.:

Qui cherchent-ils ?	*Who are they looking for?*
Qui est-ce que tu préfères ?	*Who(m) do you prefer?*

  Here, note the **que**.

- Or with a preposition. Ex.:

Avec qui parlez-vous ?	*Who are you talking with?*
Pour qui travaille-t-il ?	*Who does he work for?*
À qui apporte-t-elle les photos ?	*Who(m) is she bringing the photos to?*

■ Vocabulary

donner	*to give*
discuter	*to discuss*
avoir confiance	*to trust*
faire confiance	
compter sur	*to rely on*
régler	*to settle*
document (masc.)	*document*
affaire (fem.)	*case, matter*
mission (fem.)	*mission*
actuellement	*presently*
d'autre	*else*

B2   EXAMPLES *(A special mission)*

1. À qui téléphones-tu ?
2. À qui vas-tu donner ce document ?
3. Pour qui fais-tu ça ?
4. Pour qui est-ce que tu travailles actuellement ?
5. Pour qui travaille cet homme ?
6. Avec qui discutez-vous de cette affaire ?
7. Avec qui est-ce que vous discutez de cette affaire ?
8. En qui ont-ils confiance ?
9. À qui fais-tu confiance ?
10. À qui penses-tu pour la prochaine mission ?
11. À qui d'autre est-ce que tu penses ?
12. Sur qui comptez-vous pour régler cette affaire ?

B3 COMMENTS

■ Grammar

- Note that in questions about the indirect object, the preposition must be placed at the beginning. Ex.:

À qui penses-tu ?	*Who are you thinking of?*
Avec qui déjeunez-vous ?	*Who are you having lunch with?*
Pour qui travaille-t-il ?	*Who does he work for?*
Sur qui comptez-vous ?	*Who do you rely on?*

- Note that **compter** and **compter sur** have very different meanings.

compter	*to count*
compter sur	*to rely on*

- Note two expressions whose meanings are close:

  faire confiance <u>à</u>

  avoir confiance <u>en</u>

  Ex.: Il fait confiance **à** M. Lenoir.
  Il a confiance **en** M. Lenoir. } → *He trusts Mr. Lenoir.*

B4 TRANSLATION

1. Who are you phoning?
2. Who are you going to give this document to?
3. Who are you doing that for?
4. Who are you working for now?
5. Who is this man working for?
6. Who do you discuss this matter with?
7. Who do you discuss this matter with?
8. Who do they trust?
9. Who do you trust?
10. Who are you thinking of for the next mission?
11. Who else are you thinking of?
12. Who do you rely on to settle this matter?

C1 EXERCISES

A. ●● Change the question as in the example:
Qui chante ? / Qui est-ce qui chante ?

1. Qui habite ici ?
2. Qui écoute l'émission ?
3. Qui regarde la télévision ?
4. Qui apporte le vin ?

**B. Find the questions about the words in capital letters. Ex.:
Elle va parler AUX ÉTUDIANTS. À qui va-t-elle parler ?**

1. Ils vont parler AUX ÉLECTEURS.
2. Il prépare ce repas pour LES ENFANTS.
3. Nous voyageons avec NOS AMIS.
4. C'est la voiture DE MA FILLE.
5. Elle regarde PIERRE.
6. Je pense à VOUS.

C. Choose between qui and que:

1. Qui est-ce ... sonne ?
2. Qui est-ce ... les journalistes regardent ?
3. Qui est-ce ... tu écoutes ?
4. Qui est-ce ... va apporter les documents ?

C2 LA VIE POLITIQUE / *POLITICAL LIFE*

campagne électorale (fem.)	*election campaign*
droit de vote (masc.)	*right to vote*
voix (fem.)	*vote*
majorité (fem.)	*majority*
parti politique (masc.)	*political party*
syndicat (masc.)	*trade union*
gouvernement (masc.)	*government*
député (masc.)	*member of Parliament (US: Congress)*
roi (masc.)	*king*
reine (fem.)	*queen*
monarchie (fem.)	*monarchy*
démocratie (fem.)	*democracy*

C3 ANSWERS

A. 1. Qui est-ce qui habite ici ?
2. Qui est-ce qui écoute l'émission ?
3. Qui est-ce qui regarde la télévision ?
4. Qui est-ce qui apporte le vin ?

B. 1. À qui vont-ils parler ?
2. Pour qui prépare-t-il ce repas ?
3. Avec qui voyagez-vous ? / Avec qui voyageons-nous ?
4. À qui est la voiture ?
5. Qui regarde-t-elle ?
6. À qui pensez-vous ? / À qui penses-tu ?

C. 1. Qui est-ce qui sonne ?
2. Qui est-ce que les journalistes regardent ?
3. Qui est-ce que tu écoutes ?
4. Qui est-ce qui va apporter les documents ?

C4 ÉLECTEUR (masc.), ÉLECTRICE (fem.) / *VOTER*

- For some nouns denoting masculine persons, the ending **teur** (directeur, électeur) changes into **trice** in the feminine (**directrice, électrice**). Here are some examples:

masculine	feminine	
acteur	**actrice**	*actor, actress*
admirateur	**admiratrice**	*admirer*
auditeur	**auditrice**	*listener*
(**les auditeurs,** *the audience*)		
collaborateur	**collaboratrice**	*colleague*
conducteur	**conductrice**	*driver*
instituteur	**institutrice**	*teacher (primary school)*
spectateur	**spectatrice**	*spectator*
But:		
chanteur	**chanteuse**	*singer*

A1   PRESENTATION

■ Grammar : Possession.

- There is no form corresponding to 's in French.
    Ex.:   **La voiture de Pierre.**   *Peter's car.*
          Le sac de la secrétaire.   *The secretary's bag.*
    The form used is comparable to « the car of Peter », « the bag of
    the secretary ».

- **à qui** is the equivalent of *whose* as well as *to whom.*
    Note the construction when asking about the possessor :
    À qui est la voiture ?   *Whose car is it?*
                                  (literally : *to whom is the car?)*
    À qui sont ces vêtements ?   *Whose clothes are they?*

■ Vocabulary

P.-D.G. (Président-Directeur général) (masc.)
President and Managing Director (US : CEO, Chief Executive Officer)

employé (masc.), **employée** (fem.)	*employee*
parking (masc.)	*car park (US : parking lot)*
stylo (masc.)	*pen*
calculatrice (fem.)	*calculator*
bureau (masc.)	*desk*
dossier (masc.)	*file*
comptable (masc. and fem.)	*accountant*
salle de conférences (fem.)	*conference room*

A2   EXAMPLES *(At the office)*

1. **À qui est cette grosse voiture ? C'est la voiture du P.-D.G.**
2. **Les voitures des employés sont sur le parking.**
3. **À qui est ce stylo ? C'est le stylo de M. Lenoir.**
4. **Il est à M. Lenoir.**
5. **À qui sont ces lunettes ? Elles sont à M. Lenoir.**
6. **Ce sont les lunettes de M. Lenoir.**
7. **Est-ce que c'est la calculatrice de la secrétaire, là, sur le bureau ?**
8. **Non, c'est la calculatrice de Pierre.**
9. **Elle est à Pierre.**
10. **Le dossier « Martin » est sur le bureau de la secrétaire.**
11. **Regarde le nouvel ordinateur du comptable.**
12. **Voici la salle de conférences, elle est à côté du bureau du P.-D.G.**

A3 COMMENTS

■ Grammar

- **être à** is commonly used to answer a question starting with **à qui**.
  - Ex. : **À qui est ce livre ?** *Whose book is it?*
  - **Il est à Pierre.** *It is Peter's.*

- **du** is the contracted form of: **de le** *(of the)*.
la voiture du directeur	*the manager's car*
le bureau du président	*the president's office*
la fille du patron	*the boss's daughter*

- **des** is the contracted form of **de les**
les livres des enfants	*the children's books*
le travail des secrétaires	*the secretaries' work*

- Similarly, **à le** is contracted in **au**
  à les **aux**
Je vais au cinéma.	*I'm going to the pictures/the movies.*
Il est au bureau.	*He's at the office.*
Elle parle aux étudiants.	*She's talking to the students.*

- Note that **nouvel** is a form of the adjective **nouveau** when it precedes a masculine noun starting with a vowel or **h**.
  un nouvel ordinateur, un nouvel album, le Nouvel An.
  a new computer, a new album, the New Year.

A4 TRANSLATION

1. Who does this big car belong to? It is the Managing Director's car.
2. The employees' cars are in the car park.
3. Whose pen is this? It is Mr. Lenoir's pen.
4. It is Mr. Lenoir's. (It belongs to Mr. Lenoir.)
5. Whose glasses are these? They are Mr. Lenoir's.
6. They are Mr. Lenoir's glasses.
7. Is that the secretary's calculator there, on the desk?
8. No, it is Peter's calculator.
9. It is Peter's.
10. The « Martin » file is on the secretary's desk.
11. Look at the accountant's new computer.
12. Here is the conference room, it is next to the Managing Director's office.

B1 PRESENTATION

■ Grammar

● Possessive adjectives.

The French possessive adjectives agree in gender and number with the nouns they accompany:

masc. sg.	fem. sg.	masc. & fem. pl.	
mon	ma	mes	*my*
ton	ta	tes	*your*
son	sa	ses	*his, her, its*
notre	notre	nos	*our*
votre	votre	vos	*your*
leur	leur	leurs	*their*

■ Vocabulary

posséder	*to own*	**sud** (masc.)	*south*
venir	*to come*	**oncle** (masc.)	*uncle*
passer	*to spend*	**cousin** (masc.)	*cousin*
famille (fem.)	*family*	**entreprise** (fem.)	*firm*
père (masc.)	*father*	**affaires** (fem. pl.)	*business*
mère (fem.)	*mother*	**à l'étranger**	*abroad*

B2 EXAMPLES *(Family)*

1. Est-ce que vos parents habitent ici ?
2. Est-ce que votre famille habite près de Paris ?
3. Non, notre famille vient du sud de la France.
4. Mon père et ma mère possèdent une grande maison dans le Midi.
5. Mon oncle Pierre travaille à l'étranger, en Italie.
6. Il ne vient pas souvent voir ses enfants.
7. Mes cousins vont parfois voir leur père.
8. Sa maison est près de Rome.
9. Son entreprise est dans le centre ville.
10. Ses affaires marchent bien.
11. Ses fils vont aller travailler là-bas.
12. Nos enfants vont passer les vacances avec leur oncle à Rome cet été.

B3 COMMENTS

■ Grammar

- Note that the feminine singular possessives **ma, ta, sa** when preceding a vowel or **h** change into **mon, ton, son**.
    - Ex.: **mon amie, ton élection, son affiche, son histoire** *his/her story.* (**amie, élection, affiche, histoire** are feminine nouns.)

- **Venir** *(to come)* is an irregular verb:

Present tense			
je	**viens***	*I*	*come*
tu	**viens**	*you*	*come*
il, elle	**vient**	*he, she, it*	*comes*
nous	**venons**	*we*	*come*
vous	**venez**	*you*	*come*
ils, elles	**viennent**	*they*	*come*

- Note the change of accent in **posséder**.
  Je possède, tu possèdes, il/elle possède
  nous possédons, vous possédez, ils/elles possèdent.

- Note the particular meaning of **marcher,** *to walk* and *to be successful:* **Ça ne marche pas.** *It doesn't work.*

■ Pronunciation

* Note that **ien** in **viens, vient** or **viennent** is pronounced like *y* in *yes* followed by the sound of *an* in *bang* (see lesson 3, B3).

B4 TRANSLATION

1. Do your parents live here?
2. Does your family live near Paris?
3. No, our family comes from the south of France.
4. My father and mother own a big house in the south.
5. My uncle Pierre works abroad, in Italy.
6. He does not often come to see his children.
7. My cousins sometimes go and see their father.
8. His house is near Rome.
9. His firm is in the centre of town.
10. His business is very successful.
11. His sons are going to work there.
12. Our children are going to spend the holidays with their uncle in Rome this summer.

C1 EXERCISES

A. ●● **Modify as in the example:**
Cette voiture est à Pierre. C'est sa voiture.

1. Ce stylo est à Anne.
2. Ces lunettes sont à Marc.
3. Cette maison est à oncle Louis.
4. Ce chien est aux voisins.
5. Ces vêtements sont à Marie.

B. Fill in the blanks with du, de la, des, au, à la, aux:

1. Anne va ... théâtre samedi.
2. Écoutez le discours ... Premier ministre.
3. Nous regardons une émission ... télévision.
4. Voici la calculatrice ... secrétaire.
5. Ce sont les albums ... enfants.
6. Le président parle ... électeurs.

C. ●● **Translate into French:**

1. My son is working with his manager today.
2. His two children are students.
3. This is her house, it is near her office.
4. Her daughter lives in our flat.
5. My shirt and my shoes are new.
6. They are going to prepare their cases.
7. Our friends are going to travel with their dog.
8. Your friend isn't ready.

C2 NOTE THE USE OF **GRAND** AND **GROS** IN FRENCH

une grande église	*a big church*
une grande rue	*a wide street*
un grand écrivain	*a great writer*
une grande fille	*a tall girl, a big girl*

But:

une grosse voiture	*a big car*
un gros repas	*a big meal*
un gros gâteau	*a big cake*
un gros livre	*a big book*

C3 ANSWERS

A. 1. Ce stylo est à Anne. C'est son stylo.
2. Ces lunettes sont à Marc. Ce sont ses lunettes.
3. Cette maison est à oncle Louis. C'est sa maison.
4. Ce chien est aux voisins. C'est leur chien.
5. Ces vêtements sont à Marie. Ce sont ses vêtements.

B. 1. Anne va au théâtre samedi.
2. Écoutez le discours du Premier ministre.
3. Nous regardons une émission à la télévision.
4. Voici la calculatrice de la secrétaire.
5. Ce sont les albums des enfants.
6. Le président parle aux/des électeurs.

C. 1. Mon fils travaille avec son directeur aujourd'hui.
2. Ses deux enfants sont étudiants.
3. C'est sa maison, elle est près de son bureau.
4. Sa fille habite dans notre appartement.
5. Ma chemise et mes chaussures sont neuves.
6. Ils/elles vont préparer leurs valises.
7. Nos ami(e)s vont voyager avec leur chien.
8. Ton/votre ami(e) n'est pas prêt(e).

C4 **DIRECTIONS** / *DIRECTIONS*

nord / *north*

ouest / *west*   **est** / *east*

sud / *south*

- In **est**, **ouest**, and **sud**, the final consonants are heard.
- Notice the prepositions in some common expressions referring to places:

dans le Nord	*in the north*
dans l'Est	*in the east*
dans l'Ouest	*in the west*
dans le Sud	*in the south*
dans le Midi	*in the south (of France)*

à la mer	*at the seaside*	**en province**	*outside Paris*
à la campagne	*in the country*	**en banlieue**	*in the suburbs*
à la montagne	*in the mountains*	**en ville**	*in town*

A1 PRESENTATION

■ Grammar

- We have seen that the pronoun **on** often means *we*. It is also used to replace an indefinite subject.

  Ex.: **On sonne à la porte.**   *Someone is ringing the doorbell.*
  On n'entend rien.   *One can't hear anything.*
  On vient.   *Someone is coming.*

■ Vocabulary

sonner	*to ring (the doorbell)*
ouvrir	*to open*
appeler	*to call*
répondre	*to answer*
entendre	*to hear*
finir	*to finish*
fermer	*to close / to shut*
porte (fem.)	*door*
bruit (masc.)	*noise*
avant	*before*
ne... rien	*not anything*
ne... jamais	*never*

A2 EXAMPLES *(Calling)*

1. **On sonne ! Va ouvrir la porte, s'il te plaît !**
2. **On appelle M. ou Mme Lenoir !**
3. **On appelle Mlle Lemercier !**
4. **On appelle ; allez répondre, s'il vous plaît.**
5. **On va téléphoner.**
6. **On n'entend rien, il y a trop de bruit !**
7. **On arrive !**
8. **On arrive le 20 mars à cinq heures.**
9. **Trop tard, on ferme !**
10. **On n'a pas assez de temps.**
11. **Téléphonez après neuf heures ; on ne finit jamais avant neuf heures.**
12. **Est-ce qu'on commence bientôt ?**

A3 COMMENTS

■ Grammar

- Remember:
  on impersonal pronoun.
  ont 3rd person plural of **avoir** in the present tense.
  (The pronunciation is the same.)

- Remember that in the negative form, **ne** or **n'** is placed before the verb. Ex.: **On ne regarde pas.**
  On n'appelle pas.
  On n'arrive pas.

- Regular French verbs belong to:
  — the 1st group ending in **er: chanter** (see lesson 4, A3).
  — the 2nd group ending in **ir: finir**.
  — the 3rd group, others: **répondre, voir, ouvrir...**
  Verbs of the same group have the same conjugation.

- Note that **rien** can be used as a subject: then **ne** is placed between **rien** and the verb.
  Ex.: **Rien ne marche.** *Nothing works.*

■ Pronunciation

- Don't forget the liaison when **on** is followed by a vowel or **h**.
  Ex.: **on appelle, on arrive, on habite.**
        n   n   n

A4 TRANSLATION

1. Someone is ringing the doorbell! Go and open the door, please!
2. Someone is calling Mr. or Mrs. Lenoir!
3. Someone is calling Miss Lemercier!
4. The phone is ringing; go and answer it, please.
5. We are going to phone.
6. We can't hear anything*, there is too much noise!
7. We are coming!
8. We are coming on March 20th, at five o'clock.
9. Too late, we are closing!
10. We haven't got enough time.
11. Call after nine; we never finish before nine.
12. Are we going to start soon?

* Note that there is no equivalent of *can* in the French sentence.

143

B1 PRESENTATION

■ Grammar

- **on** is also used to express an indefinite idea.
    Ex.: **on pense que** meaning:
        people think / one thinks / they think / it is thought.

- *That* when linking two sentence units is translated by: **que** or **qu'**.
    Ex.: *I think that the computer is out of order.*
        Je pense que l'ordinateur est en panne.

    que or **qu'** can't be omitted in French.

■ Vocabulary

signaler	*to report*
conduire	*to drive*
améliorer	*to improve*
avoir le droit de	*to be allowed to*
accident (masc.)	*accident*
permis de conduire (masc.)	*driving licence*
embouteillage (masc.)	*traffic jam*
périphérique (masc.)	*ring road*
circulation (fem.)	*traffic*
travaux (masc. pl.)	*road works*
sans	*without*

B2 EXAMPLES *(Road conditions)*

1. **On signale un accident.**
2. **On signale un accident sur l'autoroute.**
3. **On a le droit de conduire à dix-huit ans.**
4. **On n'a pas le droit de conduire avant dix-huit ans.**
5. **On n'a pas le droit de conduire sans permis de conduire.**
6. **On signale des embouteillages sur le périphérique.**
7. **On signale des embouteillages en ville.**
8. **On n'aime pas rester dans les embouteillages.**
9. **On pense que les travaux vont finir bientôt.**
10. **On pense qu'on va améliorer la circulation en ville.**
11. **Est-ce qu'on va utiliser des ordinateurs ?**
12. **Oui, on pense que les ordinateurs vont améliorer la circulation.**

B3 COMMENTS

■ Grammar

• Present tense of the verbs:

2nd group, ex.: **finir**				3rd group, ex.: **entendre**			
je	finis	*I*	*finish*	j'	entends	*I*	*hear*
tu	finis	*you*	*finish*	tu	entends	*you*	*hear*
il, elle	finit	*he, she, it finishes*		il, elle	entend	*he, she, it hears*	
nous	finissons	*we*	*finish*	nous	entendons	*we*	*hear*
vous	finissez	*you*	*finish*	vous	entendez	*you*	*hear*
ils, elles	finissent	*they*	*finish*	ils, elles	entendent	*they*	*hear*

• Note that in French there is no article before the noun which follows **sans**.

Ex.: **sans permis de conduire** *without a driving licence*

• **on** can mean *we* (see lesson 4, B1).

• **on** often corresponds to the passive voice in English.

Ex.: **On signale un accident.**
An accident has been reported.

■ Pronunciation

• **ss** between two vowels is pronounced like *s* in *sun*.

Ex.: **finissez, finissons, finissent.**

B4 TRANSLATION

1. An accident has been reported.
2. An accident on the motorway has been reported.
3. You are allowed to drive at eighteen.
4. You are not allowed to drive before eighteen.
5. People are not allowed to drive without a licence.
6. Traffic jams are reported on the ring road.
7. Traffic jams are reported in town.
8. People don't like staying in traffic jams.
9. They think the road works are going to be finished soon.
10. They think they are going to improve the traffic in town.
11. Are they going to use computers?
12. Yes, it is thought that the computers will improve the traffic.

C1 EXERCISES

A. <u>on</u> / <u>ont</u>: choose the right one:

1. Ici, ... parle anglais.
2. Ils ... deux enfants.
3. Pierre et Marie ... un appartement près d'ici.
4. ... appelle la secrétaire.
5. Elles ... des valises neuves.
6. ... ne travaille pas le dimanche.

B. Use the correct form of the verb <u>finir</u>:

1. Elles ... la bouteille de vin.
2. On ... à neuf heures.
3. ... vous la tarte ?
4. Nous ... le repas.
5. Je ... les valises.

C. ●● Translate into French:

1. People think Europe is very important.
2. We think the museum is going to open at three.
3. Someone is calling in the street.
4. We are going to leave together on Thursday.
5. You are not allowed to drive at 90 kph in town.

C2 LE 1er MAI / LE 8 MAI
MAY 1ST / MAY 8TH

- To express the date in French, the ordinal number is used for the first day of the month, the cardinal for the other days.
    Ex.: **le 1er janvier, le 1er mai, le 1er août.**
    le premier janvier, le premier mai, le premier août.

    le 14 juillet, le 11 novembre, le 25 décembre.
    le quatorze juillet, le onze novembre, le vingt-cinq décembre.

- Note that: **Nous sommes le...** is the usual way to say the date. In colloquial French; **On est le...** is the usual form.
    Ex.: **Nous sommes le mardi 30 juin.**
    On est le mardi 30 juin.
    Today is Tuesday, June 30th.

C3 ANSWERS

A. 1. Ici, on parle anglais.
2. Ils ont deux enfants.
3. Pierre et Marie ont un appartement près d'ici.
4. On appelle la secrétaire.
5. Elles ont des valises neuves.
6. On ne travaille pas le dimanche.

B. 1. Elles finissent la bouteille de vin.
2. On finit à neuf heures.
3. Finissez-vous la tarte ?
4. Nous finissons le repas.
5. Je finis les valises.

C. 1. On pense que l'Europe est très importante.
2. On pense que le musée va ouvrir à trois heures.
3. On appelle dans la rue.
4. On va partir ensemble jeudi.
5. On n'a pas le droit de conduire à 90 km/h en ville.

C4 NUMÉROS DE TÉLÉPHONE
PHONE NUMBERS

- In France, phone numbers are said as follows:

42	17	19	30
quarante-deux	**dix-sept**	**dix-neuf**	**trente**
(forty two)	*(seventeen)*	*(nineteen)*	*(thirty)*
45	04	26	08
quarante-cinq	**zéro quatre**	**vingt-six**	**zéro huit**
(forty five)	*(o four)*	*(twenty six)*	*(o eight)*

●● A few words and expressions about phone calls:

une cabine	*a phone box (US : booth)*
décrocher	*to lift the receiver*
raccrocher	*to hang up*
composer le numéro	*to dial the number*
c'est occupé !	*the line is engaged! (US : busy)*
ne quittez pas !	*hold on!*

A1   PRESENTATION

■ Grammar

• To refer to a past event, the most commonly used tense is the **passé composé**. It is formed with the present tense of **avoir** and the past participle of the verb (like the present perfect).
  The endings of the past participles are:

é	for all the verbs in	**er**
i	for most verbs in	**ir**
u	for most verbs in	**oir** and **re**

➡ But some verbs are irregular.
  Ex.: **prendre - pris** *(to take - taken).*

■ Vocabulary

prendre	*to take*
louer	*to rent*
vie (fem.)	*life*
plage (fem.)	*beach*
journée (fem.)	*day*
village (masc.)	*village*
cadeau (masc.)	*present*
au bord de la mer	*at the seaside*
dernier	*last*
tout	*all, the whole*
pour	*for*

A2   EXAMPLES *(Touring)*

1. J'ai beaucoup voyagé avec Guy.
2. Nous avons visité l'Espagne et le Portugal.
3. Nous avons pris le train l'été dernier.
4. Vous avez aimé la vie à Lisbonne ?
5. Nous avons loué une maison au bord de la mer.
6. Les enfants ont joué sur la plage toute la journée.
7. Nous avons parlé avec tous les gens du village.
8. Le dernier jour, on a chanté et dansé toute la nuit.
9. Vous avez pris beaucoup de photos ?
10. Oui, et nous avons acheté des cadeaux pour toute la famille.
11. Nous avons fini les vacances dans un hôtel dans le Sud.
12. Mais Guy a oublié une valise à l'hôtel, avec toutes les photos !

A3 COMMENTS

■ Grammar

- The **passé composé** corresponds to the English simple past (preterit) as well as to the English present perfect.

  Ex.: **Il a pris le train à huit heures.**
  He took the train at eight o'clock.
  Il n'a jamais pris le train.
  He has never taken a train.

- **tout** agrees in gender and number with the noun(s) it accompanies:

singular:	**tout / toute**	*all, the whole*
plural:	**tous / toutes**	*all*

Ex.: **tout le village**   *the whole village*
     toute la ville   *the whole city*
     tous les villages   *all the villages*
     toutes les villes   *all the cities*

■ Pronunciation

- In **mer**, **er** is pronounced as in **merci**.

- **village, famille**

  Remember: **ill** is normally pronounced like *y* in *yes*, but in **village** the double **l** is pronounced like an **l**.

A4 TRANSLATION

1. I have travelled a lot with Guy.
2. We have visited Spain and Portugal.
3. We took the train last summer.
4. Did you like life in Lisbon?
5. We rented a house at the seaside.
6. The children played on the beach all day.
7. We talked to all the people in the village.
8. On the last day, we sang and danced all night.
9. Did you take many photos?
10. Yes, and we bought presents for the whole family.
11. We finished the holidays in a hotel in the south.
12. But Guy forgot a case at the hotel, with all the photos!

B1 PRESENTATION

■ Grammar

- The three usual ways of asking a question can be used with the **passé composé** :

1. **Vous avez acheté des cadeaux ?**
2. **Est-ce que vous avez acheté des cadeaux ?** → *Did you buy any gifts?*
3. **Avez-vous acheté des cadeaux ?**

Note that in 3, the auxiliary is inverted, not the verb.

■ Vocabulary

perdre	*to lose*
dire	*to say, to tell*
coin (masc.)	*corner*
objets trouvés (masc. pl.)	*lost property* (literally « found things »)
quelque chose	*something, anything*
autre chose	*something, anything else*
hier	*yesterday*
partout	*everywhere*
à propos de	*about*

B2 EXAMPLES *(Lost property)*

1. **J'ai perdu quelque chose dans le train hier.**
2. **Avez-vous regardé dans tous les coins ?**
3. **Nous avons cherché partout mais nous n'avons rien trouvé.**
4. **Quand avez-vous pris le train ?**
5. **J'ai pris le train lundi soir tard, mais j'ai oublié l'heure exacte.**
6. **Avez-vous téléphoné à la gare ?**
7. **Qu'avez-vous dit ?**
8. **Ils n'ont pas très bien compris.**
9. **Ils ont dit quelque chose à propos des objets trouvés.**
10. **Je n'ai pas bien entendu.**
11. **Est-ce que vous avez dit autre chose ?**
12. **Non, je n'ai pas eu le temps.**

B3 COMMENTS

■ Grammar

- Note the following past participles, they are irregular:
  avoir - eu *(to have - had)* (pronounced like **u** in **tu**)
  dire - dit *(to say - said)*

    Ex.: **J'ai eu dix-huit ans hier.** *I was eighteen yesterday.*
    Il a dit au revoir. *He said good bye.*

- In the negative **ne pas** or **ne rien** are on either side of the auxiliary.
    Ex.: **Nous n'avons pas acheté de cadeaux.**
    We didn't buy any gifts.
    Nous n'avons rien trouvé.
    We didn't find anything.
    Nous n'avons rien acheté.
    We didn't buy anything.
    Ils n'ont rien eu.
    They didn't get anything.

- Note that *every* + singular is usually translated by:
    tous/toutes + **les** + plural

    Ex.: **tous les coins** *every corner*
    tous les jours *every day*
    toutes les semaines *every week*

B4 TRANSLATION

1. I lost something on the train yesterday.
2. Did you look in every corner?
3. We looked everywhere, but we didn't find anything.
4. When did you take the train?
5. I took the train late on Monday night, but I've forgotten the exact time.
6. Have you phoned the station?
7. What did you say?
8. They didn't understand very well.
9. They said something about lost property.
10. I couldn't hear well.
11. Did you say anything else?
12. No, I hadn't time.

C1 EXERCISES

A. Put the verbs in the <u>passé composé</u>:

1. Elle (manger) dans un restaurant grec hier soir.
2. Nous (oublier) les parapluies.
3. Ils (finir) les travaux l'hiver dernier.
4. Les voisins (inviter) des amis.
5. Tu (avoir) peur ?

B. Put in negative, use the negation in brackets:

1. J'ai pris la voiture hier.   (ne... pas)
2. Il a répondu à Pierre.   (ne... rien)
3. Elles ont préparé le repas.   (ne... pas)
4. Nous avons eu le temps.   (ne... pas)
5. Vous avez trouvé.   (ne... rien)

C. ●● Translate into French:

1. I met Mrs. Lenoir on Tuesday.
2. We used the computer yesterday.
3. They started in August.
4. Anne has phoned.
5. He rented the flat last year.

C2 VERBS WITH IRREGULAR PAST PARTICIPLES

avoir	to have	eu	had
boire	to drink	bu	drunk
connaître	to know	connu	known
croire	to believe	cru	believed
dire	to say, to tell	dit	said, told
écrire	to write	écrit	written
être	to be	été	been
faire	to do, to make	fait	done, made
lire	to read	lu	read
mettre	to put	mis	put
ouvrir	to open	ouvert	opened
savoir	to know	su	known
venir	to come	venu	come

C3 ANSWERS

A. 1. Elle a mangé dans un restaurant grec hier soir.
2. Nous avons oublié les parapluies.
3. Ils ont fini les travaux l'hiver dernier.
4. Les voisins ont invité des amis.
5. Tu as eu peur ?

B. 1. Je n'ai pas pris la voiture hier.
2. Il n'a rien répondu à Pierre.
3. Elles n'ont pas préparé le repas.
4. Nous n'avons pas eu le temps.
5. Vous n'avez rien trouvé.

C. 1. J'ai rencontré Mme Lenoir mardi.
2. Nous avons utilisé l'ordinateur hier.
3. Ils/elles ont commencé en août.
4. Anne a téléphoné.
5. Il a loué l'appartement l'année dernière (*or* l'an dernier).

C4 COMMON EXPRESSIONS WITH **DIRE**

c'est-à-dire	*that is to say*
à vrai dire	*to tell the truth*
dis donc ! / dites donc !	*I say!*
j'ai deux mots à vous dire	*I'd like a word with you*
dire que (qu')...	*to think that...*
autrement dit	*in other words*
ça vous dit de + infinitive **?**	*do you feel like...?*
ça ne me dit rien	*I don't feel like it* / *it doesn't remind me of anything*
qu'est-ce que ça veut dire ?	*what does it mean?*

153

A1   PRESENTATION

■ Grammar

- For some verbs, the **passé composé** is formed with **être** (see list in C2).

Il est resté deux heures.	*He stayed for two hours.*
Il est allé à la campagne.	*He has gone to the country.*
Il est parti samedi matin.	*He left saturday morning.*

■ Vocabulary

skier, faire du ski	*to ski*
tomber	*to fall*
devenir	*to become*
repartir	*to go back*
retourner	*to return*
descendre	*to go down*
hôpital (masc.)	*hospital*
piste (fem.)	*trail*
endroit (masc.)	*place*
dangereux	*dangerous*
prudent	*prudent, careful*
tout de suite	*straight away, immediately*

A2   EXAMPLES *(Winter holidays)*

1. **Louis est parti en vacances le mois dernier.**
2. **Il est allé à la montagne.**
3. **Il est arrivé un dimanche.**
4. **Il a fait du ski tout de suite, mais il est allé trop vite et il est tombé.**
5. **Il n'a pas eu de chance, il est resté trois semaines à l'hôpital.**
6. **Il est sorti il y a huit jours, il va très bien.**
7. **Est-ce qu'il est reparti à la montagne ?**
8. **Oui, il est reparti il y a deux jours.**
9. **Est-il allé sur les pistes noires ?**
10. **Non, il n'est pas retourné dans les endroits dangereux.**
11. **Il est descendu lentement.**
12. **Il est devenu prudent.**

A3 COMMENTS

■ Grammar

- **il y a**, here, is the French equivalent of *ago*.
  It is placed before the expression of time.
  Ex.: **Il y a huit jours.**   *A week ago.*
  Il y a un mois.   *A month ago.*

- Note that **huit jours** is often used to mean *a week*. In the same way, **quinze jours** is often used for *two weeks*.

- Adjectives ending in **eux** change into **euse** in the feminine form.
  Ex.: **dangereux / dangereuse**   *dangerous*
  joyeux / joyeuse   *merry*
  heureux / heureuse   *happy*
  délicieux / délicieuse   *delicious*

⟶   But remember : **vieux / vieille**   *old*

- **vieil** is used instead of **vieux** in the singular before a vowel or **h**.

  un vieil ami   **un vieil hôtel**
    y   y
  an old friend   *an old hotel*

⟶   But   **de vieux amis**   **de vieux hôtels**
    z   z
  old friends   *old hotels*

  Don't forget the liaison.

A4 TRANSLATION

1. Louis went on holiday last month.
2. He went to the mountains.
3. He arrived on a Sunday.
4. He went skiing straight away, but he went too fast and he fell.
5. He was unlucky, he stayed three weeks in hospital.
6. He got out a week ago, he is fine.
7. Did he go back to the mountains?
8. Yes, he went back two days ago.
9. Has he been on the black trails?
10. No, he hasn't returned to the dangerous places.
11. He went down slowly.
12. He has become prudent.

B1 PRESENTATION

■ Grammar

- With **être** in the **passé composé**, the past participle agrees in gender and number with the subject.

    Ex.: **Elle est partie.**   *She left.*
    Ils sont tombés.   *They fell.*
    Elles sont arrivées.   *They arrived.*

■ Vocabulary

naître	*to be born*
guerre (fem.)	*war*
bébé (masc.)	*baby*
grands-parents (masc. pl.)	*grandparents*
petite-fille (fem.)	*grand-daughter*
le lendemain (masc.)	*the next day*
juste à temps	*just in time*
longtemps	*a long time*

B2 EXAMPLES *(Birth)*

1. **Marie est née en 1932 ; Philippe est né en 1931.**
2. **Ils sont nés avant la guerre.**
3. **Hélène est née la semaine dernière.**
4. **La mère est partie seule à l'hôpital.**
5. **Le père est arrivé juste à temps.**
6. **Elles sont sorties huit jours après.**
7. **Nous sommes allés voir le bébé hier, il va bien.**
8. **Nous ne sommes pas restés longtemps.**
9. **Des amies sont venues avec des cadeaux.**
10. **Les grands-parents sont venus voir leur petite-fille.**
11. **Ils sont repartis le lendemain matin.**
12. **Ils sont retournés dans le Midi.**

B3 COMMENTS

■ Grammar

● Remember:
the **passé composé** of **être** is formed with **avoir** and the past participle **été**.

Ex.: **J'ai été malade.** *I have been sick.*
Tu as été malade. *You have been sick.*
Il, elle a été malade. *He, she, it has been sick.*

● Dates:
in French dates are said like ordinary numbers.

Ex.: 1931 : **mille neuf cent trente et un** (literally: « thousand nine hundred thirty and one »).
1789 : **mille sept cent quatre-vingt-neuf.**
1900 : **mille neuf cent.**

■ Pronunciation

● In **longtemps**, **g** is not heard.

● Remember:
— **ô** in **hôpital** and **eau** in **cadeaux** are pronounced the same. They are nearly pronounced like *o* in *note*.
— **o** in **sorties** is pronounced like *o* in *not*.

B4 TRANSLATION

1. Marie was born in 1932; Philippe was born in 1931.
2. They were born before the war.
3. Hélène was born last week.
4. The mother left for the hospital alone.
5. The father arrived just in time.
6. They came out a week later.
7. We went to see the baby yesterday; she is fine.
8. We didn't stay long.
9. Friends came with presents.
10. The grandparents came to see their grand-daughter.
11. They went back the next day in the morning.
12. They returned to the south of France.

C1 EXERCISES

A. Match beginnings and ends:

	parties trop tard.
Elles sont	parti hier.
Il est	arrivées la semaine dernière.
Nous sommes	née en 1954.
Elle est	partis tôt.
Ils sont	nés après la guerre.

B. Put the verb in the passé composé:

1. M. Lenoir (repartir) à cinq heures.
2. Est-ce que Mme Lenoir (rester) à Paris ?
3. Ils (aller) sur la plage.
4. Elles (devenir) prudentes.
5. Elle (tomber) dans la rue.

C. Write these dates in full:

1. 1666	3. 1914
2. 1818	4. 1991

C2 VERBS WHOSE **PASSÉ COMPOSÉ** IS FORMED WITH **ÊTRE**

aller	to go
arriver	to arrive
descendre	to go down
devenir	to become
entrer	to enter
monter	to go up
mourir	to die
naître	to be born
partir	to leave
rentrer	to go home, to come back
rester	to stay, to remain
retourner	to return
revenir	to come back
sortir	to go out
tomber	to fall
venir	to come

C3 ANSWERS

A. Elles sont parties trop tard.
Elles sont arrivées la semaine dernière.
Il est parti hier.
Nous sommes partis tôt.
Nous sommes nés après la guerre.
Nous sommes arrivées la semaine dernière.
Nous sommes parties trop tard.
Elle est née en 1954.
Ils sont nés après la guerre.
Ils sont partis tôt.

B. 1. M. Lenoir est reparti à cinq heures.
2. Est-ce que Mme Lenoir est restée à Paris ?
3. Ils sont allés sur la plage.
4. Elles sont devenues prudentes.
5. Elle est tombée dans la rue.

C. 1. 1666 : mille six cent soixante-six.
2. 1818 : mille huit cent dix-huit.
3. 1914 : mille neuf cent quatorze.
4. 1991 : mille neuf cent quatre-vingt-onze.

C4 🔘🔘 THE WORD **TEMPS**
APPEARS IN MANY COMMON EXPRESSIONS

à temps	*in time*
de temps en temps	*from time to time*
dans le temps	*formerly*
en un rien de temps	*in no time*
prendre du bon temps	*to enjoy oneself / to have fun*
c'était le bon temps	*those were the days*
le bon vieux temps	*the good old days*
en temps voulu	*in due time*
perdre du temps	*to waste time*
gagner du temps	*to save time*

A1 PRESENTATION

■ Grammar

- The idea of duration of an action which started in the past is expressed with the **present tense** when the action is still going on. The expression of time is introduced by:

    depuis = il y a... que, cela fait... que.

    Ex.: **J'habite ici depuis 20 ans.**
    = **Il y a 20 ans que j'habite ici.** ⎤→ *I have lived here*
    = **Cela fait 20 ans que j'habite ici.** ⎦ *for 20 years.*

- When the action is finished the **passé composé** is used. The expression of time is introduced by:

    pendant or **durant**

    Ex.: **J'ai habité ici pendant 20 ans.** ⎤→ *I lived here for*
    J'ai habité ici durant 20 ans.   ⎦ *20 years.*

■ Vocabulary

connaître	*to know*
vendre	*to sell*
commerçant (masc.)	*shopkeeper*
client (masc.)	*customer*
appareil ménager (masc.)	*domestic appliance*
téléviseur (masc.)	*television set*

A2 EXAMPLES *(How long...?)*

1. **Depuis combien de temps êtes-vous commerçant ?**
2. **Je suis commerçant depuis longtemps.**
3. **Je connais mes clients depuis longtemps.**
4. **Il y a longtemps que je suis commerçant.**
5. **Il y a des années que je suis commerçant.**
6. **Cela fait des années que je connais mes clients.**
7. **Je vends des appareils ménagers depuis dix-huit ans.**
8. **Il y a dix-huit ans que je vends des appareils ménagers.**
9. **Cela fait dix-huit ans que je vends des appareils ménagers.**
10. **Ça fait trois ans que je ne vends plus de téléviseurs noir et blanc.**
11. **J'ai vendu des téléviseurs noir et blanc pendant quinze ans.**
12. **Il y a trois ans que je ne vends plus de téléviseurs noir et blanc.**

I have been a shopkeeper for a long time.

A3   COMMENTS

■ Grammar

- Remember that in colloquial French **cela** often becomes **ça**.
  - Ex.:   **Ça fait 20 ans que j'habite ici.**
    I have lived here for 20 years.

- Note that with the **passé composé** **pendant** or **durant** can be omitted.
  - Ex.:   **J'ai habité ici 20 ans.**   *I lived here for 20 years.*

⟶   Note that **durant** is less frequently used than **pendant**.

- To ask how long the action has lasted, the expression is:
  - **Depuis combien de temps...?**
    - Ex.:   **Depuis combien de temps habites-tu ici ?**
      How long have you lived here?

or   **Il y a combien de temps que... ?** (with a rising intonation)
  - Ex.:   **Il y a combien de temps que tu habites ici ?**
    How long have you lived here?

- When the action is finished the question will be:
  - **Pendant combien de temps... ?**
    - Ex.:   **Pendant combien de temps as-tu habité ici ?**
      How long did you live here?

A4   TRANSLATION

1. How long have you been a shopkeeper?
2. I have been a shopkeeper for a long time.
3. I have known my customers for a long time.
4. I have been a shopkeeper for a long time.
5. I have been a shopkeeper for years.
6. I have known my customers for years.
7. I have sold domestic appliances for eighteen years.
8. I have sold domestic appliances for eighteen years.
9. I have sold domestic appliances for eighteen years.
10. It's been three years since I sold any black and white TV sets.
11. I sold black and white TV sets for fifteen years.
12. I haven't sold any black and white TV sets for three years.

B1 PRESENTATION

■ Grammar

- To indicate the moment when the action began, **depuis** is used followed by the expression of time.

   Ex.: **J'habite ici depuis 1945 / depuis la fin de la guerre.**
   I have lived here since 1945 / since the end of the war.

- When the expression of time is a subordinate clause, **depuis que** is used:
   - if the action is still going on, the verb is in the **present tense**.

     Ex.: **Nous sommes amis depuis que je le connais.**
     We have been friends since I have known him.
   - if the action is finished, the verb is in the **passé composé**.

     Ex.: **Nous sommes amis depuis le jour où je l'ai rencontré.**
     We have been friends since the day I met him.

■ Vocabulary

réserver	to reserve, to book	**fois** (fem.)	time
		chaîne	stereo
manquer	to miss	**stéréo** (fem.)	equipment
musicien (masc.)	musician	**régal** (masc.)	treat
place (fem.)	seat	**enthousiaste**	enthusiastic
public (masc.)	audience	**extraordinaire**	extraordinary
		chaque	each

B2 EXAMPLES *(Music lovers)*

1. **Depuis quand connaissez-vous les musiciens qui jouent ce soir ?**
2. **Depuis décembre.**
3. **Depuis Noël dernier.**
4. **Depuis que nous habitons Paris.**
5. **Depuis que je connais ces musiciens, je ne manque jamais un concert.**
6. **Chaque fois qu'ils donnent un concert, je réserve des places.**
7. **Toutes les fois qu'ils donnent un concert, j'y vais.**
8. **Ils jouent à Paris depuis 1984.**
9. **Chaque fois qu'ils jouent, le public est enthousiaste.**
10. **Ils sont chaque fois extraordinaires !**
11. **J'écoute leurs disques du matin au soir depuis que je suis devenue une de leurs admiratrices.**
12. **Depuis que nous avons acheté une nouvelle chaîne stéréo, c'est un vrai régal !**

B3 COMMENTS

■ Grammar

* To ask a question about the beginning of the action the expression is **depuis quand ?** *(since when?)*

    Ex.: **Depuis quand connais-tu Pierre ?**
    Since when have you known Peter?

* Note that the idea of repetition can be expressed with:
    chaque*..., tous/toutes les..., le/l'/les...

    Ex.: **Il va au cinéma chaque lundi.**
    He goes to the pictures each Monday.
    Il va au cinéma tous les lundis.
    He goes to the pictures every Monday.
    Il va au cinéma le lundi.
    He goes to the pictures on Mondays**.

    * **Chaque** is invariable.
    ** Note the singular in French.

* **Chaque fois que...** *(each time)*, **toutes les fois que...** *(every time)* are followed:
    - by a verb in the **present tense** when the action will be repeated.
        Ex.: **Chaque fois que je vais en Espagne, je vais dans le Sud.** *Each time I go to Spain, I go to the south.*
    - by a verb in the **passé composé** when repetition in the past is referred to.
        Ex.: **Chaque fois que je suis allé en Espagne je suis allé dans le Sud.** *Each time I went to Spain, I went to the south.*

B4 TRANSLATION

1. How long have you known the musicians who are playing tonight?
2. Since December.
3. Since last Christmas.
4. Since we've lived in Paris.
5. Since I met these musicians, I never miss a concert.
6. Each time they give a concert, I book seats.
7. Everytime they give a concert, I go to it.
8. They have been playing in Paris since 1984.
9. Each time they play, the public is enthusiastic.
10. They are extraordinary each time!
11. I listen to their records from morning till night since I became an admirer of theirs.
12. Since we bought some new stereo equipment, it's a real treat!

C1   EXERCISES

A. Change as in the example:
La secrétaire utilise cet ordinateur depuis deux ans. / Il y a deux ans que la secrétaire utilise cet ordinateur. / Ça fait deux ans qu'elle utilise cet ordinateur.
1. Nous travaillons dans cette entreprise depuis des années.— 2. Je ne fume plus depuis six mois.— 3. Il ne pleut pas depuis dix jours.— 4. Louis est parti depuis dix minutes.

B. Put the verb in the correct tense:
1. Depuis que Louis (être) directeur, ses affaires (marcher) bien.— 2. Depuis qu'ils (avoir) une maison à la campagne, ils y (aller) souvent.— 3. Hélène ne (pratiquer) aucun sport depuis qu'elle (tomber) l'an dernier.— 4. Depuis que je (rencontrer) cette musicienne, je (devenir) un de ses admirateurs.

C. Change the sentences to show these things happen each time; use chaque fois que:
1. Il va à Nice - il fait beau.— 2. Nous avons voyagé en Espagne - nous avons pris le train.— 3. Je rencontre Pierre - nous parlons de politique.— 4. On téléphone - elle va répondre.

D. Find the question using <u>pendant combien de temps</u>, <u>depuis combien de temps</u> or <u>depuis quand</u>:
1. Il est président *depuis 1981.*— 2. Ils ont discuté *pendant deux heures.*— 3. Je connais Hélène *depuis qu'elle est née.*— 4. Elles sont à Paris *depuis une semaine.*

C2   CONNAÎTRE / CONNAISSANCE
    TO KNOW

- **Connaissance** (fem.) from the verb **connaître** is used in a few set expressions:
  faire connaissance avec..., faire la connaissance de...
  to meet, to make the acquaintance of...
    Ex.: **J'ai fait connaissance avec Mme Martin.**
         J'ai fait la connaissance de Mme Martin l'an dernier.
         I met Mrs. Martin last year.

         Enchanté de faire votre connaissance.
         I'm delighted to meet you.

prendre connaissance de...	*to take note of...*
perdre connaissance	*to faint*
sans connaissance	*unconscious*

C3 ANSWERS

A. 1. Il y a des années que nous travaillons dans cette entreprise.
Ça fait des années que nous travaillons dans cette entreprise.
2. Il y a six mois que je ne fume plus.
Ça fait six mois que je ne fume plus.
3. Il y a dix jours qu'il ne pleut pas.
Ça fait dix jours qu'il ne pleut pas.
4. Il y a dix minutes que Louis est parti.
Ça fait dix minutes que Louis est parti.

B. 1. Depuis que Louis est directeur, ses affaires marchent bien.
2. Depuis qu'ils ont une maison à la campagne, ils y vont souvent.
3. Hélène ne pratique aucun sport depuis qu'elle est tombée l'an dernier.
4. Depuis que j'ai rencontré cette musicienne, je suis devenu un de ses admirateurs.

C. 1. Chaque fois qu'il va à Nice, il fait beau.
2. Chaque fois que nous avons voyagé en Espagne, nous avons pris le train.
3. Chaque fois que je rencontre Pierre, nous parlons de politique.
4. Chaque fois qu'on téléphone, elle va répondre.

D. 1. Depuis quand est-il président ?
2. Pendant combien de temps ont-ils discuté ?
3. Depuis quand connaissez-vous (connais-tu) Hélène ?
4. Depuis combien de temps sont-elles à Paris ?

C4 MAGASINS / COMMERÇANTS
SHOPS / SHOPKEEPERS

épicerie (fem.), **alimentation**	*grocer's*	**épicier**
boucherie (fem.)	*butcher's*	**boucher**
boulangerie (fem.)	*baker's*	**boulanger**
librairie (fem.)	*bookshop*	**libraire**
pharmacie (fem.)	*chemist's*	**pharmacien**
	(US : *druggist's*)	
poissonnerie (fem.)	*fishmonger's*	**poissonnier**
teinturerie (fem.)	*cleaner's*	**teinturier**

A1   PRESENTATION

■ Grammar

● Strong personal pronouns can be used:

moi	toi	lui	elle	nous	vous	eux, elles
me	*you*	*him*	*her*	*us*	*you*	*them*

- to emphasize the subject.
    Ex.: **Moi, j'aime ce film.**   *I like this film.*
       Toi, tu travailles trop !   *You work too much!*
- as indirect object pronouns (with a preposition).
    Ex.: **Il est avec moi.**   *He is with me.*
       Elle parle de toi.   *She is talking about you.*

■ Vocabulary

poster	*to post (*US: *to mail)*
nouvelles (fem. pl.)	*news*
lettre (fem.)	*letter*
ligne (fem.)	*line*
télégramme (masc.)	*telegram*
facteur (masc.)	*postman (*US: *mailman)*
colis (masc.)	*parcel*
carte postale (fem.)	*postcard*
timbre (masc.)	*stamp*
paquet (masc.)	*packet*
courrier (masc.)	*mail*

A2   EXAMPLES *(Mail)*

1. **J'ai eu des nouvelles de lui hier.**
2. **Il parle de vous dans sa lettre.**
3. **Est-ce qu'il dit quelque chose de moi ?**
4. **Oui, il y a quelques lignes sur vous.**
5. **Où est Anne ? Il y a un télégramme pour elle.**
6. **Le facteur a apporté un colis pour toi.**
7. **À qui sont ces cartes postales ? — À eux.**
8. **Qui a écrit cette lettre ? — Moi.**
9. **Donne-moi des timbres, s'il te plaît.**
10. **Va poster ces lettres pour moi, s'il te plaît.**
11. **Ils ont pris le paquet avec eux.**
12. **Il n'y a pas de courrier pour nous aujourd'hui.**

A3 COMMENTS

■ Grammar

● **à moi, à toi,** etc., are commonly used to express the idea that something belongs *to me, to you,* etc.

Ex.: **C'est à moi.** *It is mine.*
Ils sont à vous. *They are yours.*
La voiture est à lui. *The car is his.*
Ces livres sont à nous. *These books are ours.*

● The same pronouns are used when standing alone without a verb.

Ex.: **Qui a dit cela ? — Moi.**
Who said that? — I did.

Qui est le patron ici ? — Lui.
Who is the boss here? — He is.

You could also say: **C'est moi.** *It's me.*
C'est lui. *It's him.*

● In the first and second person, even without a preposition, strong pronouns must be used after a command form.

Ex.: **Donne-moi.** *Give me.*
Dis-moi, dites-moi. *Tell me.*

A4 TRANSLATION

1. I had some news from him yesterday.
2. He mentions you in his letter.
3. Does he say anything about me?
4. Yes, there are a few lines about you.
5. Where is Anne? There's a telegram for her.
6. The postman has brought a parcel for you.
7. Whose postcards are these? — Theirs.
8. Who wrote this letter? — I did.
9. Give me some stamps, please.
10. Go and post these letters for me, please.
11. They have taken the packet with them.
12. There's no mail for us today.

B1 PRESENTATION

■ Grammar

• Strong personal pronouns are also used to express agreement or disagreement with what has been said:

the initial statement is	agreement	disagreement
affirmative	**moi aussi**	**pas moi** **moi non**
negative	**moi non plus**	**moi si**

Of course, the pronoun changes according to the person who agrees or disagrees.

■ Vocabulary

aimer beaucoup	*to be very fond of*
pratiquer	*to practise*
femme (fem.)	*wife*
natation (fem.)	*swimming*
mari (masc.)	*husband*
chez moi	*at home*
vrai	*real, true*
aucun(e)	*not... any*

B2 EXAMPLES *(Opinions about sports)*

1. J'aime beaucoup le sport, et toi ?
2. Moi aussi, je joue au volley tous les jours.
3. Je vais au match de football dimanche prochain.
4. Moi non, je reste chez moi.
5. Sa femme n'aime pas la natation.
6. Lui non plus.
7. Mon mari ne joue pas au tennis.
8. Nous si !
9. Je ne pratique aucun sport.
10. Moi si, je joue au basket.
11. J'ai été un vrai champion.
12. Pas moi !

B3 COMMENTS

■ Grammar

• The complement of **jouer** is generally introduced by a preposition.

If it is the name of a sport or a game, the preposition used is **à**, often contracted with the article into **au**.

Ex.:	**jouer au tennis**	*to play tennis*
	jouer au football	*to play football*
	jouer à la balle	*to play ball*

If it is followed by the name of an instrument the preposition used is **de**, often contracted with the article into **du**.

Ex.:	**jouer du piano**	*to play the piano*
	jouer de la flûte	*to play the flute*
	jouer du saxophone	*to play the saxophone*

■ Pronunciation

• **Champion:** even if the word is the same in English and French, the pronunciation is different: **ch** like *sh* in *shoe* followed by the nasal vowel **an**.

Remember that **ion** is pronounced like *y* in *yes* followed by the nasal vowel **on**.

B4 TRANSLATION

1. I am very fond of sports, what about you?
2. Me too, I play volleyball every day.
3. I'm going to the football match next Sunday.
4. I'm not, I'm staying at home.
5. His wife doesn't like swimming.
6. Neither does he.
7. My husband doesn't play tennis.
8. We do!
9. I don't practise any sport.
10. I do, I play basketball.
11. I was a real champion.
12. I wasn't!

C1 EXERCISES

A. Fill the blanks with the appropriate personal pronoun:

1. ..., je ne parle pas très bien français.
2. ..., tu as tort.
3. ..., nous allons au cinéma, et vous ?
4. ..., elle est trop jeune.
5. ..., il est journaliste.
6. ..., vous êtes très gentil.

B. Change the sentences as in the example: Pierre ne regarde pas la télévision. / Je ne regarde pas la télévision. / Pierre ne regarde pas la télévision, moi non plus.

1. Elle n'a pas d'enfants. / Il n'a pas d'enfants.
2. Anne joue au tennis. / Nous jouons au tennis.
3. Il va prendre le métro. / Je vais prendre le métro.
4. Vous allez partir. / Ils ne vont pas partir.
5. Tu as peur ? / Je n'ai pas peur.
6. Ils ont voté. / Nous avons voté.

C. Translate into French:

1. There is a telegram for you.
2. He played tennis with us.
3. Here is the teacher, I am going to speak to her.
4. The manager is here, give him those files.
5. Our friends brought this packet for us.

C2 CHEZ MOI / *AT HOME*

- **Chez** + a strong pronoun (ex.: **chez lui, chez toi, chez nous**)

  + the name of a person (ex.: **chez Pierre, chez Mme Lenoir**)

  + article or possessive or demonstrative + noun (ex.: **chez le dentiste, chez mon docteur, chez ce ministre**)

means *at* or *to somebody's place.*

Ex.: **Il est chez nous.**	*He is at our place.*
Elle rentre chez elle.	*She is going back home.*
Ils vont chez vous.	*They are going to your house.*
Nous avons dîné chez nos amis.	*We had dinner at our friends.*

C3 ANSWERS

A. 1. Moi, je ne parle pas très bien français.
2. Toi, tu as tort.
3. Nous, nous allons au cinéma, et vous ?
4. Elle, elle est trop jeune.
5. Lui, il est journaliste.
6. Vous, vous êtes très gentil.

B. 1. Elle n'a pas d'enfants, lui non plus.
2. Anne joue au tennis, nous aussi.
3. Il va prendre le métro, moi aussi.
4. Vous allez partir, eux non (pas eux).
5. Tu as peur ? Moi non (pas moi).
6. Ils ont voté, nous aussi.

C. 1. Il y a un télégramme pour toi/vous.
2. Il a joué au tennis avec nous.
3. Voici l'institutrice, je vais parler avec elle.
4. Le directeur est ici, donnez-lui ces dossiers.
5. Nos ami(e)s ont apporté ce paquet pour nous.

C4 PRONOMS POSSESSIFS
POSSESSIVE PRONOUNS

à moi	*mine*	**le mien, la mienne** **les miens, les miennes**
à toi	*yours*	**le tien, la tienne** **les tiens, les tiennes**
à lui, à elle	*his, hers, its*	**le sien, la sienne** **les siens, les siennes**
à nous	*ours*	**le nôtre*, la nôtre*** **les nôtres***
à vous	*yours*	**le vôtre*, la vôtre*** **les vôtres***
à eux, à elles	*theirs*	**le leur, la leur, les leurs**

* The **ô** is pronounced like *o* in *note*.

171

A1 PRESENTATION

■ Grammar

- Personal pronouns object.
  In the 1st and 2nd persons, the object pronouns are the same
  whether direct or indirect.

	subject		object	
singular	**je**	*I*	**me (m')**	*me*
	tu	*you*	**te (t')**	*you*
plural	**nous**	*we*	**nous**	*us*
	vous	*you*	**vous**	*you*

- With a preposition : **moi** is used instead of **me**
                    toi is used instead of **te**

■ Vocabulary

voir *	*to see*
apprendre	*to learn / to teach*
suivre	*to follow*
attendre	*to wait*
moniteur (masc.)	*instructor*
tout le monde	*everybody*
vers	*to, towards*
attentivement	*carefully*

* Irregular verb (see Grammar Summary).

A2 EXAMPLES *(Skiing lesson)*

1. **Le moniteur nous appelle.**
2. **Écoutez-moi attentivement.**
3. **Pierre, tu ne m'écoutes pas !**
4. **Regarde-moi ! Nous allons apprendre à tourner.**
5. **Suivez-moi.**
6. **Est-ce que tout le monde me voit bien ?**
7. **Nous vous attendons. Venez avec nous !**
8. **Regardez devant vous.**
9. **Ne regarde pas derrière toi !**
10. **Pierre, je ne te vois pas, viens vers moi.**
11. **Eh, attendez-moi !**
12. **Tout le monde m'a vu ? Allez-y maintenant !**

A3 COMMENTS

■ Grammar

- **me, te, nous, vous** (object) always immediately precede the verb (or auxiliary).
  - Ex.: **Tu ne m'écoutes pas.**
    You aren't listening to me.
    Tout le monde m'a vu ?
    Did everybody see me?

- In the imperative affirmative, **moi** is used instead of **me**.
  - Ex.: **Regarde-moi !**

- In the imperative affirmative, the object follows the verb and is linked to it by a hyphen.
  - Ex.: **Attendez-moi !**
    Look at me!

- Note that **apprendre à** + an infinitive is the French equivalent of
  to learn how to
  - Ex.: **Nous apprenons à skier.** *We are learning how to ski.*
    or
  to teach how to
  - Ex.: **Elle nous apprend à skier.** *She's teaching us how to ski.*

A4 TRANSLATION

1. The instructor is calling us.
2. Listen to me carefully!
3. Pierre, you aren't listening to me!
4. Look at me! We are going to learn how to turn.
5. Follow me.
6. Can everybody see me all right* ?
7. We are waiting for you. Come with us!
8. Look in front of you.
9. Don't look behind you!
10. Pierre, I can't see you, come towards me*.
11. Hey, wait for me!
12. Did everybody see me? Go ahead now!

* Note that there is no equivalent of *can* in the French sentence.

B1   PRESENTATION

■ Grammar

- Personal pronoun object
  In the 3rd person, the object pronouns are:

	direct	indirect
sing.	**le (l')** to replace a masculine noun (= *him, it*) **la (l')** to replace a feminine noun (= *her, it*)	**lui** to replace any person or animal (= *her, him, it*)
pl.	**les** to replace any noun or group of nouns (= *them*)	**leur** to replace any persons or animals (= *them*)

■ Vocabulary

commander	*to order*	**café** (masc.)	*pub*
faire signe	*to wave*	**café** (masc.)	*coffee*
sourire	*to smile*	**garçon (de café)** (masc.)	*waiter*
arrêter	⎡ *to arrest.* ⎣ *to stop*	**agent de police** (masc.) **soudain**	*policeman* *suddenly*

B2   EXAMPLES *(Detective story)*

1. Un homme entre dans un café, prend un journal et l'ouvre.
2. Il commande une boisson ; le garçon l'apporte.
3. Il y a une femme près de lui, elle le regarde.
4. Il ne la voit pas.
5. Elle appelle le garçon ; il ne l'entend pas.
6. Elle lui fait signe.
7. Des musiciens entrent. Elle leur sourit.
8. L'homme vient vers elle.
9. Il lui demande quelque chose.
10. Elle l'écoute attentivement.
11. Soudain deux agents de police vont vers eux et les arrêtent.
12. Tout le monde les regarde.

B3 COMMENTS

■ Grammar

- Personal pronouns object.
  When the indirect object is introduced by a preposition (**à, avec, devant, derrière, pour, près de, vers**...):

— **lui** *(him)*	is used for a	masculine singular
— **elle** *(her)*	" " "	feminine singular
— **eux** *(them)*	" " "	masculine plural
— **elles** *(them)*	" " "	feminine plural

Je marche devant elle.	*I'm walking in front of her.*
Parlons avec elles.	*Let's speak with them.*
Nous allons vers eux.	*We're going towards them.*
Va derrière lui.	*Go behind him.*

- Note that the personal pronoun **leur** is invariable.

B4 TRANSLATION

1. A man enters a pub, takes a newspaper and opens it.
2. He orders a drink; the waiter brings it.
3. There is a woman near him; she is looking at him.
4. He doesn't see her.
5. She calls the waiter; he doesn't hear her.
6. She waves to him.
7. Some musicians are coming in. She smiles at them.
8. The man is coming towards her.
9. He asks her something.
10. She listens to him carefully.
11. Suddenly two policemen go towards them and arrest them.
12. Everybody looks at them.

C1 EXERCISES

A. Choose the correct pronoun: le, la, l', les, leur, lui:

1. La secrétaire utilise l'ordinateur. Elle ... utilise.
2. Anne prépare le repas. Elle ... prépare.
3. Le garçon a parlé aux musiciens. Il ... a parlé.
4. Elle a dansé avec Marc. Elle a dansé avec ...
5. Nous allons voir les voisins. Nous allons ... voir.

B. ●● Put in pronouns instead of names or nouns:

1. On ne voit pas la mer.
2. Marc appelle Marie.
3. Les enfants parlent à la voisine.
4. M. et Mme Martin ont apporté le vin.
5. Nous écoutons les musiciens.

C. ●● Translate into French:

1. He is looking at me.
2. Look at me.
3. I'm speaking to you.
4. I spoke to him.
5. They spoke to her.
6. They are waiting for it.
7. Don't wait for them.

C2 VERBS ENDING WITH **VENIR**

● Here are some verbs with the same conjugation as **venir**:

- **convenir** *(to be convenient)*
  Ex.: **Est-ce que cela vous convient ?**
  Is that convenient for you?

- **devenir** *(to become)*
  Ex.: **Elle est devenue institutrice il y a un an.**
  She became a primary school teacher a year ago.

- **parvenir à** *(to reach / to succeed)*
  Ex.: **Nous ne sommes pas parvenus à un accord.**
  We couldn't reach an agreement.

➡ Remember that there is no equivalent of *can* in the French sentence.

- **prévenir** *(to warn / to let know)*
  Ex.: **Prévenez-moi avant de partir.**
  Let me know before you leave.

- **revenir** *(to come back)*
  Ex.: **Ils sont revenus en train.** *They came back by train.*

C3 ANSWERS

A. 1. La secrétaire utilise l'ordinateur. Elle l'utilise.
2. Anne prépare le repas. Elle le prépare.
3. Le garçon a parlé aux musiciens. Il leur a parlé.
4. Elle a dansé avec Marc. Elle a dansé avec lui.
5. Nous allons voir les voisins. Nous allons les voir.

B. 1. On ne la voit pas.
2. Il l'appelle.
3. Ils lui parlent.
4. Ils l'ont apporté.
5. Nous les écoutons.

C. 1. Il me regarde.
2. Regarde-moi. / Regardez-moi.
3. Je te parle. / Je vous parle.
4. Je lui ai parlé.
5. Ils lui ont parlé. / Elles lui ont parlé.
6. Ils l'attendent. / Elles l'attendent.
7. Ne les attends pas. / Ne les attendez pas.

C4 PASSÉ RÉCENT / *RECENT PAST*

- **Venir de** + infinitive is used to refer to what has just happened or been done.
  Ex.: **Il vient de partir.**
  He has just left.
  Nous venons de le voir.
  We have just seen him.
  Ils viennent d'arriver.
  They have just arrived.

- But: **venir de** + the name of a place is the French equivalent of *to come from.*
  Ex.: **Il vient de Londres.**
  He comes from London.
  Je viens d'Allemagne.
  I come from Germany.
  Elle vient de la campagne.
  She comes from the country.

29 Quand la cérémonie a-t-elle lieu ?

A1 PRESENTATION

■ Grammar

- In addition to the three interrogative forms already seen, there is a fourth one, which is used in more elegant French.

   Ex.: **Les enfants sont-ils dans le jardin ?**
   Are the children in the garden?
   Pierre va-t-il acheter une voiture ?
   Is Pierre going to buy a car?
   Ta mère vient-elle demain ?
   Is your mother coming tomorrow?
   Vos amies repartent-elles bientôt ?
   Are your friends going back soon?
   Pierre et toi connaissez-vous Rome ?
   Do Pierre and you know Rome?

   In this form you can find both a subject and a pronoun which recalls it, following the verbal form:

   | Subject + Verbal Form + Pronoun + ... |

■ Vocabulary

avoir lieu	*to take place*
cérémonie (fem.)	*ceremony*
sœur (fem.)	*sister*
frère (masc.)	*brother*
fleur (fem.)	*flower*
couple (masc.)	*couple*
voyage de noces (masc.)	*honeymoon (trip)*

A2 EXAMPLES *(A wedding ceremony)*

1. **À quelle heure les gens arrivent-ils ?**
2. **Quand la cérémonie a-t-elle lieu ?**
3. **Les parents vont-ils venir ensemble ?**
5. **Anne va-t-elle venir seule ?**
6. **Antoine vient-il avec elle ?**
7. **Ton frère arrive-t-il par le train ?**
8. **Quelqu'un va-t-il le chercher à la gare ?**
9. **Ta sœur a-t-elle commandé les fleurs ?**
10. **Où les invités vont-ils danser ?**
11. **Quelqu'un a-t-il pensé à la musique ?**
12. **Où le jeune couple part-il en voyage de noces ?**

A3 COMMENTS

■ Grammar

● Remember that when the verb is inverted in this interrogative form it is joined to the pronoun by a hyphen.

Ex.: **Les invités arrivent-ils ?** *Are the guests arriving?*

If the verb ends with a vowel, **t** is introduced between the verb and the pronoun.

Ex.: **Pierre va-t-il venir ?** *Is Peter going to come?*
Antoine arrive-t-il ? *Is Antoine arriving?*

● If the verb is in the **passé composé**, the pronoun is placed between the auxiliary and the past participle.

Ex.: **Quelqu'un a-t-il pensé à la musique ?**
Has someone thought about the music?
Ta sœur est-elle arrivée ?
Has your sister arrived?

■ Pronunciation

● Remember:
— **g** followed by **e**, **i** or **y** is pronounced like *su* in *pleasure*: **gens, voyage**.
— **g** followed by another vowel is pronounced like *g* in *good*: **gare**.

A4 TRANSLATION

1. What time are the people coming?
2. When is the ceremony taking place?
3. Are the relatives coming together?
5. Is Anne coming alone?
6. Is Antoine coming with her?
7. Is your brother coming by train?
8. Is someone going to meet him at the station?
9. Did your sister order the flowers?
10. Where are the guests going to dance?
11. Has someone thought about the music?
12. Where are the young couple going on their honeymoon?

B1 PRESENTATION

■ Grammar

- A reported question is generally introduced by the verb **demander**.

  Ex. : **Pierre : « Est-ce qu'il fait froid ? »**
  Pierre demande s'il fait froid.

  Pierre : « Anne va-t-elle venir ? »
  Pierre demande si Anne va venir.

- As the reported question is a statement, **est-ce que** or the inverted form disappear. The intonation, of course, is not rising.

- When the expected answer is yes or no, the reported question is introduced by : **si** = *if*.

■ Vocabulary

changer	*to exchange*	**banque** (fem.)	*bank*
recevoir	*to receive*	**chéquier** (m.)	*cheque book*
devoir	*must, to have to*	**carte de**	
remplir	*to fill in, to fill*	**crédit** (f.)	*credit card*
touriste (m., f.)	*tourist*	**compte (en**	
bureau de	*foreign exchange*	**banque)** (m.)	*account*
change (m.)	*office*	**formulaire** (m.)	*form*

B2 EXAMPLES *(At the bank)*

1. **Une femme : « Est-ce que la banque ferme à midi ? »**
2. **Une femme demande si la banque ferme à midi.**
3. **Un touriste : « Est-ce qu'il y a un bureau de change ? »**
4. **Un touriste demande s'il y a un bureau de change.**
5. **Un client : « Est-ce qu'il y a un chéquier pour moi ? »**
6. **Un client demande s'il y a un chéquier pour lui.**
7. **Une cliente : « Pourquoi est-ce que je n'ai pas reçu ma carte de crédit ? »**
8. **Une cliente demande pourquoi elle n'a pas reçu sa carte de crédit.**
9. **Un jeune homme : « Que dois-je faire pour ouvrir un compte ? »**
10. **Un jeune homme demande ce qu'il doit faire pour ouvrir un compte.**
11. **Un commerçant : « Dois-je remplir un formulaire ? »**
12. **Un commerçant demande s'il doit remplir un formulaire.**

B3 COMMENTS

■ Grammar

- To convey the idea of obligation, it is possible to use the verb **devoir** followed by an infinitive.
    Ex.: **Je dois aller à la gare.**
      I must go to the station. / I have to go to the station.

Present tense						
je	**dois**	*I*	*must*	**nous**	**devons**	*we must*
tu	**dois**	*you*	*must*	**vous**	**devez**	*you must*
il, elle	**doit**	*he, she, it must*		**ils, elles**	**doivent**	*they must*
Past participle : **dû**						

- Note that most interrogative words or expressions remain the same in a reported question except: **que** which becomes **ce que**.
    Ex.: **Anne : « Que fait Pierre ? »**
      Anne: "What is Pierre doing?"
      Anne demande ce que fait Pierre.
      Anne asks what Pierre is doing.

- If the direct question starts with **qu'est-ce qui** or **qu'est-ce que**, only **ce qui** or **ce que** remain in the reported question.
    Ex.: **Qu'est-ce qui manque ?**
      What is missing?
      On demande ce qui manque.
      Someone asks what is missing.

B4 TRANSLATION

1. A woman: "Does the bank close at twelve?"
2. A woman asks if the bank closes at twelve.
3. A tourist: "Is there a foreign exchange office?"
4. A tourist asks if there is a foreign exchange office.
5. A customer: "Is there a cheque book for me?"
6. A customer asks if there is a cheque book for him.
7. A customer: "Why haven't I received my credit card?"
8. A customer asks why she hasn't received her credit card.
9. A young man: "What must I do to open an account?"
10. A young man asks what he must do to open an account.
11. A shopkeeper: "Do I have to fill in a form?"
12. A shopkeeper asks if he has to fill in a form.

181

C1 EXERCISES

A. ⚫⚫ **Transform using both a subject and a pronoun to recall it:**
1. Est-ce que ton frère aime le football ?
2. Est-ce que le facteur a apporté une lettre pour moi ?
3. Est-ce que vos amis vivent à Paris ?
4. Est-ce que les enfants ont appris leurs leçons ?
5. Est-ce que Pierre et Jeanne connaissent ta sœur ?
6. Est-ce qu'Hélène et Agnès vont sortir ce soir ?

B. Use the verb <u>devoir</u> in the correct form:
1. Je ... repartir demain.
2. Pourquoi ...-tu aller à la banque ?
3. Que ... -nous dire ?
4. Elle ... prendre l'avion.
5. Vous ... téléphoner au directeur.
6. Combien de temps ...-on attendre ?
7. Quand ...-ils commencer ?

C. Turn into reported questions:
1. L'étudiant : « Est-ce qu'on doit écrire l'adresse sur le formulaire ? »
2. La secrétaire : « Depuis combien d'années cet employé travaille-t-il ? »
3. Le moniteur : « Quel sport préférez-vous ? »
4. Une étudiante : « Que dois-je faire pour avoir une carte de crédit ? »
5. Un touriste : « À quelle heure ouvrent les bureaux de change ? »
6. Le directeur : « Y a-t-il des télégrammes pour moi ? »

C2 ⚫⚫ **DEVOIR** = *MUST* / **DEVOIR** = *TO OWE*

- The word **devoir** has several meanings and is used in many expressions:

Combien je vous dois ?	*How much do I owe you?*
Nous devons de l'argent à quelqu'un.	*We owe someone money.*
Avec tout le respect qui lui/leur est dû.	*With due respect.*
Comme il se doit.	*As it should be.*
Ce doit être vrai.	*It must be true.*
Il a fait son devoir.	*He has done his duty.*
Il a fait ses devoirs.	*He has done his homework.*

C3 ANSWERS

A. 1. Ton frère aime-t-il le football ?
2. Le facteur a-t-il apporté une lettre pour moi ?
3. Vos amis vivent-ils à Paris ?
4. Les enfants ont-ils appris leurs leçons ?
5. Pierre et Jeanne connaissent-ils ta sœur ?
6. Hélène et Agnès vont-elles sortir ce soir ?

B. 1. Je dois repartir demain.
2. Pourquoi dois-tu aller à la banque ?
3. Que devons-nous dire ?
4. Elle doit prendre l'avion.
5. Vous devez téléphoner au directeur.
6. Combien de temps doit-on attendre ?
7. Quand doivent-ils commencer ?

C. 1. L'étudiant demande si on doit écrire l'adresse sur le formulaire.
2. La secrétaire demande depuis combien d'années cet employé travaille.
3. Le moniteur demande quel sport je préfère (*or* nous préférons, vous préférez).
4. Une étudiante demande ce qu'elle doit faire pour avoir une carte de crédit.
5. Un touriste demande à quelle heure ouvrent les bureaux de change.
6. Le directeur demande s'il y a des télégrammes pour lui.

C4 **C'EST LE MOMENT DE PAYER** ●●
IT'S TIME TO PAY

● Here are useful expressions to ask how much you have to pay :

Quel est le prix de... ?	*What's the price of...?*
Combien coûte(nt)... ?	*How much is/are...?*
Combien vaut/valent... ?	*How much is/are... worth?*
Combien fait/font... ?	*How much is/are...?*

In colloquial French you will often hear :

Combien ça coûte ?
Combien ça vaut ?
Combien ça fait ? → *How much is it?*
C'est combien ?

A1 PRESENTATION

■ Grammar

- In French, the idea of possibility is expressed by: **pouvoir**. Here is its conjugation:

Present			
je	**peux**	*I*	*can*
tu	**peux**	*you*	*can*
il, elle	**peut**	*he, she, it*	*can*
nous	**pouvons**	*we*	*can*
vous	**pouvez**	*you*	*can*
ils, elles	**peuvent**	*they*	*can*
Past participle: **pu**			

- **pouvoir** is followed by an infinitive.
  - Ex.: **Vous pouvez venir.** *You can come.*
  - **Ils peuvent rester.** *They can stay.*

■ Vocabulary

épeler	*to spell*	**occupé**	*busy*
rappeler	*to call back*	**désolé**	*sorry*
rendez-vous (masc.)	*appointment*	**possible**	*possible*
problème (masc.)	*problem*	**tout à fait**	*quite*
répondeur (masc.)	*answering machine*	**à partir de**	*from*
		d'accord	*all right*

A2 EXAMPLES *(Making an appointment)*

1. Est-ce que le docteur peut me voir demain ?
2. Pouvez-vous venir l'après-midi ? À quatorze heures par exemple ?
3. Désolé, je ne peux pas venir, je suis occupé.
4. Il ne pourra pas vous voir plus tard, il est occupé.
5. Est-ce possible mardi soir ?
6. Oui, c'est tout à fait possible, vous pouvez avoir un rendez-vous à partir de dix-sept heures.
7. D'accord, je peux venir à dix-sept heures trente.
8. Pouvez-vous me donner votre nom ?
9. Je ne vous entends pas très bien. Pouvez-vous l'épeler ?
10. Vous m'entendez mieux ?
11. Puis-je vous rappeler s'il y a un problème ?
12. On peut rappeler n'importe quand : il y a un répondeur.

A3   COMMENTS

■ Grammar

● Note that with verbs like: **entendre**   *to hear*
                        voir   *to see*
                        sentir   *to smell, to feel*
the idea of possibility is never expressed in French.
> Ex.:   **J'entends.**   *I can hear.*
>   **Je vois.**   *I can see.*

● Note that in a question in the 1st person singular where the verb is inverted, **puis** is used instead of **peux**.
> Ex.:   **Puis-je vous aider ?**
>   *Can I help you?*
>   **Que puis-je faire pour vous ?**
>   *What can I do for you?*

● **Pouvoir** is often used to make an order more polite.
> Ex.:   **Pouvez-vous me donner votre nom ?**
>   *Can you give me your name?*
>   **Peux-tu m'aider ?**
>   *Can you help me?*
>   **Pouvez-vous venir ?**
>   *Can you come?*

A4   TRANSLATION

1. Can the doctor see me tomorrow?
2. Can you come in the afternoon? At two p.m. for instance.
3. Sorry, I can't come, I'm busy.
4. He won't be able to see you later, he's busy.
5. Is Tuesday evening possible?
6. Yes, it's quite possible, you can have an appointment from five onward.
7. All right, I can come at five thirty.
8. Can you give me your name?
9. I can't hear you very well. Can you spell it?
10. Can you hear me better?
11. Can I call back if there's a problem?
12. You can call back any time, there's an answering machine.

B1 PRESENTATION

■ Grammar

- A possibility which is the result of capacity + training is expressed in French by **savoir**, *to know*. Here is its conjugation:

Present			
je	sais	*I*	*know*
tu	sais	*you*	*know*
il, elle	sait	*he, she, it*	*knows*
nous	savons	*we*	*know*
vous	savez	*you*	*know*
ils, elles	savent	*they*	*know*

- **savoir** is followed by an infinitive.
  - Ex.: **Je sais conduire.** *I know how to drive.*
  - **Ils savent lire et écrire.** *They can read and write.*

■ Vocabulary

taper à la machine	to type	**message** (masc.)	*message*
se servir de	to use	**langue** (fem.)	*language*
quitter	to leave	**salaire** (masc.)	*salary*
gagner	to earn	**idée** (fem.)	*idea*
traitement de		**moyen**	*average*
texte (masc.)	*word processor*	**exactement**	*exactly*

B2 EXAMPLES *(Questions when applying for a job)*

1. **Quand pouvez-vous commencer à travailler ?**
2. **Je peux commencer tout de suite.**
3. **Savez-vous taper à la machine ?**
4. **Oui, et je sais me servir d'un traitement de texte.**
5. **Comprenez-vous bien le français, pouvez-vous prendre des messages au téléphone ?**
6. **Pouvez-vous quitter la France facilement ?**
7. **Savez-vous conduire ?**
8. **Non, je ne sais pas.**
9. **Savez-vous parler plusieurs langues ?**
10. **Pouvons-nous parler du salaire ?**
11. **Je ne peux pas vous dire exactement combien vous allez gagner.**
12. **Je peux vous donner une idée du salaire moyen pour ce travail.**

B3 COMMENTS

■ Grammar

● Verbs indicating the beginning, the continuation, or the end of an action are followed by a preposition and an infinitive:

$$\begin{matrix} \textbf{commencer} \\ \textbf{continuer} \end{matrix} + \textbf{à} + \text{infinitive}$$

Ex.: **Il a commencé à lire il y a une heure.**
He started reading an hour ago.
Il a commencé à pleuvoir.
It's started to rain.

$$\begin{matrix} \textbf{arrêter} \\ \textbf{finir} \end{matrix} + \textbf{de} + \text{infinitive}$$

Ex.: **Il a arrêté de fumer il y a un mois.**
He stopped smoking a month ago.
J'ai fini d'écrire mon livre.
I've finished writing my book.

● **Pouvez-vous quitter la France ?**
Note that when the name of a country is subject or object, it is necessary to use the article.

Ex.: **La Grèce a rejoint l'Europe en 1981.**
Greece joined Europe in 1981.
Je ne connais pas le Danemark.
I don't know Denmark.
Je connais bien les États-Unis.
I know the United States well.

B4 TRANSLATION

1. When can you start work?
2. I can start straight away.
3. Do you know how to type?
4. Yes, and I can use a word processor.
5. Do you understand French well, can you take messages on the phone?
6. Are you free to travel? (Literally: Can you leave France easily?)
7. Can you drive?
8. No, I can't.
9. Can you speak several languages?
10. Can we talk about the salary?
11. I can't tell you exactly how much you are going to earn.
12. I can give you an idea of the average salary for this job.

C1 EXERCISES

A. Write the correct form of the verb:

je (pouvoir) - tu (pouvoir) - vous (pouvoir)
il (savoir) - elle (pouvoir) - tu (savoir)
nous (pouvoir) - elles (savoir) - je (savoir)

B. ●● Translate into French:

1. This student can speak several languages.
2. Pierre can't drive.
3. Can you help me?
4. Our manager can make superb speeches.
5. Can you see him?
6. I can play the piano.

C. Put in the correct preposition:

1. Je m'arrête ... travailler à sept heures du soir.
2. À cinq ans, mon fils commençait ... lire.
3. La secrétaire finit ... taper une lettre à la machine.
4. Ses parents continuent ... s'occuper de la ferme.
5. Mon mari a arrêté ... écrire des articles pour ce journal.

D. Write the article before the name of the country when necessary:

1. J'ai visité ... France il y a trois ans.
2. Tu fais tes études en ... Italie ?
3. L'avion quittera ... Belgique à six heures.
4. ... Danemark est plus petit que ... Angleterre.
5. Nous revenons de ... France.

C2 PROBABILITÉ - PERMISSION
PROBABILITY - PERMISSION

- **pouvoir** can also express an idea of probability; it is then an equivalent of *may*. Ex.:

Un accident peut toujours arriver.	*An accident can always happen.*
Il peut y avoir une grève.	*There may be a strike.*
Il peut arriver n'importe quoi.	*Anything may happen.*
Le train peut arriver en retard.	*The train may arrive late.*

- **pouvoir** is used to express permission. Ex.:

Vous pouvez sortir.	*You may go.*
Puis-je vous emprunter votre stylo?	*May I borrow your pen?*

C3 ANSWERS

A. je peux - tu peux - vous pouvez
il sait - elle peut - tu sais
nous pouvons - elles savent - je sais

B. 1. Cet étudiant sait parler plusieurs langues.— 2. Pierre ne sait pas conduire.— 3. Est-ce que vous pouvez m'aider ?— 4. Notre directeur sait faire de superbes discours.— 5. Est-ce que vous le voyez ?— 6. Je sais jouer du piano.

C. 1. Je m'arrête de travailler à sept heures du soir.
2. À cinq ans, mon fils commençait à lire.
3. La secrétaire finit de taper une lettre à la machine.
4. Ses parents continuent à s'occuper de la ferme.
5. Mon mari a arrêté d'écrire des articles pour ce journal.

D. 1. J'ai visité la France il y a trois ans.— 2. Tu fais tes études en Italie ?— 3. L'avion quittera la Belgique à six heures.— 4. Le Danemark est plus petit que l'Angleterre.— 5. Nous revenons de France.

C4 SAVOIR / CONNAÎTRE
TO KNOW

- **savoir** and **connaître** have close meanings but can't always be used one for the other.

— **savoir** means to have information about facts, to know how to; it is generally followed by an infinitive or a subordinate clause.

Ex.: **Il sait tout faire.** *He can do anything.*
Il sait lire. *He can read.*
Savez-vous quand elle arrive ?
Do you know when she is coming?
Savent-ils où nous sommes ?
Do they know where we are?
On ne sait pas ce qu'il a dit.
We don't know what he said.

— **connaître** means to have knowledge of things, to be acquainted with persons, places.

Ex.: **Je connais cette chanson.**
I know that song.
Est-ce qu'elle connaît le président ?
Does she know the president?
Je ne connais pas l'Italie.
I don't know Italy.

189

A1 PRESENTATION

■ Grammar

- The **imparfait** is a past tense used to express what was taking place or what used to happen.
  It is formed by dropping the ending **ons** of the 1st person plural of the present tense and adding the following endings to the stem.
  Ex.: **marcher,** *to walk*

sing.				
-ais	je	marchais	*I was walking*
-ais	tu	marchais	or *I used to walk,*
-ait	il, elle	marchait	etc.
plur.				
-ions	nous	marchions	
-iez	vous	marchiez	
-aient	ils, elles	marchaient	

⟶ It is the same for all verbs, except **être**.

■ Vocabulary

faire ses		**manifestation** (fem.)	*demonstration*
études	*to study*	**réunion** (fem.)	*meeting*
défiler	*to march*	**bagarre** (fem.)	*fight*
éclater	*to break out*	**transistor** (masc.)	*transistor*
brûler	*to burn*	**pendant**	*for*
faculté (fem.)	*college*	**pendant que**	*while*

A2 EXAMPLES *(Those were the days)*

1. **En 68, je faisais mes études à Paris.**
2. **J'avais les cheveux longs.**
3. **J'allais à la « fac » tous les jours.**
4. **Nous parlions beaucoup.**
5. **En mai, pendant les manifestations, il y avait beaucoup de réunions.**
6. **Nous discutions politique pendant des heures.**
7. **Dans les rues, les étudiants défilaient.**
8. **On les entendait de loin.**
9. **La police essayait de les arrêter.**
10. **Un soir, pendant qu'ils défilaient, une bagarre a éclaté.**
11. **Des voitures brûlaient au quartier Latin.**
12. **Les gens écoutaient les nouvelles sur leurs transistors.**

We used to discuss politics for hours.

A3 COMMENTS

■ Pronunciation

- **ais, ait** and **aient** are pronounced like **è**.

■ Grammar

- The **imparfait** is often used in past description to describe a state of affairs
    Ex.: **Il faisait chaud.**   *It was hot.*
  or an action taking place when something else happened. The action taking place is in the **imparfait**, what happened is in the **passé composé**.
    Ex.: **J'écoutais les nouvelles quand il est entré.**
        I was listening to the news when he came in.
        Il travaillait quand elle a appelé.
        He was working when she called.

- In colloquial French, some long words are shortened to one or two syllables.
    Ex.: **fac**   for **faculté**
        manif   for **manifestation**
        métro   for **métropolitain**
        pub   for **publicité** *(advert* or *advertising)*

- **police** is followed by a verb in the singular, as is **gouvernement**.

- When the stem of the verb ends with **t**, note that in the 1st person plural of the imperfect **tions** is pronounced **tion** with the sound **t**.
    Ex.: **arrêtions, quittions, partions.**

A4 TRANSLATION

1. In 68, I was studying in Paris.
2. I had long hair.
3. I used to go to college everyday.
4. We talked a lot.
5. In May, during the demonstrations, there were a lot of meetings.
6. We used to discuss politics for hours.
7. In the streets the students were marching.
8. You could hear them from far away.
9. The police were trying to stop them.
10. One evening, while they were marching, a fight broke out.
11. Cars were burning in the Latin Quarter.
12. People were listening to the news on their transistor radios.

B1 PRESENTATION

■ Grammar

- **Être** *(to be)*

Imparfait			
j'	**étais**	*I*	*was*
tu	**étais**	*you*	*were*
il, elle	**était**	*he, she, it*	*was*
nous	**étions**	*we*	*were*
vous	**étiez**	*you*	*were*
ils, elles	**étaient**	*they*	*were*

■ Vocabulary

s'échapper	*to get away, to escape*
aider	*to help*
enfance (fem.)	*childhood*
ferme (fem.)	*farm*
champ (masc.)	*field*
forêt (fem.)	*forest*
devoirs (masc. pl.)	*homework*
tracteur (masc.)	*tractor*
cheval (masc.)	*horse*
écurie (fem.)	*stable*
brun	*dark-haired*
différent	*different*
autrefois	*in the past*

B2 EXAMPLES *(Childhood)*

1. Quand j'étais jeune, mon père me parlait de son enfance.
2. C'était un petit garçon aux yeux noirs et aux cheveux bruns.
3. Il avait deux frères, ils vivaient dans une ferme.
4. Ils étaient souvent dans les champs.
5. Ils n'étaient pas très riches.
6. Leur ferme n'était pas très grande.
7. La forêt était tout près.
8. Leur mère était toujours occupée.
9. Autrefois, la vie à la campagne était très différente.
10. Quand il avait fait ses devoirs, il aidait ses parents.
11. Il n'y avait pas de tracteur, ils avaient des chevaux.
12. Un jour, pendant qu'il était en train de jouer dans l'écurie, les chevaux s'étaient échappés.

B3 COMMENTS

■ Grammar

- To insist on the action taking place, the expression:
  être en train de + infinitive is sometimes used.
  Ex.: **Il jouait.**
  Il était en train de jouer. ⎤→ *He was playing.*

  J'écoutais les nouvelles.
  J'étais en train d'écouter les nouvelles.
  I was listening to the news.

NB: the same expression can be used in the present.
  Ex.: **Il joue.**
  Il est en train de jouer. ⎤→ *He is playing.*

- The **imparfait** of **être** or **avoir** + the past participle of a verb form the **plus-que-parfait**.
  The **plus-que-parfait** is the same in usage as the pluperfect in English.
  Ex.: **Il avait fini quand elle a appelé.**
  He had finished when she called.
  Nous étions partis quand vous êtes arrivés.
  We had left when you arrived.

- As for the **passé composé**, the past participle agrees with the subject when the auxiliary is **être**.

B4 TRANSLATION

1. When I was young, my father used to tell me about his childhood.
2. He was a dark-eyed, dark-haired little boy.
3. He had two brothers, they used to live on a farm.
4. They were often in the fields.
5. They were not very rich.
6. Their farm was not very big.
7. The forest was near by.
8. Their mother was always busy.
9. In the past, life in the country was very different.
10. When he had finished his homework, he used to help his parents.
11. There were no tractors, they had horses.
12. One day, while he was playing in the stable, the horses escaped.

C1 EXERCISES

A. Put the verb in the correct form of the _imparfait_:

1. Où (être) tu ?
2. Que (faire) vous ?
3. Il ne (travailler) pas à Paris.
4. Autrefois, les femmes (porter) des jupes longues.
5. Les vacances (finir) en octobre quand j' (être) jeune.
6. Que (chercher) ils ?
7. Nous (regarder) des albums pendant des heures.

B. Use the _imparfait_ or _passé composé_:

1. Pendant que je (faire) une promenade, je (rencontrer) Pierre.
2. Pendant qu'ils (regarder) la télévision, le téléphone (sonner).
3. Quand vous (arriver), nous (discuter).

C. ●● Insist on the action taking place:

1. Je parlais.
2. Tu travaillais.
3. Il faisait un discours.
4. Nous jouions.

D. Don't insist on the action taking place:

1. Vous étiez en train de manger.
2. Ils étaient en train de lire.
3. J'étais en train d'écrire.
4. Elle était en train de chanter.

C2 SOME WORDS ARE USUALLY IN THE PLURAL IN FRENCH

cheveux (masc. pl.) _hair_

Others have different meanings in the singular and in the plural:

devoir (masc.)	_duty_	**devoirs**	_homework_
lunette (masc.)	_telescope_	**lunettes**	_glasses_
course (fem.)	_race_	**courses**	_shopping_
vêtement (masc.)	_garment_	**vêtements**	_clothes_

C3 ANSWERS

A. 1. Où étais-tu ?
2. Que faisiez-vous ?
3. Il ne travaillait pas à Paris.
4. Autrefois, les femmes portaient des jupes longues.
5. Les vacances finissaient en octobre quand j'étais jeune.
6. Que cherchaient-ils ?
7. Nous regardions des albums pendant des heures.

B. 1. Pendant que je faisais une promenade, j'ai rencontré Pierre.
2. Pendant qu'ils regardaient la télévision, le téléphone a sonné.
3. Quand vous êtes arrivé (arrivée, arrivés, arrivées), nous discutions.

C. 1. J'étais en train de parler.
2. Tu étais en train de travailler.
3. Il était en train de faire un discours.
4. Nous étions en train de jouer.

D. 1. Vous mangiez.
2. Ils lisaient.
3. J'écrivais.
4. Elle chantait.

C4 PHYSICAL OR MORAL DESCRIPTIONS

- The equivalents of the compound adjectives: *fair-haired, blue-eyed,* etc., are expressions with:

à la, au, aux + noun + adjective

Ex.: **un garçon aux yeux noirs**   *a dark-eyed boy*
une fille aux cheveux blonds   *a fair-haired girl*
un bébé à la peau douce   *a soft-skinned baby*
un garçon au nez pointu   *a sharp-nosed boy*
un homme à l'œil brillant   *a bright-eyed man*
une personne à l'esprit étroit   *a narrow-minded person*

A1 PRESENTATION

■ Grammar

- When the same person is both the subject and the object of the action, the verb is called a reflexive verb.
  Reflexive verbs must be used with special reflexive pronouns:

> **me, m'**
> **te, t'**
> **se, s'**
> **nous**
> **vous**
> **se, s'**

- The reflexive pronoun precedes the verb or auxiliary except in the imperative.

  Ex.: **Je me dépêche / Dépêchez-vous.**
  I'm hurrying! / Hurry up!

- **s'appeler**, the equivalent of *his, her, its name is...*, is a reflexive verb.

■ Vocabulary

se lever	*to get up*	**se faire mal**	*to hurt oneself*
se raser	*to shave*	**se dépêcher**	*to hurry*
s'habiller	*to dress,*	**se disputer**	*to quarrel*
	to dress up	**se tromper**	*to be mistaken*
se laver	*to wash*	**d'habitude**	*usually*
se préparer	*to get ready*		

A2 EXAMPLES *(Everyday life)*

1. Je m'appelle Pierre Lebon.
2. Je me lève tous les jours à sept heures.
3. Je me rase avant de partir.
4. D'habitude, il s'habille pour le dîner.
5. Les enfants se lavent.
6. Elle se prépare pour le dîner.
7. On se prépare pour sortir.
8. Nous nous levons tard le dimanche.
9. Tu t'es fait mal ?
10. Ils se dépêchent pour prendre le bus.
11. Les enfants se disputent beaucoup, mais ils s'entendent bien.
12. Tu te trompes !

A3 COMMENTS

■ Grammar

me	French equivalent of	*myself*
te		*yourself*
se	*himself, herself, itself, themselves*	
nous		*ourselves*
vous		*yourselves*

Ex.: **Je me regarde.** *I'm looking at myself.*
Il s'est fait mal. *He hurt himself.*

- **nous, vous, se, s'** are the equivalents of *each other* or *one another*.
  Ex.: **Ils se regardent.**
  They are looking at each other.
  Nous nous comprenons.
  We understand one another.

- Note the different uses of the singular and plural in French and English:

  tous les jours *every day*
  le dimanche *on Sundays*

A4 TRANSLATION

1. My name is Pierre Lebon.
2. I get up at seven every day.
3. I shave before leaving.
4. He usually dresses up for dinner.
5. The children are washing.
6. She is getting ready for dinner.
7. We're getting ready to go out.
8. We get up late on Sundays.
9. Did you hurt yourself?
10. They're hurrying to take the bus.
11. The children quarrel a lot, but they get on well.
12. You are mistaken!

B1 PRESENTATION

■ Grammar

- In the imperative, the reflexive pronoun is a « strong » one :

> **moi**
> **toi**
> **nous**
> **vous**

Ex.: **Habillez-vous !** *Get dressed!*
Lève-toi ! *Get up!*

- For all reflexive verbs, the **passé composé** is formed with **être**, and the past participle agrees with the subject.

Ex.: **Ils ne se sont pas reposés.**
They didn't rest.

■ Vocabulary

s'asseoir	*to sit down*	**petit déjeuner** (masc.)	*breakfast*
s'amuser	*to have fun*		
se coucher	*to go to bed*	**chemin** (masc.)	*way*
se réveiller	*to wake up*	**demi-heure** (fem.)	*half an hour*
se promener	*to go for a walk*		
s'occuper de	*to look after*	**de bonne heure**	*early*
se reposer	*to rest*	**prêt**	*ready*

B2 EXAMPLES *(Sleeping late)*

1. **Levez-vous, il est sept heures !**
2. **Dépêche-toi, le petit déjeuner est prêt.**
3. **Dépêchez-vous, il est huit heures et demie !**
4. **Asseyez-vous, je vous en prie.**
5. **Vous vous êtes bien amusés hier soir ?**
6. **Oui, on s'est couché à minuit moins le quart.**
7. **On s'est trompé de chemin pour revenir.**
8. **Tu t'es réveillé de bonne heure ?**
9. **Oui, je me suis promené dans le jardin une demi-heure.**
10. **Je me suis occupé des fleurs.**
11. **Nous nous sommes reposés une heure.**
12. **Habillez-vous, nous allons nous promener.**

B3 COMMENTS

■ Grammar

- For a negative command, the reflexive pronoun precedes the verb.
  Ne vous dépêchez pas. *Don't hurry.*
  Ne te trompe pas. *Don't make a mistake.*
  Ne t'occupe pas des fleurs. *Don't take care of the flowers.*

- **Se tromper de** + noun is the French equivalent of:

  to take
  to have ⎤→ *the wrong* + noun
  to get

  Ex.: **se tromper de bus** *to take the wrong bus*
  se tromper de numéro *to get a wrong number*

- Note the difference between:
  une demi-heure *half an hour*
  une heure et demie *an hour and a half*
  un quart d'heure *a quarter of an hour*
  une heure et quart *an hour and a quarter*

■ Pronunciation

- In **asseyez**, the first **e** is pronounced **é**.

B4 TRANSLATION

1. Get up, it is seven o'clock!
2. Hurry up, breakfast is ready.
3. Hurry up, it is half past eight!
4. Do sit down (literally: Sit down I pray you).
5. Did you have fun last night?
6. Yes, we went to bed at a quarter to twelve.
7. We took the wrong way back.
8. Did you wake up early?
9. Yes, I went for a walk in the garden for half an hour.
10. I looked after the flowers.
11. We rested for an hour.
12. Get dressed, we are going for a walk.

C1 EXERCISES

A. Match:

te		asseyons
je	me	regardes
tu	se, s'	assoit
il, elle	vous	disputent
nous	nous	promenez
vous		dépêchez
ils, elles		rase

B. ●● **Put in the imperative form:**

1. Tu te lèves.
2. Tu t'occupes des enfants.
3. Nous nous reposons.
4. Vous vous habillez.
5. Vous vous amusez bien.

C. ●● **Translate into French:**

1. I get up at nine o'clock.
2. She is hurrying.
3. I'm getting ready.
4. We are taking the wrong car.
5. Did you hurt yourselves?

C2 SOYONS POLIS / LET'S BE POLITE

Here are some useful expressions:

- to apologize:
  pardon, excusez-moi, je suis désolé(e), je suis navré(e).

- to say: *it doesn't matter*
  de rien, je vous en prie, ce n'est rien.

- to insist politely on an order:
  je vous en prie.

  Ex.: a. **Je suis désolée d'être en retard !**   *I'm sorry, I'm late!*
  b. **Je vous en prie !**   *It's all right!*

  a. **Asseyez-vous, je vous en prie !**   *Do sit down!*
  b. **Merci beaucoup !**   *Thanks a lot!*
  a. **De rien !**   *Don't mention it!*

C3 ANSWERS

A. je me rase — il se rase — tu te regardes — il, elle s'assoit
nous nous asseyons — vous vous promenez
vous vous dépêchez — ils, elles se disputent

B. 1. Lève-toi !
2. Occupe-toi des enfants.
3. Reposons-nous.
4. Habillez-vous.
5. Amusez-vous bien !

C. 1. Je me lève à neuf heures.
2. Elle se dépêche.
3. Je me prépare.
4. Nous nous trompons de voiture.
5. Vous vous êtes fait mal ? / Est-ce que vous vous êtes fait mal ? /
Vous êtes-vous fait mal ?

C4 NOM, PRÉNOM ●●
NAME, FIRST NAME

- To introduce oneself or somebody else, the commonly used
  expression is :

Je m'appelle*...	*My name is... (literally : I call myself...)*
Tu t'appelles*...	*Your name is...*
Il, elle s'appelle*...	*His, her, its name is...*
Nous nous appelons...	*Our names are...*
Vous vous appelez...	*Your names are..., your name is...*
Ils, elles s'appellent*...	*Their names are...*

- **Comment vous appelez-vous ?**
  Comment tu t'appelles ? ⎤→ *What's your name?*

* Notice the double **l** : in that case, the first **e** is pronounced like *e* in *pet*.
In **appelons** and **appelez**, only one **l** and the **e** is glided over.

201

A1 PRESENTATION

■ Grammar

- Remember we have seen: **aller** + infinitive to express a future action. Here is the future tense as such. Its construction is:

  (sing.) infinitive + **-ai**   (pl.) infinitive + **-ons**
                    -as   **-ez**
                    -a   **-ont**

  Ex.: **je sortirai, tu parleras, il jouera,**
         nous finirons, vous partirez, ils donneront.

- When the infinitive ends in **-re**, the **e** is dropped.
  Ex.: **je conduirai, tu prendras, il rira.**

■ Vocabulary

décoller	*to take off*	**directeur**	*marketing*
se poser	*to land*	**commercial** (masc.)	*manager*
emmener à	*to take to*	**renseignement** (masc.)	*information*
prendre		**contrat** (masc.)	*contract*
contact	*to contact*	**de toute façon**	*anyway*
signer	*to sign*		
accepter	*to accept*		

A2 EXAMPLES *(Business trip)*

1. À quelle heure décollera l'avion ?
2. Il décollera à neuf heures et se posera à Tokyo seize heures plus tard.
3. Quand vous sortirez de l'aéroport, une voiture vous attendra.
4. Elle vous emmènera à votre hôtel dans le centre ville.
5. Notre directeur commercial prendra contact avec vous.
6. Quand vous connaîtrez votre planning, vous nous appellerez.
7. S'il y a un problème, nous vous donnerons des renseignements.
8. Quand vous rencontrerez nos clients, vous leur direz que le contrat est prêt.
9. Quand le patron arrivera, il le signera.
10. J'espère qu'ils accepteront nos conditions.
11. Vous n'aurez sûrement pas le temps de visiter la ville.
12. De toute façon, nous y retournerons ensemble l'an prochain.

A3 COMMENTS

■ Grammar

- Note that to indicate the idea of future action, a sentence starting with **quand** must be in the future.

  Ex.: **Quand vous sortirez de l'aéroport, vous trouverez une voiture.**

  When you come out of the airport, you'll find a car.

- Other conjunctions of time follow the same rule:

dès que	*as soon as*
aussitôt que	*as soon as*
au moment où	*the moment when*

- Note that the English word *planning* is commonly used in French meaning *schedule* or *programme* or *calendar*.

- Note that **renseignement** is often used in the plural.

■ Pronunciation

- In A2, you see many words with a circumflex accent: **hôtel, connaîtrez, prêt, sûrement**.

  Remember it doesn't alter the pronunciation of the vowel.

A4 TRANSLATION

1. What time will the plane take off?
2. It'll take off at nine, and land in Tokyo sixteen hours later.
3. When you come out of the airport, a car will be waiting for you.
4. It'll take you to your hotel in the centre of town.
5. Our marketing manager will contact you.
6. You'll call us when you know your schedule.
7. If there's a problem, we'll give you information.
8. When you meet our customers, you'll tell them the contract is ready.
9. When the boss arrives, he'll sign it.
10. I hope they'll accept our conditions.
11. You surely won't have time to visit the city.
12. We'll go back there together next year anyway.

B1   PRESENTATION

■ Grammar

• Irregular verbs in the future (see also B3)

	être *to be*	avoir *to have*
je	serai	aurai
tu	seras	auras
il/elle	sera	aura
nous	serons	aurons
vous	serez	aurez
ils/elles	seront	auront

■ Vocabulary

découvrir	*to discover*	**médicament** (masc.)	*medicine*
espérer	*to hope*	**maladie** (fem.)	*disease*
éviter	*to avoid*	**technologie** (fem.)	*technology*
espace (masc.)	*space*	**pollution** (fem.)	*pollution*
navette (fem.)	*shuttle*	**paix** (fem.)	*peace*
lune (fem.)	*moon*	**peut-être**	*perhaps*
planète (fem.)	*planet*	**grâce à**	*thanks to*
génération (f.)	*generation*	**jusqu'à quand**	*until when*

B2   EXAMPLES *(In 2010)*

1. Un jour viendra où nous irons très loin dans l'espace.
2. Il y aura des navettes entre les planètes.
3. Nous ferons des voyages extraordinaires.
4. On se promènera sur la Lune.
5. Nous voyagerons de plus en plus loin.
6. Nous découvrirons d'autres mondes.
7. On découvrira de nouveaux médicaments, mais il y aura peut-être plus de maladies.
8. Grâce aux technologies nouvelles, on sera en contact avec le monde entier à tout moment.
9. On trouvera peut-être des solutions au problème de la pollution.
10. L'homme vivra peut-être de plus en plus longtemps.
11. Jusqu'à quand évitera-t-on la guerre ?
12. Espérons que les générations futures vivront en paix.

B3 COMMENTS

■ Grammar

- Note that in such expressions of time as **un jour viendra où** *(a day will come when)*, **le jour où** *(the day when)*, **au moment où** *(the moment when)*, the word **où** is used meaning *WHEN* and not *WHERE*.

- Before nouns *more* is translated by **plus de**.
    - Ex.: **Il y a plus de pollution à Paris que dans les Alpes.**
      There's more pollution in Paris than in the Alps.

- Remember that in an interrogative form with an inverted verb, if it ends with a vowel, **t** must be placed before **il, elle** or **on**:
    - Ex.: **Évitera-t-on ? Viendra-t-elle ? Partira-t-il ?**

- Irregular verbs in the future:

	aller *to go*	faire *to do / to make*	venir *to come*
je/j'	irai	ferai	viendrai
tu	iras	feras	viendras
il/elle	ira	fera	viendra
nous	irons	ferons	viendrons
vous	irez	ferez	viendrez
ils/elles	iront	feront	viendront

B4 TRANSLATION

1. A day will come when we go very far into space.
2. There'll be shuttles between the planets.
3. We'll take extraordinary trips.
4. We'll walk on the moon.
5. We'll travel farther and farther.
6. We'll discover other worlds.
7. New medicines will be discovered, but there will perhaps be more diseases.
8. Thanks to new technologies, we'll be in contact with the whole world at all times.
9. Maybe solutions to the problem of pollution will be found.
10. Man will perhaps live longer and longer.
11. Until when will we avoid war?
12. Let's hope future generations will live in peace.

C1 EXERCISES

A. Put into the future:

1. Je vous (rejoindre).
2. Tu (accepter) les conditions.
3. Elle nous (emmener).
4. Nous (prendre contact).
5. Il (aller) loin.
6. Vous (signer) le contrat.
7. Ils (découvrir) le pays.
8. Elles (venir) avec nous.

B. Put in the correct order:

1. nous / promener / vous / nous / avec / forêt / irons / la / dans.
2. il / sept / sera / quand / heures / nouvelles / les / nous / écouterons.
3. avion / viendra / navette / dès que / l' / la / se posera / chercher / vous.

C. Take the odd one out:

1. irons - prendrons - avons - viendrons - découvrirons.
2. seront - font - sortiront - traverseront - entendront.
3. pleurez - claquerez - traverserez - possèderez - connaîtrez.

D. Translate into French:

1. Please call me as soon as you arrive.
2. When the boss sees her, he'll give her the contract.
3. When I'm eighty five, I'll write the story of my life.

C2 HOW TO EXPRESS THE NEAR FUTURE

bientôt	*soon*
demain	*tomorrow*
après-demain	*the day after tomorrow*
tout à l'heure	*in a moment*
plus tard	*later*
sous peu	*before long*
d'ici...	*within...*

C3 ANSWERS

A. 1. Je vous rejoindrai.
2. Tu accepteras les conditions.
3. Elle nous emmènera.
4. Nous prendrons contact.
5. Il ira loin.
6. Vous signerez le contrat.
7. Ils découvriront le pays.
8. Elles viendront avec nous.

B. 1. Nous irons nous promener avec vous dans la forêt.
2. Quand il sera sept heures, nous écouterons les nouvelles. /
Nous écouterons les nouvelles quand il sera sept heures.
3. Dès que l'avion se posera, la navette viendra vous chercher. /
La navette viendra vous chercher dès que l'avion se posera.

C. 1. avons.
2. font.
3. pleurez.

D. 1. S'il vous plaît, appelez-moi dès que vous arriverez.
2. Quand le patron la verra, il lui donnera le contrat.
3. Quand j'aurai quatre-vingt-cinq ans, j'écrirai l'histoire de ma vie.

C4 COMPARATIVE EXPRESSIONS

- Double comparisons like *faster and faster* or *more and more comfortable* are translated by
de plus en plus rapide / confortable.
The equivalent of *less and less* is **de moins en moins**.

- Useful expressions:
The sooner the better.   **Le plus tôt sera le mieux.**
The more the merrier.   **Plus on est de fous plus on rit.**
(Literally: the more madmen there are the more they laugh.)

But: *Sooner or later.*   **Tôt ou tard.**

A1 PRESENTATION

■ Grammar

- **en** and **y** are pronouns used to avoid repeating the name of a place introduced by a preposition.

  Ex.: **Est-ce que tu vas <u>à la gare</u> ? — Oui, j'<u>y</u> vais.**
  On va <u>au cinéma</u> ? — Oui, on <u>y</u> va.
  Est-ce que tu viens <u>de la campagne</u> ? — Oui, j'<u>en</u> viens.

  Note that **à** (or the contracted forms **au, aux**) + noun = **y**
  de (or the contracted forms **du, des**) + noun = **en**

- **y** is also used to replace a complement (whether a noun or an infinitive) introduced by the preposition **à**. Ex.:
  Tu penses à ton travail ? — Oui, j'y pense.
  Est-ce que tu as pensé à prendre les livres ? — Oui, j'y ai pensé.

■ Vocabulary

sortir	*to go out,* *to come out*	**agence de voyages** (fem.)	*travel agency*
passer par	*to go via*	**liste** (fem.)	*list*
s'arrêter	*to stop*	**piscine** (fem.)	*swimming pool*
se renseigner	*to ask for information*	**ce soir**	*tonight*
choisir	*to choose*		

A2 EXAMPLES *(Booking)*

1. **Est-ce que tu es allé à l'agence de voyages pour prendre les billets ?**
2. **Oui, j'en viens.**
3. **Quand y es-tu allé ?**
4. **J'y suis allé à l'heure du déjeuner.**
5. **Il n'y avait personne, et j'en suis sorti cinq minutes plus tard.**
6. **On passe par Athènes ; est-ce que tu sais si l'avion s'y arrête ?**
7. **Non, je n'en sais rien, mais je peux me renseigner.**
8. **As-tu pensé à réserver l'hôtel ?**
9. **J'y ai pensé mais j'ai préféré attendre pour choisir avec toi.**
10. **L'agence m'a donné des listes d'hôtels, on en choisira un ce soir.**
11. **On en prendra un avec piscine ?**
12. **Pourquoi pas ? J'y pense depuis longtemps !**

A3 COMMENTS

■ Grammar

- Note that **y** can never be used for a person.

  Je pense à mon examen.   **J'y pense.**
  I'm thinking about my exam.   *I'm thinking about it.*

  Je pense à mon oncle.   **Je pense à lui.**
  I'm thinking about my uncle.   *I'm thinking about him.*

- On the contrary, **en** can be used for a person.

  Je rêve de mes vacances.   **J'en rêve.**
  I'm dreaming about my holidays.   *I'm dreaming about there.*

  J'ai rêvé de mes enfants.   **J'en ai rêvé.**
  I dreamed about my children.   *I dreamed about them.*

- **un** and **une** are not only indefinite articles. They are also pronouns. They are the French equivalent of *one*, but they are always used with **en**. Ex.:

  Tu prends un sac ? — Oui, j'en prends un.
  Are you taking a bag? — Yes, I'm taking one.

  Tu as réservé une chambre ? — Oui, j'en ai réservé une.
  Did you reserve a room? — Yes, I reserved one.

- Note a few set expressions where a noun is used without any article:

avec piscine	*with a swimming pool*
avec vue	*with a view*
avec salle de bains	*with a bathroom*

A4 TRANSLATION

1. Did you go to the travel agency to get the tickets?
2. Yes, I've just been there.
3. When did you go*?
4. I went at lunch time*.
5. There was nobody, and I came out five minutes later*.
6. We go via Athens; do you know whether the plane stops there?
7. No, I have no idea, but I can ask.
8. Did you think of reserving the hotel?
9. I thought of it, but I prefered to wait to choose with you.
10. The agency gave me lists of hotels, we'll choose one tonight.
11. Shall we take one with a swimming pool?
12. Why not? I've been thinking about it for a long time!

* Note that **y** or **en** can't be omitted in French whereas *there* can be in English.

B1 PRESENTATION

■ Grammar

- **en** as a pronoun is used to avoid repeating a partitive construction with **de, du, de la, de l', des.**
  - Ex.: **Avez-vous acheté du vin ? — Oui, j'en ai acheté.**
    Did you buy any wine? — Yes, I bought some.
    A-t-elle lu des livres de science-fiction ?
    Has she read science fiction books?
    Non, elle n'en a jamais lu.
    No, she has never read any.

- It is also used to avoid repeating the complement of an expression of quantity : **beaucoup de** *(a lot of)*, **un peu de** *(a little)*, **trop de** *(too much/many).*
  - Ex.: **Il a beaucoup d'amis. — Oui, il en a beaucoup.**
    He has a lot of friends. — Yes, he has many.
    Ils ont trop de travail. — Oui, ils en ont trop.
    They have too much work. — Yes, they have too much.

■ Vocabulary

château (masc.)	*castle*
usine (fem.)	*factory*
fortune (fem.)	*fortune*
milliardaire (masc.)	*multimillionaire*
héritier (masc.)	*heir*
projet (masc.)	*plan*
immense	*huge*

B2 EXAMPLES *(After a rich man's death)*

1. Est-ce qu'il avait beaucoup d'argent ?
2. Oui, il en avait beaucoup.
3. Possédait-il des châteaux ?
4. Oui, il en avait trois.
5. Avait-il aussi des usines ?
6. Oui, il en possédait en France et à l'étranger.
7. Parlait-il souvent de sa fortune ?
8. Non, il n'en parlait jamais.
9. Connaissait-il d'autres milliardaires ?
10. Il en connaissait, mais il ne les aimait pas.
11. Ses héritiers font-ils des projets ?
12. Oui, ils en font beaucoup : leur fortune est immense !

B3 COMMENTS

■ Grammar

● Note that **en** and **y** precede the verbal form, except in the imperative. Ex.:
Est-ce qu'il prend du thé le matin ? — Oui, il en prend.
Does he have tea in the morning? — Yes, he does.
Prends du thé !   **Prends-en !**
Have some tea!   *Have some!*
J'y vais.   *I am going there.*
Vas-y !   *Go there!*

● In the negative, **en** and **y** always precede the verbal form.
Il n'en parle pas.   *He doesn't speak about it.*
Il n'en a pas parlé.   *He didn't speak about it.*
N'en parle pas.   *Don't speak about it.*
Elle n'y pense pas.   *She doesn't think about it.*
N'y pense pas.   *Don't think about it.*
Je n'en sais rien.   *I know nothing about it.*

■ Pronunciation

● Remember that **im** is pronounced **in**, at the beginning of a word.
    Ex.: **imperméable, impossible, important**,
but when the **m** is doubled, **im** is pronounced **i + m**.
    Ex.: **immeuble, immense**.

B4 TRANSLATION

1. Did he have much money?
2. Yes, he had a lot.
3. Did he own castles?
4. Yes, he had three.
5. Did he also have factories?
6. Yes, he owned some, in France and abroad.
7. Did he often speak about his fortune?
8. No, he never spoke about it.
9. Did he know other multimillionnaires?
10. He knew a few but he did not like them.
11. Are his heirs making plans?
12. Yes, they are making many, they have a huge fortune!

C1 EXERCISES

A. Complete the answers using the pronoun en:

1. Est-ce que tu as des cigarettes ? — Oui, ...
2. Est-ce qu'elle a des nouvelles de son mari ? — Non, ...
3. As-tu pris de l'argent ? — Oui, ...
4. A-t-il peur des serpents ? — Oui, ...
5. Tu as envie de café ? — Non, ...
6. Est-ce que vous venez de la plage ? — Oui, ...

B. Choose between y or en:

1. Je pense souvent à ce film. J'... pense souvent.
2. Anne ne parle pas beaucoup de ses amis. Elle n'... parle pas beaucoup.
3. Elle rêve d'habiter Athènes. Elle ... rêve.
4. Ne faisons pas attention à la pluie ! N'... faisons pas attention !
5. Ils discutent de leur contrat. Ils ... discutent.
6. Pensez à réserver votre hôtel ! Pensez-... !

C. ●● Translate into French:

1. Have you got magazines? — I have got one.
2. Did you write postcards? — I wrote one.
3. Can I have a glass of whisky? — Of course, have one.
4. Where are the plates? Bring me one please.
5. Will you buy presents? — Yes, I'll buy one for our friends.

C2 SOME VERBAL EXPRESSIONS ARE FOLLOWED BY A COMPLEMENT INTRODUCED BY DE

avoir envie de	*to feel like*
avoir besoin de	*to need*
avoir peur de	*to be afraid of*
avoir honte de	*to be ashamed of*

- **en** makes it possible to avoid repeating the complement with these expressions:

  As-tu envie de jouer au tennis ? — Oui, j'en ai envie.
  Do you feel like playing tennis? — Yes, I do.

- Remember: **J'en ai assez.**   *I'm fed up.*
                J'en ai assez de...   *I'm fed up with...*

C3 ANSWERS

A. 1. Est-ce que tu as des cigarettes ? — Oui, j'en ai. 2. Est-ce qu'elle a des nouvelles de son mari ? — Non, elle n'en a pas. 3. As-tu pris de l'argent ? — Oui, j'en ai pris. 4. A-t-il peur des serpents ? — Oui, il en a peur. 5. Tu as envie de café ? — Non, je n'en ai pas envie. 6. Est-ce que vous venez de la plage ? — Oui, nous en venons/j'en viens.

B. 1. Je pense souvent à ce film. J'y pense souvent.— 2. Anne ne parle pas beaucoup de ses amis. Elle n'en parle pas beaucoup.— 3. Elle rêve d'habiter Athènes. Elle en rêve.— 4. Ne faisons pas attention à la pluie ! N'y faisons pas attention !— 5. Ils discutent de leur contrat. Ils en discutent.— 6. Pensez à réserver votre hôtel ! Pensez-y !

C. 1. Avez-vous/As-tu des magazines ? — J'en ai un.
2. Avez-vous/As-tu écrit des cartes postales ? — J'en ai écrit une.
3. Puis-je avoir un verre de whisky ? — Bien sûr, prenez-en un.
4. Où sont les assiettes ? Apporte-m'en une s'il te plaît. / Apportez-m'en... 5. Achèterez-vous/achèteras-tu des cadeaux ? — Oui, j'en achèterai un pour nos amis.

C4 ARGENT / *MONEY*

monnaie (courante) (fem.) *currency*   **monnaie** (fem.) *change*
- **billet** (masc.) *note (US: bill)*

un billet	de 500 F (cinq cents francs)	
	de 200 F (deux cents francs)	
	de 100 F (cent francs)	← These are the French
	de 50 F (cinquante francs)	notes in circulation.
	de 20 F (vingt francs)	

- **pièce** (fem.) *coin*

une pièce	de 10 F (dix francs)	
	de 5 F (cinq francs)	
	de 2 F (deux francs)	
	de 1 F (un franc)	
	de 50 c (cinquante centimes)	← These are the French
	de 20 c (vingt centimes)	coins in circulation.
	de 10 c (dix centimes)	
	de 5 c (cinq centimes)	

There are 100 **centimes** in one **franc**.

A1 PRESENTATION

■ Grammar

- **Je lis en écoutant la radio.**
  I'm reading and listening to the radio.

  To express the idea that two (or more) actions with the same subject are taking place simultaneously, the construction is:

action A (conjugated verb)	+ **en** +	action B (verb in the **participe présent**)
Je lis	**en**	**écoutant**

- The **participe présent** *(present participle)* is formed by adding **ant** or **issant** to the stem of the verb (see p. 266).

■ Vocabulary

traverser	*to cross*	**carrefour** (masc.)	*intersection*
renverser	*to run over*	**piéton** (masc.)	*pedestrian*
remonter la rue	*to go up the street*	**ambulance** (fem.)	*ambulance*
courir	*to run*	**infirmière** (fem.)	*nurse*
poser des questions	*to ask questions*	**témoin** (masc.)	*witness*
soigner	*to take care of, to treat*	**inquiet**	*anxious, worried*
		avec inquiétude	*anxiously*

A2 EXAMPLES *(An accident)*

1. Mon mari et moi avons vu un accident en nous promenant dans la rue.
2. En traversant le carrefour, une voiture a renversé un piéton.
3. Le conducteur avait l'air inquiet en sortant de sa voiture.
4. Il a traversé la rue en courant.
5. Il était très inquiet en appelant l'ambulance.
6. L'ambulance allait très vite en remontant la rue.
7. Tout en soignant le piéton, le médecin lui posait des questions.
8. Il répondait en le regardant avec inquiétude.
9. Une infirmière lui parlait doucement en le soignant.
10. Un agent de police allait d'un témoin à l'autre en posant des questions.
11. Un témoin répondait en donnant des précisions.
12. Nous sommes rentrés chez nous en discutant de l'accident.

A3 COMMENTS

■ Grammar

- To emphasize the idea of simultaneity **tout** can be placed before **en**.
  - Ex.: **Je lis tout en écoutant la radio.**
    I'm reading while listening to the radio.

- Note irregular **participes présents**:

être	étant	*being*
avoir	ayant	*having*
savoir	sachant	*knowing*

- The construction **en + participe présent** often conveys the idea expressed in English by a prepositional verb.
  - Ex.: **Il est parti en courant.**   *He ran away.*
    Il est monté en courant.   *He ran up.*
    Il est descendu en courant.   *He ran down.*
    Il est sorti en courant.   *He ran out.*

- Note that **moi, toi, lui, elle, nous, vous, eux, elles** are also used as unemphasized subjects when linked to other subjects by **et**.
  - Ex.: **Pierre et moi sommes amis.**
    Peter and I are friends.
    Lui et moi sommes amis.
    He and I are friends.
    Ton frère et toi viendrez demain.
    You brother and you will come tomorrow.

- **Avec inquiétude**: note that the article is omitted (see C4).

A4 TRANSLATION

1. My husband and I saw an accident as we were walking in the street.
2. As it was crossing the intersection, a car ran over a pedestrian.
3. The driver seemed worried as he got out of his car.
4. He ran across the street.
5. He was very worried when he was calling the ambulance.
6. The ambulance went up the street very fast.
7. While treating the pedestrian, the doctor asked him some questions.
8. He answered, looking at him anxiously.
9. A nurse was talking to him quietly as she was taking care of him.
10. A policeman was going from one witness to the other, asking questions.
11. A witness was answering, giving details.
12. We went home talking about the accident.

B1 PRESENTATION

■ Grammar

- **En + participe présent** does not only express simultaneity :
    Ex.: **Elle est sortie en riant.** *She went out laughing.*
    Il a ouvert la porte en tournant la poignée.
    He opened the door by turning the knob.

- The **participe présent** is invariable, but the **ant** form can also be used as an adjective ; it then agrees in gender and number with the noun it refers to.
    Ex.: **un livre intéressant** *an interesting book*
    des livres intéressants *interesting books*
    une femme charmante *a charming woman*
    des amies charmantes *charming friends*

■ Vocabulary

(se) perfectionner	*to improve*	**expression** (fem.)	*expression*
se distraire	*to have fun*	**régulièrement**	*regularly*
cassette (fem.)	*cassette*	**couramment**	*fluently*
		sans peine	*easily*

B2 EXAMPLES *(Learning languages)*

1. **On apprend une langue en utilisant des livres, des cassettes, etc.**
2. **Mais on apprend aussi une langue en la pratiquant.**
3. **En la pratiquant régulièrement, on oublie moins.**
4. **Que faire pour parler couramment ?**
5. **Bien sûr, en allant dans le pays, vous parlerez de mieux en mieux.**
6. **En écoutant la radio, vous améliorerez votre français.**
7. **Comment apprendre une langue sans dire un mot ?**
8. **En discutant avec vos voisins, vous vous perfectionnerez sans peine.**
9. **Vous apprendrez des expressions utiles en lisant les journaux.**
10. **Regarder la télévision vous aidera à mieux comprendre.**
11. **Voir des films en français peut vous aider.**
12. **C'est une façon d'apprendre une langue en se distrayant.**

B3 COMMENTS

■ Grammar

- Note that **en** is the only preposition which is followed by a **participe présent**; all the others are followed by an infinitive.

  Ex.: **sans parler** *without speaking*
  pour oublier *in order to forget*
  après manger *after eating*

- Remember the spelling of:

voir	: **voyant**
se distraire	: **se distrayant**
avoir	: **ayant**
s'asseoir	: **s'asseyant**

■ Pronunciation

- Remember **an, en, em, am** are pronounced the same: nasal vowel **an** except for **am** when it is followed by a vowel.

  Ex.: **ami, améliorer, s'amuser, américain** *(American).*
  couramment is pronounced **coura/ment.**

B4 TRANSLATION

1. You learn a language using books, cassettes, etc.
2. But you also learn a language by practising it.
3. By practising regularly you forget less.
4. What can you do to speak fluently?
5. Of course, by going to the country, you'll speak better and better.
6. By listening to the radio, you'll improve your French.
7. How can you learn a language without saying a word?
8. By talking with your neighbours, you will improve easily.
9. You will learn useful expressions by reading the newspapers.
10. Watching television will help you to understand better.
11. Seeing films in French can help you.
12. It is a way to learn a language and have fun at the same time.

C1 EXERCISES

A. Put in the participe présent:

1. habiter
2. ouvrir
3. aller
4. rire
5. dire
6. venir

B. Change as in the example: Il mange et il regarde la télévision. / Il mange en regardant la télévision.

1. Je lis mon journal et j'attends le bus.
2. Les enfants marchent et ils s'amusent.
3. Nous discutons et nous préparons le repas.
4. La secrétaire répond au téléphone et elle écrit.
5. Ils regardent le château et ils font des projets.
6. Mon fils traverse la rue et il se dépêche.

C. Choose the infinitive or present participle:

1. Il est parti sans (perdre / perdant) une minute.
2. Il est parti en (oublier / oubliant) son dossier.
3. Nous avons acheté une carte postale pour l'(envoyer / envoyant) à Louis.
4. La secrétaire travaille en (utiliser / utilisant) un ordinateur.
5. Venez me voir avant de (partir / partant).

D. Give the correct form of the adjective:

1. C'est une émission (distrayant).
2. Je ne comprends pas les expressions (courant).
3. Est-ce que ces cassettes sont (intéressant) ?
4. Cet ami écrit des histoires (amusant).
5. J'ai passé mes vacances dans un endroit (charmant).

C2 PARTICIPE PRÉSENT AND PAST PARTICIPLE

- One might expect the **participe présent** to be used to express physical attitudes, but in that case, the past participle is used in French:

assis	*sitting*
allongé	*lying down*
couché	*lying down*
penché	*leaning*
accroupi	*squatting*
agenouillé	*kneeling*

C3 ANSWERS

A.
1. habiter / habitant
2. ouvrir / ouvrant
3. aller / allant
4. rire / riant
5. dire / disant
6. venir / venant

B.
1. Je lis mon journal en attendant le bus.
2. Les enfants marchent en s'amusant.
3. Nous discutons en préparant le repas.
4. La secrétaire répond au téléphone en écrivant.
5. Ils regardent le château en faisant des projets.
6. Mon fils traverse la rue en se dépêchant.

C.
1. Il est parti sans perdre une minute.
2. Il est parti en oubliant son dossier.
3. Nous avons acheté une carte postale pour l'envoyer à Louis.
4. La secrétaire travaille en utilisant un ordinateur.
5. Venez me voir avant de partir.

D.
1. C'est une émission distrayante.
2. Je ne comprends pas les expressions courantes.
3. Est-ce que ces cassettes sont intéressantes ?
4. Cet ami écrit des histoires amusantes.
5. J'ai passé mes vacances dans un endroit charmant.

C4 SANS RANCUNE... / *NO HARD FEELINGS...*

- In prepositional expressions, the article is omitted, which is unusual in French:

avec plaisir	*with pleasure*
avec joie	*with pleasure*
avec peine	*with difficulty*
sans arrêt	*endlessly*
sans crainte	*without fear*
sur place	*on the spot*
sur mesure	*tailored*
au fur et à mesure	*as, progressively*
par exemple	*for example*
par hasard	*by chance*

A1 PRESENTATION

■ Grammar

• The idea of a condition is most often conveyed by: **si**

> **si** + subordinate clause + main clause
> présent   future

with a high degree of certainty about the result.

Ex.: **Si vous venez à midi, nous déjeunerons ensemble.**
If you come at noon, we'll have lunch together.
S'il fait beau, nous irons à la campagne.
If the weather is nice, we'll go to the country.
S'il ne pleut pas, ils feront une promenade.
If it doesn't rain, they'll go for a walk.

■ Vocabulary

permettre	to allow	**être le/la**	
être pressé	to be in a hurry	**bienvenu(e)**	to be welcome
se baigner	to go swimming	**villa** (fem.)	house, cottage
se régaler	to have a real treat	**clef** (fem.)	key
		carte (fem.)	card
arriver à	to manage	**poisson** (masc.)	fish
se libérer	to free oneself	**absent**	absent, not at home

A2 EXAMPLES *(Summer plans)*

1. Si nous achetons une maison, nous irons chaque été au bord de la mer.
2. Si tu viens, tu seras le bienvenu.
3. Si nous sommes absents, tu pourras prendre la clef chez la voisine.
4. Si tu as le temps, tu passeras quelques jours avec nous.
5. Si tu n'es pas trop pressé, tu pourras prendre le train.
6. Si tu prends le TGV, le voyage te prendra six heures.
7. Si le temps le permet, nous ferons du bateau.
8. Nous nous baignerons s'il ne pleut pas.
9. S'il pleut, nous lirons ou nous jouerons aux cartes.
10. Si tu aimes le poisson, tu te régaleras.
11. S'il fait beau, nous resterons une semaine de plus.
12. Si tu n'arrives pas à te libérer en août, tu pourras venir en septembre.

A3 COMMENTS

■ Grammar

- Note that **si** becomes **s'** before **il** or **ils**, but doesn't change before **elle** or **elles**.

  Ex.: **s'il vient...**   **s'ils viennent...**
  si elle vient...   **si elles viennent...**

- The subordinate clause introduced by **si** can be placed either before or after the main clause.

  Ex.: **Nous ferons du bateau si le temps le permet. /**
  Si le temps le permet, nous ferons du bateau.

- **faire** is used in many expressions where it has no equivalent in English:

faire du vélo	*to ride (a bike)*
faire du cheval	*to ride (a horse)*
faire du ski	*to ski*
faire du surf	*to windsurf*
faire de la voile	*to sail*
faire de la voiture	*to drive*
faire de l'auto-stop	
faire du stop	*to hitchhike*

A4 TRANSLATION

1. If we buy a house, we'll go to the seaside every summer.
2. If you come, you'll be welcome.
3. If we're not at home, you can get the key from the neighbour.
4. If you have the time, you can spend a few days with us.
5. If you're not in too big a hurry, you can take the train.
6. If you take the high speed train, the trip will take you six hours.
7. Weather permitting, we'll go sailing.
8. We'll go swimming if it doesn't rain.
9. If it rains, we'll read or play cards.
10. If you like fish, you're in for a real treat.
11. If the weather is nice, we'll stay a week longer.
12. If you can't manage to be free in August, you could come in September.

36 | Que ferais-tu si tu étais riche ?

B1 PRESENTATION

■ Grammar

- The present tense of the conditional is used when the condition is expressed in the **imparfait**:

> **si** + subordinate clause + main clause
> **imparfait**   conditional

The conditional is formed with the infinitive + -ais   -ions
                                            -ais   -iez
                                            -ait   -aient

Ex.: **Si vous veniez à midi, nous déjeunerions ensemble.**
If you came at noon, we would have lunch together.
S'ils avaient de l'argent, ils voyageraient.
If they had money, they would travel.

■ Vocabulary

dépenser	*to spend*
avoir les moyens de	*to be able to afford*
faire un effort	*to make an effort*
se rendre compte de	*to realize*
gros lot (masc.)	*top prize in the lottery*
importance (fem.)	*importance*
tant de	*so much, so many*

B2 EXAMPLES *(Dreams)*

1. Si je gagnais le gros lot, je serais millionnaire.
2. Que ferais-tu si tu étais riche ?
3. Moi, je dépenserais tout !
4. Moi, je ferais des cadeaux à tout le monde.
5. Si j'en avais les moyens, j'achèterais des tableaux.
6. Si j'avais beaucoup d'argent, j'ouvrirais un compte en banque en Suisse.
7. Si je n'avais pas besoin de gagner ma vie, je passerais mon temps à lire.
8. Si c'était possible, j'arrêterais de travailler.
9. Si j'étais riche, je n'aurais pas besoin de travailler.
10. S'ils se rendaient compte de l'importance des problèmes, les pays riches aideraient les pays pauvres.
11. Si tout le monde faisait un effort, on trouverait des solutions.
12. Les gens seraient peut-être plus heureux si l'argent n'avait pas tant d'importance.

B3   COMMENTS

■ Grammar

- Note that when the infinitive ends with an **e**, the **e** is dropped in the conditional. Ex.:

lire	*to read*	**je lirais**	*I would read*
écrire	*to write*	**j'écrirais**	*I would write*
prendre	*to take*	**je prendrais**	*I would take*
descendre	*to go down*	**je descendrais**	*I would go down*

Conditional of:	to have	to be	to do	can
	avoir	**être**	**faire**	**pouvoir**
	I would have etc.	*I would be etc.*	*I would do etc.*	*I could etc.*
je, j'	aurais	serais	ferais	pourrais
tu	aurais	serais	ferais	pourrais
il, elle	aurait	serait	ferait	pourrait
nous	aurions	serions	ferions	pourrions
vous	auriez	seriez	feriez	pourriez
ils, elles	auraient	seraient	feraient	pourraient

- The conditional of **pouvoir** is used in questions to make orders more polite. Ex.: **Pourriez-vous me passer le pain ?**
  Could you pass me the bread?

- Note that the subordinate clause needn't be repeated (see B2, 3 and 4).

B4   TRANSLATION

1. If I won the top prize in the lottery, I would be a millionaire.
2. What would you do if you were rich?
3. I would spend all my money!
4. I would give everybody presents.
5. If I could afford it, I'd buy paintings.
6. If I had a lot of money, I'd open a bank account in Switzerland.
7. If I didn't need to earn my living, I'd spend my time reading.
8. If it were possible, I'd stop working.
9. If I were rich, I wouldn't need to work.
10. If they realized the importance of the problems, the rich countries would help the poor countries.
11. If everybody made an effort, we could find solutions.
12. People would perhaps be happier if money weren't so important.

C1 EXERCISES

A. ●● **Put the subordinate in the imparfait and make the necessary changes:**

1. Si tu rencontres Pierre, tu pourras l'inviter.
2. Si vous ne prenez pas ce médicament, vous serez malade.
3. Ils viendront si nous leur faisons signe.
4. S'il sait se servir d'un traitement de texte, ça ira plus vite.
5. Si ce tableau n'est pas cher, je le prendrai.

B. Put the verb in the correct tense:

1. Si mon ami avait un mois de vacances, il (partir) en Grèce.
2. Si vous faisiez un discours, que (dire)-vous ?
3. Anne ne (être) pas toujours en retard si elle se levait plus tôt !
4. Si vous (rester) chez moi, nous écouterions des disques.

C. Translate into French:

1. If your son phoned the doctor now, he would have an appointment for next Monday.
2. If we were famous singers, we would earn a lot of money.
3. They would learn a lot of things if they talked more with Pierre.
4. If you spoke less quickly, I would understand!
5. If you came to Paris, you could meet my students.

C2 CELA PRENDRA DU TEMPS
IT'LL TAKE TIME

- **prendre** + expression of time   *take* + expression of time

Cela prendra deux jours.   *It'll take two days.*
Cela prend des années.   *That takes years.*
Cela a pris beaucoup de temps.   *It took a lot of time.*

- Another way of conveying the same meaning is to use the verb **mettre**:

> **On mettra deux jours à peindre les fenêtres.**
> *We'll spend two days painting the windows.*
> **On met des mois à apprendre une langue.**
> *One spends months learning a language.*
> **On a mis beaucoup de temps à trouver la solution.**
> *We spent a lot of time finding the solution.*

C3 ANSWERS

A.
1. Si tu rencontrais Pierre, tu pourrais l'inviter.
2. Si vous ne preniez pas ce médicament, vous seriez malade.
3. Ils viendraient si nous leur faisions signe.
4. S'il savait se servir d'un traitement de texte, ça irait plus vite.
5. Si ce tableau n'était pas cher, je le prendrais.

B.
1. Si mon ami avait un mois de vacances, il partirait en Grèce.
2. Si vous faisiez un discours, que diriez-vous ?
3. Anne ne serait pas toujours en retard si elle se levait plus tôt !
4. Si vous restiez chez moi, nous écouterions des disques.

C.
1. Si ton/votre fils téléphonait au docteur maintenant, il aurait un rendez-vous pour lundi prochain.
2. Si nous étions des chanteurs célèbres, nous gagnerions beaucoup d'argent.
3. Ils/elles apprendraient beaucoup de choses s'ils/si elles discutaient plus avec Pierre.
4. Si vous parliez/tu parlais moins vite, je comprendrais !
5. Si vous veniez/tu venais à Paris, vous pourriez/tu pourrais rencontrer mes étudiants.

C4 HOW TO EXPRESS A CONDITION

- Besides **si**, other expressions can be used to express conditions.

au cas où pour le cas où dans le cas où	+	verb in the conditional in the subordinate clause	*in case*
en cas de	+	substantive	*in case of*
à condition de	+	infinitive	*providing*

Au cas où il y aurait des grèves, nous viendrions en voiture.
In case there were strikes, we would come by car.
En cas de grèves, nous viendrions en voiture.
In case of strikes, we would come by car.
À condition de partir tôt, vous serez à l'heure.
Providing you leave early, you'll be on time.

en cas d'urgence	*in case of emergency*
en cas de besoin	*in case you need...*
en cas d'accident	*in case of accident*
en cas de malheur	*in case something terrible happened*

225

A1 PRESENTATION

■ Grammar

- The French equivalent of to want is **vouloir**. It is used to express either will or wish.

	Présent	Imparfait	Futur
	I want, etc.	*I wanted*, etc.	*I shall want*, etc.
je	veux	voulais	voudrai
tu	veux	voulais	voudras
il, elle	veut	voulait	voudra
nous	voulons	voulions	voudrons
vous	voulez	vouliez	voudrez
ils, elles	veulent	voulaient	voudront
Past participle : **voulu** *(wanted)*			

■ Vocabulary

rester	*to be left*
accompagner	*to go with, to accompany*
menu (masc.)	*menu*
plat du jour (masc.)	*the day's special*
comme	*as, whatever*
ensuite	*next*

A2 EXAMPLES *(At the restaurant)*

1. Bonjour ! Voulez-vous jeter un coup d'œil au menu ?
2. Nous voulions goûter votre plat du jour.
3. Qu'est-ce que vous voulez boire ?
4. Tu veux encore un peu de viande ?
5. Il reste des légumes, tu en veux ?
6. Non, merci, je n'en veux plus.
7. Qu'est-ce que tu veux faire ensuite ?
8. Comme tu voudras !
9. Je vais demander à Hélène ce qu'elle veut faire.
10. Qu'est-ce que tu veux dire ?
11. Je vais lui demander si elle veut nous accompagner.
12. On ne peut pas toujours faire ce qu'on veut !

A3 COMMENTS

■ Grammar

- **vouloir** can be followed by a noun or an infinitive.
  - Ex.: **Pierre veut un nouvel appareil photo.**
    Pierre wants a new camera.
    Mes enfants veulent des disques de jazz.
    My children want jazz records.
    Nous voulions partir de bonne heure.
    We wanted to leave early.

- Remember that in reported speech **qu'est-ce que** becomes **ce que**.
  - Ex.: (direct speech) **Qu'est-ce que tu veux .**
    What do you want?
    (indirect speech) **Dis-moi ce que tu veux.**
    Tell me what you want.

- **est-ce que** becomes **si** :

Est-ce qu'elles viennent ?   *Are they coming?*
Demande-leur si elles viennent. *Ask them if they are coming.*

- Note the impersonal form of **il reste...** meaning *...left*.
  - Ex.:

Il reste du pain.	*There is some bread left.*
Il reste de la place.	*There is some room left.*
Il reste des places.	*There are some seats left.*
Il ne me reste pas d'argent.	*I have no money left.*
Il ne nous reste pas beaucoup de temps.	*We haven't much time left.*

A4 TRANSLATION

1. Good afternoon! Would you like to have a look at the menu?
2. We would like to try today's special.
3. What would you like to drink?
4. Do you want a little more meat?
5. There are some vegetables left, do you want some?
6. No, thank you, I don't want any more.
7. What do you want to do next?
8. Whatever you like!
9. I'm going to ask Hélène what she wants to do.
10. What do you mean?
11. I'm going to ask her if she wants to go with us.
12. You can't always do what you want!

B1 PRESENTATION

■ Grammar

● **vouloir** in the conditional:

je	**voudrais**	I	would	like
tu	**voudrais**	you	would	like
il, elle	**voudrait**	he, she	would	like
nous	**voudrions**	we	would	like
vous	**voudriez**	you	would	like
ils, elles	**voudraient**	they	would	like

● The conditional is often used:
— to make a request more polite. Ex.:
Je voudrais emprunter ce livre, voudriez-vous me le prêter ?
I would like to borrow this book, would you lend it to me?
— to express a wish. Ex.:
Je voudrais devenir célèbre.
I would like to become famous.

■ Vocabulary

réussir	to succeed, to be successful	**ennui** (masc.)	trouble, problem
		avenir (masc.)	future
attendre de	to expect from	**succès** (masc.)	success
atteindre	to reach	**but** (masc.)	goal, purpose
gâcher	to ruin	**heureux**	happy

B2 EXAMPLES *(Hopes)*

1. Beaucoup de gens voudraient réussir dans la vie.
2. Ils voudraient aussi être heureux et faire ce qu'ils veulent.
3. Ils ne voudraient pas avoir d'ennuis.
4. Les uns voudraient ceci, les autres voudraient cela.
5. Certains voudraient tout avoir !
6. Et vous, que voudriez-vous faire ? Si vous nous disiez ce que vous attendez de l'avenir ?
7. Vous voudriez peut-être avoir du succès ?
8. Expliquez-nous ce que vous voudriez faire.
9. Dites-nous le but que vous voudriez atteindre.
10. Parfois on voudrait pouvoir revenir en arrière.
11. On voudrait être et avoir été.
12. On ne voudrait pas gâcher sa vie !

B3 COMMENTS

■ Grammar

● Note the masculine and feminine forms :

l'un... l'autre / l'une... l'autre	*one... the other*
les uns... les autres / les unes... les autres	*some... others*

● **si** followed by a subject and a verb in the imperfect conveys the meaning of : *what about, how about* followed by a verb. Ex. :

Si nous partions ?	*How about leaving?*
Si on allait au cinéma ?	*What about going to the pictures?*

● **et** followed by a noun or pronoun conveys the meaning of : *what about, how about* followed by a noun or pronoun.

Ex. :	**Et Anne ?**	*What about Anne?*
	Et vous ?	*What about you?*
	Et toi ?	*What about you?*
	Et lui ?	*What about him?*
	Et eux ?	*What about them?*

● Note that the expression **vouloir bien** has a different meaning according to the tense.

— **vouloir bien** in the present means :	*to be happy to*
— **vouloir bien** in the conditional means :	*would like*

> Ex. : **Je veux bien t'accompagner.**
> *I'll be happy to go with you.*
> **Je voudrais bien t'accompagner.**
> *I would like to go with you.*

B4 TRANSLATION

1. Many people would like to succeed in life.
2. They would also like to be happy and do what they want.
3. They don't want to have problems.
4. Some would like this, others would like that.
5. Some want to have it all!
6. What about you, what would you like to do? How about telling us what you expect from the future.
7. Perhaps you want to be successful?
8. Explain to us what you would like to do.
9. Tell us the goal you would like to reach.
10. Sometimes one wants to be able to go back and start over.
11. One wants to be and to have been.
12. One doesn't want to ruin one's life!

C1 EXERCISES

A. Fill in the blanks with correct form of <u>vouloir</u>:

1. Mes étudiants ... voyager à l'étranger.
2. Sa fille ... louer un studio.
3. Téléphone-lui si tu ... discuter avec lui.
4. Que ... -il comme cadeau de Noël ?
5. Je ... visiter ce musée hier.
6. Demande leur s'ils ... sortir avec nous.
7. Que ...-vous faire aujourd'hui ?
8. Nous ... passer par Paris.

B. ●● Make the following commands more polite using <u>vouloir</u> or <u>pouvoir</u>:

1. Prêtez-moi votre stylo.
2. Donnez-lui le menu.
3. Passez-nous le sucre.
4. Ouvre-nous la porte !

C. ●● Translate into French:

1. Ask them what they want.
2. I wish I were twenty !
3. Would you like to live in France?
4. Would you lend me your camera, please?

C2 JE NE VOULAIS PAS... / *I DIDN'T MEAN TO...*

- **Vouloir** in the **imparfait** or **passé composé**, negative form, conveys the meaning of: *didn't mean to, didn't intend to, had no intention of.*

    Ex.: **Il n'a pas voulu vous faire mal.**
    He didn't intend to hurt you.

    Je ne voulais pas vous déranger.
    I didn't mean to disturb you.

    Je n'ai pas voulu la contrarier !
    I didn't mean to annoy her!

C3 ANSWERS

A. 1. Mes étudiants veulent/voudraient voyager à l'étranger.
2. Sa fille veut/voudrait louer un studio.
3. Téléphone-lui si tu veux discuter avec lui.
4. Que veut/voudrait-il comme cadeau de Noël ?
5. Je voulais visiter ce musée hier.
6. Demande-leur s'ils veulent sortir avec nous.
7. Que voulez-vous faire aujourd'hui ?
8. Nous voulons/voudrions passer par Paris.

B. 1. Pourriez-vous me prêter votre stylo ?
   Voudriez-vous me prêter votre stylo ?
2. Pourriez-vous lui donner le menu ?
   Voudriez-vous lui donner le menu ?
3. Pourriez-vous nous passer le sucre ?
   Voudriez-vous nous passer le sucre ?
4. Pourrais-tu nous ouvrir la porte ?
   Voudrais-tu nous ouvrir la porte ?

C. 1. Demande-leur ce qu'ils veulent.
   Demandez-leur ce qu'ils veulent.
2. Je voudrais avoir vingt ans !
3. Voudrais-tu habiter/vivre en France ?
   Voudriez-vous habiter/vivre en France ?
4. Voudrais-tu me prêter ton appareil-photo s'il te plaît ?
   Voudriez-vous me prêter votre appareil-photo s'il vous plaît ?

C4 MORE ABOUT WILL AND WISH

- **en vouloir à**
  Ex.: **J'en veux à Pierre !** *I've got a grudge against Peter!*
- **ne pas vouloir de**
  Ex.: **Je ne veux pas de ça !** *I won't have it!*

désirer	*to desire*	**désir** (masc.)	*desire*
espérer	*to hope*	**espoir** (masc.)	*hope*
souhaiter	*to wish*	**souhait** (masc.)	*wish*
volonté (fem.)	*will*	**bonne volonté** (fem.)	*willingness*
vœu (masc.)	*wish*		

volontiers	*willingly / with pleasure*
(in)volontairement	*(un)intentionally / on purpose*
à volonté	*at will*
bon gré mal gré	*willy nilly*

231

A1 PRESENTATION

■ Grammar

- When **vouloir** is followed by **que** and a subordinate, the verb in the subordinate clause is in a present tense called: **présent du subjonctif**.

  Ex.: **Nous voulons qu'ils écoutent.** *We want them to listen.*

- **Présent du subjonctif:**

Verbs of the 1st and 3rd group		Verbs of the 2nd group	
stem +	-e -es -e -ions -iez -ent	stem +	-isse -isses -isse -issions -issiez -issent

■ Vocabulary

construire	*to build*	**habitant** (masc.)	*inhabitant*
organiser	*to organize*	**maire** (masc.)	*mayor*
agrandir	*to enlarge,*	**école** (fem.)	*school*
	to extend	**entrée** (fem.)	*admission*
interdire	*to forbid*	**marché** (masc.)	*market*
stationner	*to park*	**gratuit**	*free (of charge)*
		au contraire	*on the contrary*

A2 EXAMPLES *(Town management)*

1. **Les habitants de notre ville veulent que ça change !**
2. **Ils veulent que le maire se rende compte des problèmes.**
3. **Ils veulent que l'on construise un nouvel hôpital.**
4. **Ils voudraient qu'on finisse rapidement les travaux.**
5. **Ils voudraient qu'on agrandisse l'ancienne école.**
6. **Ils ne veulent pas qu'on la ferme.**
7. **Les jeunes voudraient qu'on organise des concerts.**
8. **Les familles voudraient que l'entrée à la piscine soit gratuite.**
9. **Beaucoup de gens voudraient qu'on interdise la circulation dans le centre ville.**
10. **Certains ne veulent pas que les voitures stationnent près du marché.**
11. **D'autres veulent, au contraire, qu'on agrandisse le parking.**
12. **Les commerçants voudraient qu'on agrandisse la zone piétonne.**

A3 COMMENTS

■ Grammar

● Irregular verbs (subjunctive present):

		être	avoir	pouvoir
(que)	je, j'	sois	aie	puisse
"	tu	sois	aies	puisses
"	il, elle	soit	ait	puisse
"	nous	soyons	ayons	puissions
"	vous	soyez	ayez	puissiez
"	ils, elles	soient	aient	puissent

● Note that **vouloir que**, whatever the tense of **vouloir**, is always followed by a subjunctive.

● Remember that **que l'on** is often used instead of **qu'on** in elegant speech.

● The **présent du subjonctif** will be found often in French. It is always used in subordinate clause generally expressing wish or will after verbs such as:

souhaiter (que)	*to wish*
espérer (que)	*to hope*
vouloir (que)	*to want*

A4 TRANSLATION

1. The inhabitants of our town want things to change!
2. They want the mayor to be aware of the problems.
3. They want a new hospital to be built.
4. They want the construction work to be finished rapidly.
5. They want the old school to be extended.
6. They don't want it to be closed.
7. The young people want concerts to be organized.
8. The families want admission to the swimming pool to be free.
9. Many people want traffic to be forbidden in the centre of town.
10. Some people don't want cars to be parked near the market.
11. Others, on the contrary, want the car park to be extended.
12. The shopkeepers want the pedestrian zone to be extended.

B1 PRESENTATION

■ Grammar

- The **présent du subjonctif** is always used after the expression: **il faut que.**

  Il faut que conveys the idea of obligation, of necessity. It is an impersonal expression similar to *it is necessary that*.

  Ex.: **Il faut que vous partiez.**
  You must leave.
  Il faut que les documents soient prêts à midi.
  The documents must be ready by twelve.

■ Vocabulary

décider	*to make a decision*
correspondre aux besoins	*to meet the requirements*
besoin (masc.)	*need*
candidat (masc.)	*applicant*
expérience (fem.)	*experience*
CV (curriculum vitae) (masc.)	*CV (US: resume)*
entretien (masc.)	*interview*
compétent	*competent*
efficace	*efficient*
au moins	*at least*

B2 EXAMPLES *(A man to meet our requirements)*

1. **Il faut que nous choisissions un nouveau directeur commercial.**
2. **On n'a pas de temps à perdre, il faut qu'on décide rapidement.**
3. **Il faut que la personne corresponde à nos besoins.**
4. **Il faut que le candidat ait au moins dix ans d'expérience.**
5. **Il faut qu'il soit compétent et efficace.**
6. **Il faut qu'il soit prêt à travailler en équipe.**
7. **Il ne faut pas qu'il ait plus de quarante-cinq ans.**
8. **Il ne faut pas qu'il soit trop jeune non plus.**
9. **S'ils sont intéressés, il faut que les candidats écrivent, il ne faut pas qu'ils téléphonent.**
10. **Il faut qu'ils envoient un CV et une photo.**
11. **Il faut qu'ils puissent se libérer d'ici à un mois.**
12. **Il faut que le P.-D.G. ait un entretien avec chaque candidat.**

B3 COMMENTS

■ Grammar

- Note that **il faut** can be followed by an infinitive when there is no specific subject.

    Ex.: **Il faut faire attention.**
    One must pay attention. / One must be careful.

    or when the subject is understood as **nous** or **on**.

    Ex.: **C'est trop loin, il faut prendre un taxi.**
    It is too far, we have to take a taxi.

- In the conditional **il faut** becomes **il faudrait** and is followed by a subjunctive.

    Ex.: **Il faudrait que nous partions de bonne heure.**
    We'll have to leave early.

    or an infinitive.

    Ex.: **Il faudrait partir de bonne heure.**
    We'll have to leave early.

Il faudrait is used to give advice.

B4 TRANSLATION

1. We must choose a new marketing manager.
2. There's no time to lose, we have to make a decision quickly.
3. The person must meet our requirements.
4. The applicant has to have at least ten years' experience.
5. He or she has to be competent and efficient.
6. He or she has to be willing to work as a member of a team.
7. The applicant mustn't be more than 45 years old.
8. The applicant mustn't be too young, either.
9. If the job interests them, applicants must write; they mustn't telephone.
10. They must send a CV and a photo.
11. They must be free within a month's time.
12. The President and Managing Director has to interview every applicant.

235

C1 EXERCISES

A. Put the verbs in brackets in the correct form:

1. Ma mère ne veut pas que je (parler) pendant des heures au téléphone.
2. Les commerçants voudraient qu'il y (avoir) plus de zones piétonnes dans leur ville.
3. Certains veulent qu'on (interdire) de fumer dans les avions.
4. Je ne veux pas que tu te (lever) trop tard demain matin.
5. La secrétaire voudrait que vous (choisir) vite le nouvel ordinateur.
6. Le maire ne veut pas que nous (construire) de nouveaux immeubles ici.
7. Tout le monde veut que la piscine (être) gratuite !

B. Transform the sentences using il faut or il ne faut pas as in the example : Dépêche-toi. Il faut que tu te dépêches.

1. Choisissez une carte. — 2. N'utilise pas la voiture.
3. Repose-toi un peu. — 4. Téléphonez au directeur de l'agence.
5. Attends quelques minutes. — 6. Ne soyez pas en retard !
7. Prépare-toi.

C. ●● Translate into French:

1. I must send my CV as soon as possible. — 2. They must organize an election to have a new mayor. — 3. Don't park here, you mustn't leave your car in front of the hospital. — 4. Do you want us to wait for you? — 5. I would like her to avoid the town centre.

C2 J'EN DOUTE / *I DOUBT IT*

- Verbs or verbal expressions conveying an idea of doubt, wish or regret are followed by a subordinate in the subjunctive. Ex.:

Je doute qu'elle soit mariée.
    I doubt she is married.

Je ne crois pas qu'elle soit mariée.
    I don't believe she is married.

Je ne pense pas qu'il ait plus de trente ans.
    I don't think he is more than thirty.

Je n'ai pas l'impression que cela puisse correspondre à nos besoins.
    I don't feel it can meet our requirements.

→ Note the negation to express doubt.

Je souhaite qu'ils réussissent.	*I hope they succeed.*
Je regrette que vous soyez malade.	*I am sorry you are ill.*

C3 ANSWERS

A. 1. Ma mère ne veut pas que je parle pendant des heures au téléphone.
2. Les commerçants voudraient qu'il y ait plus de zones piétonnes dans leur ville.
3. Certains veulent qu'on interdise de fumer dans les avions.
4. Je ne veux pas que tu te lèves trop tard demain matin.
5. La secrétaire voudrait que vous choisissiez vite le nouvel ordinateur.
6. Le maire ne veut pas que nous construisions de nouveaux immeubles ici.
7. Tout le monde veut que la piscine soit gratuite !

B. 1. Il faut que vous choisissiez une carte. — 2. Il ne faut pas que tu utilises la voiture. — 3. Il faut que tu te reposes un peu. — 4. Il faut que vous téléphoniez au directeur de l'agence. — 5. Il faut que tu attendes quelques minutes. — 6. Il ne faut pas que vous soyez en retard ! — 7. Il faut que tu te prépares.

C. 1. Il faut que j'envoie mon CV dès que possible. — 2. Il faut qu'ils organisent des élections pour avoir un nouveau maire. — 3. Ne stationnez pas ici, il ne faut pas que vous laissiez votre voiture devant l'hôpital. — 4. Voulez-vous que nous vous attendions ? *or* Est-ce que vous voulez que nous vous (*or* t') attendions ? — 5. Je voudrais qu'elle évite le centre ville.

C4 QUELQUES PANNEAUX D'INTERDICTION ●●
SOME WARNING SIGNS

Interdit de fumer.	*No smoking.*
Stationnement interdit.	
Interdit de stationner.	*No parking.*
Entrée interdite.	*No entrance.*
Jeux de ballons interdits.	*Ball games forbidden.*
Feux interdits.	*No fires.*
Il est interdit de marcher sur les pelouses.	*Keep off the grass.*
Ne pas se pencher au dehors.	*Do not lean out of the window.*
Défense d'entrer.	*No trespassing.*
Défense d'afficher.	*Post no bills.*
Défense de déposer des ordures.	*No dumping.*

In 1968, you could read graffiti on the walls of Paris:
« **Il est interdit d'interdire.** »   *"It is forbidden to forbid."*

A1 PRESENTATION

■ Grammar

- When there are two personal pronouns (a direct and an indirect object) in a sentence, the pronouns must be placed before the verbal form in a given order: <u>indirect object + direct object</u>. Ex.:

Pierre nous donne un livre. *Pierre gives us a book.*
Pierre nous le donne. *Pierre gives it to us.*

- When the indirect object pronoun is **lui** or **leur** this rule doesn't apply. The order is: <u>direct object + indirect objet</u>. Ex.:

Pierre donne un livre à son amie. *Pierre gives a book to his friend.*
Pierre le lui donne. *Pierre gives it to her.*
Pierre donne un livre aux enfants. *Pierre gives the children a book.*
Pierre le leur donne. *Pierre gives it to them.*

■ Vocabulary

envoyer	*to send*	**hebdomadaire** (m.)	*weekly*
montrer	*to show*	**abonnement** (masc.)	*subscription*
rendre	*to turn in,*	**rédacteur en**	
	to give back	**chef** (masc.)	*editor*
exemplaire (masc.)	*copy*	**article** (masc.)	*article*
numéro (masc.)	*issue*	**d'urgence**	*urgently*

A2 EXAMPLES *(A weekly paper)*

1. **Un libraire demande dix exemplaires du dernier numéro.**
2. **Il faut les lui envoyer d'urgence.**
3. **Est-ce qu'on a envoyé un exemplaire du nouvel hebdomadaire à tous les clients ?**
4. **Est-ce qu'on le leur a envoyé avec des formulaires d'abonnement ?**
5. **Si le facteur apporte du courrier, vous devez le donner à Mme Martin.**
6. **Vous le lui donnerez dès qu'il sera arrivé.**
7. **Quand va-t-on montrer les photos au rédacteur en chef ?**
8. **Il faut les lui montrer dès qu'elles arriveront.**
9. **Il faut que les journalistes nous rendent leurs articles avant cinq heures.**
10. **Il ne faut pas qu'il nous les rendent plus tard.**
11. **Pouvez-vous dire à la secrétaire de m'apporter les articles qu'elles a tapés ?**
12. **Pouvez-vous lui dire de me les apporter immédiatement ?**

A3   COMMENTS

■ Grammar

• **Vous le lui donnerez dès qu'il <u>sera arrivé</u>.**

The compound tense used here is called **futur antérieur**.
It is used in a subordinate clause when the main clause is in the future. It refers to an action which will happen in the future but before the main action.

Ex.: **Quand il aura fini, il rendra son article.**
When he has finished, he'll turn in his article.
(Literally: When he will have finished, he'll turn in his article.)

• The **futur antérieur** is formed with:

> **avoir** or **être**
> in the future + past participle of the verb

• The **futur antérieur** is very much like the **passé composé**.
Avoir is used with most verbs, but with some of them (see list in lesson 25, C2), **être** is necessary.

Ex.: **Je lirai son roman quand il l'aura écrit.**
I'll read his novel when he has written it.
Dès qu'il sera parti, quelqu'un prendra sa place.
As soon as he leaves, someone will take his place.

With **être** the past participle agrees with the subject.

Ex.: **Dès qu'elle sera partie, quelqu'un prendra sa place.**
As soon as she leaves, someone will take her place.

A4   TRANSLATION

1. A bookseller wants ten copies of the last issue.
2. They must be sent to him urgently.
3. Did we send a copy of the new weekly to all the customers?
4. Did we send it to them with the subscription forms?
5. If the postman brings the mail, you must give it to Mrs. Martin.
6. Give it to her as soon as it arrives.
7. When are we going to show the photos to the editor?
8. We must show them to him as soon as they arrive.
9. The journalists must turn their articles in to us before five o'clock.
10. They mustn't give them in to us any later.
11. Can you tell the secretary to bring me the articles that she typed?
12. Can you tell her to bring them to me immediately?

B1   PRESENTATION

■ Grammar

- With an imperative form, the pronouns must be placed after the verb; the order is : <u>direct object / indirect object</u>.

    Ex.:   **Envoyez-le-moi.**   *Send it to me.*

- With a negative command, the pronouns are placed before the verb and the order is inverted.

    Ex.:   **Ne me l'envoyez pas.**   *Don't send it to me.*
    Ne nous les envoyez pas.   *Don't send them to us.*

- But with **lui** and **leur** this rule doesn't apply ; the order must be :

    ne + indirect object + direct object + verb

    Ex.:   **Ne le lui envoyez pas.**   *Don't send it to him/her.*
    Ne le leur envoyez pas.   *Don't send it to them.*

■ Vocabulary

insister	*to insist*	**réveillon** (masc.)	*Christmas*
aller	*to fit*	**(de Noël)**	*Eve party*
renvoyer	*to send back*	**(du 1ᵉʳ de l'an)**	*New Year's*
plaire*	*to please*		*Eve party*
ne pas se ⎤	*not to hesitate,*	**gilet** (masc.)	*cardigan*
gêner (pour) ⎦	*to feel free to*	**même**	*even*
ennuyer ⎤⎦	*to bother,* *to annoy*	**en recommandé**	*registered post*

* see C4.

B2   EXAMPLES *(Granny and Grandpa can't come for Christmas)*

1. **Nous ne pourrons pas venir pour Noël, explique-le aux enfants.**
2. **Explique-le-leur.**
3. **Ne leur montre pas les cadeaux.**
4. **Ne les leur montre pas encore.**
5. **Ne leur dis pas ce que c'est.**
6. **Ne le leur dis pas, même s'ils insistent.**
7. **Donne-les-leur le soir du réveillon.**
8. **Essaye le gilet que je t'ai fait ; s'il ne te va pas, renvoie-le-moi.**
9. **Ne me le renvoie pas trop tard, s'il te plaît.**
10. **S'il ne te plaît pas, dis-le-moi, ne te gêne pas.**
11. **N'oubliez pas de prendre des photos, envoyez-les-nous vite.**
12. **Envoyez-les-nous en recommandé, si cela ne vous ennuie pas.**

B3 COMMENTS

■ Grammar

- **Ne leur dis pas ce que c'est. Ne le leur dis pas.**
  Note that in **Ne le leur dis pas,** *Don't tell them,*
      or **Dis-le-leur,** *Tell them,*
           Dis-le-moi, *Tell me,*
           Dis-le-lui, *Tell him/her,*

  le, meaning *it*, summing up a whole sentence, has no equivalent in the English expression, but it should not be omitted in French although you may sometimes hear **Dis-lui** or **Dis-leur** in familiar speech.

- **S'il ne te plaît pas beaucoup...** *If you don't like it very much...*
  But remember that *very* has no equivalent here, **très** doesn't appear in the French sentence.
      Ex.: **Merci beaucoup !** *Thank you very much!*

- **Si cela ne vous ennuie pas.** *If it's not too much bother/trouble.*
                    (Literally: if it doesn't annoy you.)
  Note the construction of the French expression.

- For verbs ending in **-oyer** or **-uyer** in the infinitive (ex.: **envoyer, ennuyer**), there is a change of spelling when the ending of the conjugation is a silent **e**: **e / es / ent**.
      Ex.: **Tu envoies, ennuies / il envoie, ennuie
           elles envoient, ennuient.**

B4 TRANSLATION

1. We can't come for Christmas; explain this to the children.
2. Explain it to them.
3. Don't show them the presents.
4. Don't show them to them yet.
5. Don't tell them what they are.
6. Don't tell them, even if they insist.
7. Give them to them on Christmas Eve.
8. Try on the cardigan that I made for you; if it doesn't fit, send it back to me.
9. Don't send it back to me too late, please.
10. If you don't like it, tell me so, don't hesitate to be frank.
11. Don't forget to take photos, send them to us quickly.
12. Send them to us by registered post, if it's not too much bother.

C1 EXERCISES

A. Replace the nouns by pronouns:

1. Grand-mère raconte une histoire à ses petites-filles.
2. Il faut envoyer un formulaire aux étudiants.
3. Le journaliste doit donner son article au rédacteur en chef.
4. Tu peux rendre ces dossiers à la directrice aujourd'hui.
5. Je te renvoie un exemplaire du journal.
6. Pierre doit 300 F à Antoine.
7. Elle a oublié de me donner la date de la cérémonie.

B. Same exercice as A:

1. Ne montre pas cette lettre à ton fils.
2. Donnez les résultats des élections aux journalistes.
3. Ne vends pas ta voiture à cette personne.
4. Apporte ces fleurs à tes parents.
5. Ne loue pas ton appartement à cet homme.
6. Achetez-nous les billets.

C. 🔵🔵 Translate into French:

1. When you have finished your article, we'll go and see the editor.
2. If he doesn't like your article very much, he'll tell you at once.
3. Send me a copy of your new novel, if it's not too much bother.
4. I am going to meet some journalists, I would like to show it to them.

C2 LA PRESSE / *THE PRESS*

quotidien (masc.)	*daily*
hebdomadaire (masc.)	*weekly*
revue (fem.)	*review, magazine*
nouvelles (fem. pl.)	*news*
faits divers (masc. pl.)	*news in brief*
titre (masc.)	*headline*
petites annonces (fem. pl.)	*classified ads*
dessin humoristique (masc.) ⎤	
caricature (fem.) ⎦ →	*cartoon*

C3 ANSWERS

A. 1. Elle la leur raconte.
2. Il faut le leur envoyer.
3. Il doit le lui donner.
4. Tu peux les lui rendre aujourd'hui.
5. Je te le renvoie.
6. Il les lui doit.
7. Elle a oublié de me la donner.

B. 1. Ne la lui montre pas.
2. Donnez-les-leur.
3. Ne la lui vends pas.
4. Apporte-les-leur.
5. Ne le lui loue pas.
6. Achetez-les-nous.

C. 1. Quand tu auras (vous aurez) fini ton (votre) article, nous irons voir le rédacteur en chef.
2. Si ton (votre) article ne lui plaît pas beaucoup, il te (vous) le dira tout de suite.
3. Envoie (envoyez) -moi un exemplaire de ton (votre) dernier roman, si cela ne t' (vous) ennuie pas.
4. Je vais rencontrer des journalistes, je voudrais le leur montrer.

C4 CE LIVRE VOUS PLAÎT ? ●●
DO YOU LIKE THIS BOOK?

- The verb **plaire** is frequently used in French to convey the meaning of *to like*.

  Ex.: **Ce livre me plaît.**   *I like this book.*
  Cet appartement leur plaît.   *They like this flat.*
  Vous lui plaisez.   *He/she likes you.*
  Il ne me plaît pas.   *I don't like him.*
  Est-ce que ça vous plaît ?   *Do you like it?*

- **plaire** is found in the different tenses.

  Ex.: **Est-ce que ça vous a plu ?**   *Did you like it?*
  Vous lui plaisiez beaucoup.   *He liked you very much.*
  Comme il vous plaira.   *As you like it.*

- It is also found of course in: **s'il te plaît, s'il vous plaît.**

A1 PRESENTATION

■ Grammar

- **Pour que, pour qu'...** conveys the meaning of *so that*.
  Bien que, bien qu'... conveys the meaning of *though*.

- Both conjunctions are followed by the **subjonctif** in French.
  Ex.: **Je lui écris pour qu'elle vienne à Noël.**
  I am writing to her so that she comes at Christmas.
  Bien qu'il soit très jeune, il a réussi son examen.
  Though he is very young he passed his exam.

■ Vocabulary

passer devant	*to walk by*
faire attention	*to pay attention*
attirer l'attention	*to draw attention*
se souvenir	*to remember*
remarquer	*to notice*
slogan (masc.)	*slogan*
œuvre d'art (fem.)	*work of art*
efficace	*effective*
vif (masc.)/**vive** (fem.)	*bright*
presque	*nearly*
donc	*therefore*

A2 EXAMPLES *(Posters)*

1. **Que faut-il pour que les affiches soient efficaces ?**
2. **Bien qu'il y en ait presque partout dans les villes, les gens ne les voient pas toujours.**
3. **Bien qu'ils passent devant plusieurs fois par jour, ils n'y font pas attention.**
4. **Pour qu'on les voie que faut-il faire ?**
5. **Que faut-il faire pour qu'on s'en souvienne ?**
6. **Bien que les gens ne les regardent pas vraiment, elles doivent attirer leur attention.**
7. **Elles doivent attirer leur attention pour qu'ils achètent.**
8. **Il faut donc des couleurs vives pour qu'on les remarque.**
9. **Il faut un slogan simple pour que les gens s'en souviennent.**
10. **Pour qu'on puisse le lire vite et facilement.**
11. **Il vaut mieux qu'il soit drôle pour plaire à tous.**
12. **Bien qu'elles soient faites pour vendre, les affiches peuvent être des œuvres d'art.**

A3 COMMENTS

■ Grammar

● Note that, with **pour**, when the subject is the same in the main clause and in the subordinate, the infinitive is used, not the subjunctive. Ex.:

> **Il nous écrit pour donner des nouvelles.**
> *He is writing to tell us how he is.*

but **Il nous écrit pour que nous donnions de nos nouvelles.**
> *He is writing us to know how we are.*
> (Literally: *So that we give news.*)

● Remember that **être fait pour** is the French equivalent of *to be meant for* or *to be fit for.*

C'est fait pour être vu.	*It is meant to be seen.*
Il n'est pas fait pour ce travail.	*He's not fit for this job.*

● **vif, vive**: all adjectives ending in **f** in the masculine change into **ve** in the feminine. Ex.: **naïf, naïve**.

● We have already seen words which are the same in French and in English; **slogan** is another one; so are: **sandwich, barman, babysitter, interview...**
But some words borrowed from English have been slightly altered:

parking	means	*car park,*
camping	"	*camp ground, site.*

A4 TRANSLATION

1. What is necessary for posters to be effective?
2. Though they are nearly everywhere in the cities, people don't always see them.
3. Though they walk by them several times a day, they don't pay any attention to them.
4. What must be done so that they are seen?
5. What must be done so that they are remembered?
6. Though people don't really look at them, they must draw their attention.
7. They must draw people's attention so that they buy.
8. Therefore they need to have bright colours so that they are noticed.
9. They need a simple slogan so that people can remember it.
10. So that people can read it quickly and easily.
11. It is better if it is funny so that everyone likes it.
12. Though they are meant to sell, posters can be works of art.

B1 PRESENTATION

■ Grammar

- **avant que** conveys the meaning of *before* followed by a subordinate clause;
  en attendant que, jusqu'à ce que both convey the meaning of *till, until.*
  Both conjunctions are followed by the **subjonctif** in French.

  Ex.: **Je prépare tout avant qu'ils ne soient là.**
  I prepare everything before they are there.
  Jouons aux cartes en attendant qu'ils viennent.
  Let's play cards till they come.

■ Vocabulary

décorer	*to decorate*	**tombée** (fem.)	*fall*
bavarder	*to chat*	**feu d'artifice** (masc.)	*fireworks*
façade (fem.)	*front*	**foule** (fem.)	*crowd*
drapeau (masc.)	*flag*	**bal** (masc.)	*ball, dance*
défilé (masc.)	*parade*	**fête** (fem.)	*feast,*
rang (masc.)	*row*		*holiday*
		en attendant	*meanwhile*

B2 EXAMPLES *(Bastille Day, July 14th)*

1. **Les façades sont décorées de drapeaux avant que les cérémonies n'aient lieu.**
2. **Le matin, un défilé est organisé dans chaque ville ; les gens sont déjà là avant qu'il ne commence.**
3. **Tout le monde se dépêche pour être au premier rang avant que passe le défilé.**
4. **Il ne commencera pas avant que le maire ne soit là.**
5. **Les gens bavardent en attendant.**
6. **Il y aura des feux d'artifice après la tombée de la nuit.**
7. **La foule se promène dans les rues en attendant qu'il fasse nuit.**
8. **S'il y a un orage on attendra jusqu'à ce qu'il ne pleuve plus !**
9. **Il y a aussi des bals presque partout ; les musiciens bavardent en attendant que les gens arrivent.**
10. **Ils joueront jusqu'à ce qu'il n'y ait plus personne.**
11. **Ils joueront jusqu'à ce que tout le monde s'en aille.**
12. **On entendra de la musique jusqu'à ce que la fête finisse.**

B3   COMMENTS

■ Grammar

• **Les façades sont décorées de drapeaux. Un défilé est organisé**, those sentences are in the passive.
  Its construction is: subject + **être** + past participle.
  This form is less often used in French than it is in English as **on** and an active voice usually express what is expressed in English by a passive.
    Ex.: **On a volé un tableau célèbre.**
        A famous painting has been stolen.
  However, the passive is found in French to emphasize the result of an action.

• **avant que passe le défilé**, note that the verb can precede the subject.

• **avant qu'il ne commence, avant que le maire ne soit là.**
  Note that, even in a statement, you can find **ne** between the subject and the verbal form in subordinate clauses introduced by **avant que**.

• Note that **en attendant que** is followed by a subjonctive.
    Ex.: **En attendant qu'il vienne.**

  en attendant de is followed by an infinitive.
    Ex.: **En attendant de partir.**

B4   TRANSLATION

1. The house fronts are decorated with flags before the ceremonies take place.
2. In the morning, a parade is organized in every city; people are already there before it starts.
3. Everyone hurries to be in the front row before the parade passes by.
4. It won't start before the mayor is there.
5. Meanwhile people are chatting.
6. There will be fireworks after nightfall.
7. The crowd strolls in the streets till it is dark.
8. If there is a storm, they will wait until it stops raining.
9. There are also balls nearly everywhere; the musicians chat while waiting for people to come.
10. They will play till there is no one left.
11. They will play till everyone goes.
12. Music will be heard until the holiday's over.

C1 EXERCISES

A. Put the verb in the correct form:

1. Téléphone-leur avant qu'ils ne (partir) de chez eux. — 2. Le client doit attendre jusqu'à ce qu'on lui (donner) sa carte de crédit. — 3. Restons là en attendant qu'il (faire) beau. — 4. J'envoie un colis aujourd'hui pour qu'elle l' (avoir) avant mardi. — 5. Bien qu'elle n' (aller) pas très loin, elle prendra l'avion.

B. Transform the sentence using jusqu'à ce que and a verbal form:

1. Nous attendrons jusqu'à la fin du spectacle. — 2. Ils restent ici jusqu'à la tombée de la nuit. — 3. Il faut que les portes soient fermées jusqu'à leur arrivée. — 4. Ne vous levez pas jusqu'à l'arrêt du bus.

C. Put the verb in the right form:

1. Une nouvelle étoile vient d'être (découvrir). — 2. Ces lettres ont été (écrire) il y a cent ans. — 3. Une église va être (construire) près de la gare. — 4. La circulation devrait être (interdire) ici. — 5. Est-ce que la piscine est (ouvrir) le dimanche ? — 6. Les listes n'ont pas encore été (faire).

D. ●● Translate into French:

1. She should take a taxi to arrive at the station before the train leaves. — 2. You'd better sign your articles so that people know who wrote them. — 3. He calls the travel agency ten times a day to know if his tickets are ready.

C2 IL ÉTAIT UNE FOIS... / *ONCE UPON A TIME...*

Plusieurs fois par jour is the equivalent of *several times a day*; note the presence of **par** and the absence of an article (literally: *several times by day*). Similar expressions:

Une fois par an	*Once a year*
Deux fois par semaine	*Twice a week*
Dix fois par jour	*Ten times a day*

Expressions:

Combien de fois ?	*How many times?*
Encore une fois	*Once more*
À la fois	*At the same time*
Pour une fois	*For once*
Une fois pour toutes	*Once and for all*

C3 ANSWERS

A. 1. Téléphone-leur avant qu'ils ne partent de chez eux.
2. Le client doit attendre jusqu'à ce qu'on lui donne sa carte de crédit.
3. Restons là en attendant qu'il fasse beau.
4. J'envoie un colis aujourd'hui pour qu'elle l'ait avant mardi.
5. Bien qu'elle n'aille pas très loin, elle prendra l'avion.

B. 1. Nous attendrons jusqu'à ce que le spectacle finisse.
2. Ils restent ici jusqu'à ce que la nuit tombe.
3. Il faut que les portes soient fermées jusqu'à ce qu'ils/elles arrivent.
4. Ne vous levez pas jusqu'à ce que le bus s'arrête.

C. 1. Une nouvelle étoile vient d'être découverte.
2. Ces lettres ont été écrites il y a cent ans.
3. Une église va être construite près de la gare.
4. La circulation devrait être interdite ici.
5. Est-ce que la piscine est ouverte le dimanche ?
6. Les listes n'ont pas encore été faites.

D. 1. Il faudrait qu'elle prenne un taxi pour arriver à la gare avant que le train ne parte / avant le départ du train.
2. Il vaudrait mieux signer vos articles pour que les gens sachent qui les a écrits.
3. Il téléphone à l'agence de voyages dix fois par jour pour savoir si ses billets sont prêts.

C4 **PRENDRE CONGÉ...** ●●
TO TAKE LEAVE...

In addition to **au revoir**, here are some expressions to take leave of someone :

Je vous laisse, je vous quitte.	*I'm leaving (you).*
Adieu	*Farewell*
À bientôt	*See you soon*
Au plaisir de vous revoir	*I hope we shall meet again*

GRAMMAR SUMMARY

Content   Pages

1 - STATEMENTS

As far as the construction of simple statements is concerned, there are few differences between French and English.

Ex.: **Pierre est français.**	*Pierre is French.*
Il habite à Paris.	*He lives in Paris.*

Of course the structures can be more complex and this grammar summary will help you to construct them.

2 - NEGATIVE STATEMENTS

Negative statements are formed with **ne ... pas** on either side of the verb.

Ex.: **Je ne fume pas.**	*I don't smoke.*
Ce n'est pas* difficile.	*It isn't difficult.*

* **n' ... pas** is used when the verb starts with a vowel or **h**.

Ne/n' ... rien, **ne/n' ... plus,** **ne/n' ... jamais,**
not anything *no more/no longer* *never,*
are used in the same way.

Ex.: **Je n'achète rien.**	*I don't buy anything.*
Nous ne travaillons plus.	*We no longer work.*
Ils ne sortent jamais.	*They never go out.*

3 - QUESTIONS

In a question the intonation is always rising.
To turn a statement into a question:

1. You may simply modify the intonation of the statement without changing the structure (see lesson 3, A3).

Ex.: **Tu chantes ?**	*Do you sing?*

2. **Est-ce que** can be placed at the beginning of the statement.

Ex.: **Est-ce que tu chantes ?**	*Are you singing?*
Est-ce que c'est cher ?	*Is it expensive?*

3. When the subject is a pronoun, the subject and the verb can be inverted (mostly with: **vous, il, elle, ils, elles**).

Ex.: **Chantez-vous ?**	*Are you singing?*
Prennent-ils le train ?	*Do they take the train?*

   When the verb is inverted, it is joined to the pronoun by a hyphen.

Ex.: **Parlez-vous français ?**	*Do you speak French?*

   If the verb ends with a vowel, **t** is introduced between the verb and **il** or **elle**.

Ex.: **Parle-t-elle français ?**	*Does she speak French?*

4. In more elegant French, you can find both a subject and a pronoun which recalls it following the verbal form:

subject + verbal form + pronoun + ...

Ex.: **Pierre va-t-<u>il</u> parler ?**
Is Pierre going to speak?
Ta sœur vient-<u>elle</u> demain ?
Is your sister coming tomorrow?

---

4 - NOUNS

■ GENDER

- All nouns in French are either masculine or feminine. For persons or animals this corresponds to male or female.

- For things or concepts, there is no real rule; for instance, trains are masculine and cars are feminine; it is therefore best to learn the gender when you learn the word. In this book, (masc.) or (fem.), after the noun, indicate the gender. This will help you to memorize the noun with an article. For nouns indicating persons or animals, the feminine can be formed:

1. by adding **e** to the masculine.
Ex.: **ami - amie** (the pronunciation doesn't change);
client - cliente, candidat - candidate (the final consonant is heard);
chat - chatte (the final consonant is doubled and heard);

2. by changing the ending.
Ex.: **directeur - directrice**   *manager*
chanteur - chanteuse   *singer*

- Some nouns remain the same in the masculine and the feminine.
Ex.: **secrétaire, journaliste, artiste.**
secretary, journalist, artist.

- Some are completely different.
Ex.: **homme - femme**   *man - woman*
mari - femme   *husband - wife*
frère - sœur   *brother - sister*

■ NUMBER

- The plural of nouns is generally formed by adding **s** to the singular:
un ami - des amis - une amie - des amies,
a friend - friends
un livre - des livres
a book - books

- For most nouns ending with **eau, eu, x** is added instead of **s**.
Ex.: **un oiseau - des oiseaux**   **un cheveu - des cheveux**
a bird - birds   *a hair - hairs*

- For most nouns ending with **al** or **ail** the ending changes into **aux** in the plural.

  Ex.: **un cheval - des chevaux** *a horse - horses*
  un travail - des travaux *work - works*

- Nouns ending with **s, z,** and **x** in the singular do not change in the plural.

  Ex.: **un nez - des nez** *a nose - noses*
  un repas - des repas *a meal - meals*
  un prix - des prix *a price - prices*

- Generally family names do not change in the plural.

  Ex.: **les Lenoir, les Martin.**

---

5 - ARTICLES

In French the article agrees in gender and number with the noun it accompanies.

■ DEFINITE AND INDEFINITE ARTICLES

	Indefinite		Definite		
	masc.	fem.	masc.	fem.	contract. (with **à** & **de**) masc. fem.
sing.	**un**	**une**	**le (l')**	**la (l')**	**à + le = au** **de + le = du**
plur.	**des**		**les**		**à + les = aux** **de + les = des**

Remember that it is practically impossible to use a noun alone in French, an article (or a partitive, possessive, demonstrative, numeral, etc.) is almost always necessary.

■ PARTITIVE ARTICLES

The partitive construction requires: **de** + the appropriate singular definite article:

AFFIRMATIVE		NÉGATIVE
fem.	masc.	masc. fem.
de la salade **de l'**eau	**du** vin **de l'**argent	pas **de** café pas **d'**eau

In the plural, only one possibility:

des légumes   **pas de légumes**
des enfants   **pas d'enfants**

In English the partitive article is often omitted; in French it must always be expressed. Ex.: **Nous avons du vin et de l'eau.**
We have got wine and water.

6 - NUMBER AND QUANTITY

- To ask a question about either a number or a quantity, the interrogative word is: **combien de/d'** *how many / how much?*

Countable nouns

For a large number	For a small number
beaucoup de/d' + plur. *a lot of, many*	**peu de/d'** + plur. *few* **quelques** + plur. *a few, some*

Non-countable nouns

For a large quantity	For a small quantity
beaucoup de/d' + sing. *a lot of, much*	**peu de/d', un peu de/d'** + sing. *little, a little*

- A subjective judgment about a number or a quantity can be expressed by:

trop de/d'	*too many, too much*
assez de/d'	*enough*
pas assez de/d'	*not enough*

Ex. **beaucoup d'amis, peu d'amis, quelques amis, beaucoup de courage, peu de courage, pas assez de courage.**

7 - ADJECTIVES

■ AGREEMENT

- The adjective <u>always agrees</u> in gender and number with the noun it accompanies.
  - Ex.: **un hiver froid, une nuit froide**
    a cold winter, a cold night
    des hivers froids, des nuits froides
    cold winters, cold nights

- When an adjective refers to several nouns, and at least one of them is masculine, the form of the adjective is masculine plural.

■ FEMININE

- To form a feminine adjective, the usual rule is to add **e** to the masculine form.
  - Ex.: **joli - jolie** *pretty*
    bleu - bleue *blue*
  (The pronunciation doesn't change.)

- When the masculine adjective ends with an **e** there is no change in the feminine.

  Ex.: **jeune**   *young*
       moderne   *modern*

- When the masculine adjective ends with a consonant which is not heard, the rule applies and the final consonant is then heard, the **e** is glided over.

  Ex.: **grand - grande**   *big, great*
       intelligent - intelligente   *intelligent*

- If the final consonant is an **x**, it generally turns into **se** in the feminine.

  Ex.: **joyeux - joyeuse**   *merry*
       délicieux - délicieuse   *delicious*

  (But **doux - douce** *soft, mild.*)

- If the final consonant is an **f** it generally turns into **ve** in the feminine.

  Ex.: **vif - vive**   *bright*
       neuf - neuve   *new*

- Other minor changes of spelling (ex.: final consonant doubled in **gentil - gentille**) are systematically indicated when a new adjective appears in the lessons.

- Here are some adjectives with a particular feminine form:

      beau - belle   *beautiful*
      nouveau - nouvelle   *new*
      vieux - vieille   *old*

■ PLURAL

- To form the plural of an adjective, the usual rule is to add **s** to the singular, whether masculine or feminine.

  Ex.: **joli - jolis**   *pretty*
       jolie - jolies   *pretty*
       triste - tristes   *sad*

  (Remember that the final consonant is not heard.)

- Adjectives ending with **eau** in the singular add **x** instead of **s** in the plural.

  Ex.: **beau - beaux**   *beautiful*
       nouveau - nouveaux   *new*

- Adjectives ending with **s** or **x** in the singular do not change in the plural.

  Ex.: **gris - gris**   *grey*
       vieux - vieux   *old*

■ PLACE

Most adjectives are placed <u>after the noun</u> they accompany.
However some short, commonly used adjectives are placed before the
noun. Here are the most frequently met:

masc.	fem.	
bon	**bonne**	*good*
cher	**chère**	*dear*
grand	**grande**	*tall, big, great*
jeune	**jeune**	*young*
joli	**jolie**	*pretty*
long	**longue**	*long*
mauvais	**mauvaise**	*bad*
petit	**petite**	*little*
vieux/vieil	**vieille**	*old*
nouveau	**nouvelle**	*new*

---

8 - ADVERBS

Most adverbs are formed by adding **ment** to the feminine adjective.

Ex.: masc. sing.	fem. sing.	adverb
lent *(slow)*	**lente**	**lentement** *(slowly)*
rapide *(fast)*	**rapide**	**rapidement** *(fast)*

But not all adverbs end in **ment**, especially adverbs of:

<u>time</u>:	**souvent**	*often*
	maintenant	*now*
	parfois	*sometimes*
<u>place</u>:	**ici**	*here*
	là	*there*
	loin	*far*
and	**bien**	*well*
	mal	*badly*

All adverbs are <u>invariable</u>.

■ PLACE

Adverbs are usually placed <u>after the verb</u> they modify.

Ex.: **Elle parle lentement.**
She speaks slowly.
Ils viennent souvent.
They often come.
Tu danses bien.
You dance well.

9 - COMPARATIVES AND SUPERLATIVES

■ COMPARATIVES

With adjectives and adverbs the comparative form is as follows:

+	**plus**	adjective/adverb	**que/qu'**
=	**aussi**	....	**que/qu'**
–	**moins**	....	**que/qu'**

Ex.: **Pierre est <u>plus</u> jeune <u>que</u> Louis.**
Pierre is younger than Louis.

Il est <u>plus</u> intelligent <u>que</u> Louis.
He is more intelligent than Louis.

Anne est <u>aussi</u> jolie <u>qu'</u>Hélène.
Anne is as pretty as Hélène.

Louis est <u>moins</u> riche <u>que</u> Pierre.
Louis is less rich than Pierre.

The pronoun after **que/qu'** must be a strong pronoun: **moi, toi, lui, elle, eux.**

Ex.: **Pierre est plus petit que moi.**   *Pierre is smaller than me.*

With nouns the comparative form is as follows:

+	**plus**	**de/d'**	+ noun
=	**autant**	**de/d'**	....
–	**moins**	**de/d'**	....

Ex.: **plus d'argent, autant d'argent, moins d'argent**
more money, as much money, less money.

■ SUPERLATIVES

The superlative is formed by placing:

le, la, les plus...   *the most*
le, la, les moins...   *the least*

before the adjective.

Ex.: **C'est <u>la plus</u> intelligente.**
She is the most intelligent.
C'est <u>le plus</u> drôle.
He is the funniest.
Ce livre est <u>le moins</u> cher.
This book is the least expensive.

After a superlative, the complement is introduced by **de** or the contracted form **du**.

Ex.: **le plus grand immeuble de la ville.**
the tallest building in town.
la plus belle fille du monde.
the most beautiful girl in the world.

■ IRREGULAR COMPARATIVES AND SUPERLATIVES

bon *(good):*
meilleur (masc. sg.) **... que,**   **meilleure** (fem. sg.) **... que**
meilleurs (masc. pl.) **... que,**   **meilleures** (fem. pl.) **... que**
                                      = *better than...*
le, la, les meilleur(e)(s)   = *the best...*

bien *(well):*   **mieux que** = *better... than*
              le mieux   = *the best*

mauvais *(bad):* **pire que** = *worse than* (both masc. and fem.)
                le pire   = *the worst*

---

10 - DEMONSTRATIVES

■ ADJECTIVES

	masc.	fem.	
sg.	**ce**	**cette**	*this / that*
plur.	**ces**		*these / those*

Ex.: **ce garçon**   *this (that) boy*
   cette femme   *this (that) woman*
   ces amis   *these (those) friends*

Ce becomes **cet** before a vowel or **h** : **cet ami, cet homme.**

■ PRONOUNS

The demonstrative pronoun agrees in gender and number with the noun it refers to:

(masc. sg.)	**celui**	(fem. sg.)	**celle**
(masc. pl.)	**ceux**	(fem. pl.)	**celles**

-ci can be added to the pronoun
   celui-ci   **celle-ci**   *this (one)*
   ceux-ci   **celles-ci**   *these (ones)*

-là can be added to the pronoun
   celui-là   **celle-là**   *that (one)*
   ceux-là   **celles-là**   *those (ones)*

Ex.:
Est-ce que vous utilisez un ordinateur ?   **Oui, celui-ci.**
Are you using a computer?   *Yes, this one.*
Est-ce que vous avez une voiture ?   **Oui, c'est celle-ci.**
Have you got a car?   *Yes, it is this one.*

Ceci is the French equivalent of *this* used alone.

Cela is the French equivalent of *that* used alone.
In colloquial French **cela** is frequently contracted to **ça.**

Ex.: **Je n'aime pas cela/ça.**   *I don't like that (it).*

---

11 - POSSESSION

In French, possession is generally expressed with the preposition **de** followed by the name of the possessor.
There is no form corresponding to the possessive case.

Ex.: **la voiture de Pierre**   *Peter's car*
      le sac de la secrétaire   *the secretary's bag*

It is comparable to « the car of Peter », « the bag of the secretary ».

À qui ? is the equivalent of *whose?*

Ex.: **À qui est la voiture ?**   *Whose car is it?* (literally: to whom is the car?)

      À qui sont ces vêtements ?   *Whose clothes are they?*

Être à is commonly used to answer a question starting with **À qui.**

Ex.: **À qui est ce livre ?**   *Whose book is it?*
      Il est à Pierre.   *It is Peter's.*

■ POSSESSIVE ADJECTIVES

The French possessive adjective <u>agrees in gender and number</u> with the noun it accompanies:

masc. sg.	fem. sg.	masc. & fem. plural	
mon	**ma**	**mes**	*my*
ton	**ta**	**tes**	*your*
son	**sa**	**ses**	*his, her, its*
notre	**notre**	**nos**	*our*
votre	**votre**	**vos**	*your*
leur	**leur**	**leurs**	*their*

ma, ta, sa change into **mon, ton, son** when preceding a vowel or **h.**

Ex.: **mon amie, son histoire**   *my friend, his/her story*
(**amie, histoire** are feminine nouns.)

■ POSSESSIVE PRONOUNS

le mien, la mienne **les miens, les miennes**	à moi	*mine*
le tien, la tienne **les tiens, les tiennes**	à toi	*yours*
le sien, la sienne **les siens, les siennes**	à lui, à elle	*his, hers, its*
le nôtre, la nôtre **les nôtres**	à nous	*ours*
le vôtre, la vôtre **les vôtres**	à vous	*yours*
le leur, la leur, les leurs	à eux, à elles	*theirs*

Ex.:

Ce livre est à elle ; c'est <u>le sien</u>.	*It is hers.*
Ces livres sont à elle ; ce sont <u>les siens</u>.	*They are hers.*
Ce livre est à nous ; c'est <u>le nôtre</u>.	*It is ours.*
Ces livres sont à nous ; ce sont <u>les nôtres</u>.	*They are ours.*

---

12 - PERSONAL PRONOUNS

		Subject	Direct object	Indirect object (without preposition)	Indirect object (with preposition)
S I N G.	1ʳᵉ	**je/j'**	**me, m'**	**me**	**moi**
	2ᵉ	**tu**	**te, t',**	**te**	**toi**
	3ᵉ	**il** **elle** **on****	**le, l', se*, s'**** **la, l', se*, s'**** **le, la, l', se, s'**	**lui, se** **en, y**	**lui** **elle** **lui, elle, soi**
P L U R.	1ʳᵉ	**nous**	**nous**	**nous**	**nous**
	2ᵉ	**vous**	**vous**	**vous**	**vous**
	3ᵉ	**ils** **elles**	**les, se, s'**	**leur, se** **en, y**	**eux** **elles**

Remember that **tu/te/toi** are used for a child, a person you know very well, a relative or a friend.

* **se/s'** is a reflexive pronoun.

  Ex.: **Il <u>se</u> lave.**   *He washes (himself).*

** **on** is an impersonal pronoun used when the subject is unknown or when the speaker is more interested in *what is/was done* than in *who does/did it*; it is therefore a frequent equivalent of the English passive.

Ex.: **On vient.**   *Someone is coming.*
     On a ouvert un nouveau musée.
     A new museum has been opened.

In colloquial French **on** is often used instead of **nous**.
     Ex.: **On part à 5 heures.** *We are leaving at 5 o'clock.*

- Remember that **quelqu'un** = *somebody, anybody,* **personne** = *nobody* are indefinite personal pronouns.

- **En** and **y** can be indefinite personal pronouns used as indirect objects.
     Ex.: **Il parle de sa femme, il en parle.**
          He speaks about her.
          Il pense à son avenir, il y pense.
          He thinks of it.

■ PLACE AND ORDER

1	2	3	
je, tu **on, il, elle** **nous, vous** **ils, elles**	**me, m', te, t'** **nous, vous** **le, la, les** **lui, leur** **m', t', nous, vous**	**le, la, les** **en** **lui, leur, en** **en**	**verb**

Ex.:
Je te le donne, nous le lui donnons, elles vous les donnent
I give it to you, we give it to him/her/it, they give them to you

For the order with the imperative see lesson 39, B1, B3.

13 - RELATIVE PRONOUNS

The relative pronouns which are most often used are:

		simple forms		compound forms
subject	**qui**	*who, that, which*	**ce qui**	*what*
direct object	**que/qu'**	*whom, that, which*	**ce que**	*what*

qui and **que** may refer to a masculine or feminine, singular or plural noun. Both may refer to persons or things. Ex.:

Écoute l'homme qui parle.	*Listen to the man who is speaking.*
L'homme que vous voyez est anglais.*	*The man you see is English.*
Donne-moi le livre qui est là.	*Give me the book which is there.*
Où est le livre qu'Anne lisait ?*	*Where is the book Anne was reading?*
Regarde ce qui est ici.	*Look what is here.*
Regarde ce que j'ai.	*Look what I've got.*

* Remember that **que/qu'** <u>cannot be omitted</u> in French.

14 - INTERROGATIVE WORDS

■ ADJECTIVES

masc. sing.	**quel**	fem. sing.	**quelle**	*what, which*
masc. plur.	**quels**	fem. plur.	**quelles**	*what, which*

- Remember that, in French, adjectives always agree with the noun they accompany.

Ex.:

Quel livre lis-tu ?	*Which book are you reading?*
Quels livres lis-tu ?	*Which books are you reading?*
Quelle voiture préfères-tu ?	*Which car do you prefer?*
Avec **quelles** amies pars-tu ?	*Which friends are you going with?*

■ PRONOUNS

	Persons	Things
subject	**qui ?** *who*	**qu'est-ce qui ?** *what*
direct object	**qui ?** *who*	**que ?** *what*
indirect object (with preposition)	**qui ?** *who*	**quoi ?** *what*

Ex.:

Qui est-ce ?	*Who is it?*
Qui est-ce qui parle ?	*Who is talking?*
Qui regardent-ils ?	*Who are they looking at?*
Qui est-ce que tu préfères ?	*Who(m) do you prefer?*
À quoi est-ce que vous pensez ?	*What are you thinking about?*
Que manges-tu ? ⎫	
Qu'est-ce que tu manges ? ⎭ →	*What are you eating?*

- The interrogative pronoun corresponding to **quel** is **lequel**, it also agrees in gender and number with the noun it refers to.

masc. sing. **lequel**	fem. sing. **laquelle**
masc. plur. **lesquels**	fem. plur. **lesquelles**

Ex.: **Lequel préfères-tu ?**   *Which one do you prefer?*
Lesquelles préfères-tu ?   *Which ones do you prefer?*

■ ADVERBS

combien ?	*how much, how many?*
comment ?	*how?*
où ?	*where?*
pourquoi ?	*why?*
quand ?	*when?*

15 - VERBS

Regular French verbs belong to:

the <u>1st group</u> ending in **er**: **parler**;
the <u>2nd group</u> ending in **ir**: **finir**;
the <u>3rd group</u>: other endings: **répondre, entendre, ouvrir**.

Verbs of the same group have the same conjugation.
In French, the endings of verbs vary according to the subject.

- **Présent** - *Present tense*

	1st group	2nd group	3rd group		
	Parler *(to speak)*	**Finir** *(to finish)*	**Voir** *(to see)*	**Entendre** *(to hear)*	**Ouvrir** *(to open)*
je, j'	parle	finis	vois	entends	ouvre
tu	parles	finis	vois	entends	ouvres
il, elle, on	parle	finit	voit	entend	ouvre
nous	parl**ons**	finiss**ons**	voy**ons**	entend**ons**	ouvr**ons**
vous	parl**ez**	finiss**ez**	voy**ez**	entend**ez**	ouvr**ez**
ils, elles	parl**ent**	finiss**ent**	voi**ent**	entend**ent**	ouvr**ent**

The French **présent** corresponds to the English simple present as well
as to the progressive present.

- **Impératif** - *Imperative*

   Only 3 persons, no subject (see lessons 1 and 2).

   Ex.: **parle, parlons, parlez.**

■ TO REFER TO A PAST EVENT

- **Imparfait** - *Imperfect*

   A past tense used to express what was taking place or what used
   to happen.
   It is formed by dropping the ending **ons** of the 1st person plural
   of the present tense and adding: **-ais**
                                   -ais
                                   -ait
                                   -ions
                                   -iez
                                   -aient

   to the stem.

   Ex.: **je marchais, tu finissais, nous prenions.**

   It is the same for all verbs, except **être**.

- **Passé composé**

  It corresponds to the English simple past as well as to the English present perfect. For most verbs it is formed with the present tense of

  avoir + past participle

  Ex.: **Il a travaillé hier.**   *He worked yesterday.*

  Il n'a jamais travaillé. *   He has never worked.*

  * In compound tenses, the negation is placed on either side of the auxiliary.

- For some verbs (see list in lesson 25, C2) the **passé composé** is formed with

  être + past participle

  Ex.: **Il est resté, il est parti.**

  With this auxiliary, the <u>past participle agrees</u> with the subject.

  Ex.: **Elle est restée, elle est partie.**

- **Plus-que-parfait** - *Pluperfect*

  It is formed like the **passé composé** with

  imperfect of **être** or **avoir** + past participle

  The **plus-que-parfait** is the same in usage as the pluperfect in English.

  Ex.: **Il avait fini quand elle a appelé.**

  He had finished when she called.

  Nous étions partis quand vous êtes arrivés.

  We had left when you arrived.

  As for the **passé composé**, the past participle agrees with the subject when the auxiliary is **être**.

  The endings of the past participles are:

  é for all the verbs in **er** (parler - parlé)

  i for most verbs in **ir** (finir - fini)

  u for most verbs in **oir** or **re** (voir - vu, entendre - entendu)

  But some verbs are irregular.

■ MAIN IRREGULAR PAST PARTICIPLES

aller → allé	**dormir** → dormi	**plaire** → plu
apprendre → appris	**écrire** → écrit	**pleuvoir** → plu
asseoir (s') → assis	**entendre** → entendu	**pouvoir** → pu
attendre → attendu	**être** → été	**prendre** → pris
avoir → eu	**faire** → fait	**recevoir** → reçu
boire → bu	**falloir** → fallu	**répondre** → répondu
choisir → choisi	**finir** → fini	**réussir** → réussi
comprendre → compris	**interdire** → interdit	**rire** → ri
conduire → conduit	**lire** → lu	**savoir** → su
connaître → connu	**mettre** → mis	**sentir** → senti
construire → construit	**mourir** → mort	**sortir** → sorti
croire → cru	**offrir** → offert	**vendre** → vendu
découvrir → découvert	**ouvrir** → ouvert	**venir** → venu
devenir → devenu	**partir** → parti	**vivre** → vécu
devoir → dû	**perdre** → perdu	**voir** → vu
dire → dit	**permettre** → permis	**vouloir** → voulu

■ TO EXPRESS A FUTURE ACTION

- **Aller** + infinitive.

  It is the equivalent of *to be going to* + infinitive.

  > Ex. **Je vais acheter une nouvelle voiture.**
  > *I am going to buy a new car.*

- **Futur** - *Future*

  Its construction is infinitive + -**ai**
  > -**as**
  > -**a**
  > -**ons**
  > -**ez**
  > -**ont**

  > Ex.: **Je sortirai, tu parleras, il jouera, nous finirons.**

  When the infinitive ends in **re**, the **e** is dropped.

  > Ex.: **conduire - je conduirai.** *I'll drive.*
  > **prendre - tu prendras.** *you'll take.*

- The **futur antérieur** is used for a future action preceding another future action (see lesson 39).

  > Ex.: **Dès qu'il sera parti, quelqu'un prendra sa place.**
  > *As soon as he leaves, someone will take his place.*

  It is formed with
  > **être** or **avoir** in the future + past participle.

- **Conditionnel** - *Conditional*

  The conditional is formed with the infinitive + -**ais**
  > -**ais**
  > -**ait**
  > -**ions**
  > -**iez**
  > -**aient**

  > Ex.: **Il parlerait, nous dormirions.**

- When the infinitive ends with an **e**, it is dropped in the conditional.

  > Ex.: **lire**   **je lirais**
  > **prendre**   **je prendrais**

- The present tense of the conditional is used when the condition is expressed in the **imparfait**.

  > **si/s'** + subordinate clause + main clause

  > Ex.: **Si vous veniez à midi, nous déjeunerions ensemble.**
  > *If you came at noon, we would have lunch together.*

- **Présent du subjonctif**

	1st and 3rd group		2nd group
	e		**isse**
	es		**isses**
	e		**isse**
stem +	ions	stem +	**issions**
	iez		**issiez**
	ent		**issent**

Ex.: **Que vous parliez, que tu finisses, qu'ils entendent.**

It is mainly used after **vouloir que/qu'** *to want someone to*
il faut que/qu' *it is necessary that*

after conjunctions such as

avant que/qu'	*before*
en attendant que/qu'	*till*
pour que/qu'	*so that*
bien que/qu'	*though*

and to express an idea of *doubt, wish* or *regret* (see lessons 38, 39, 40).

Ex.: **Je veux que vous veniez.** *I want you to come.*
Il faut que vous partiez. *You have to go.*

---

16 - CONJUGATIONS

■ <u>1st GROUP</u> - **Aimer** *(To love)*

INDICATIF				SUBJONCTIF	
Présent *I love*		**Passé composé** *I loved, I have loved*		**Présent** *I love*	
j'	aime	j'	ai aimé	que j'	aime
tu	aimes	tu	as aimé	que tu	aimes
il	aime	il	a aimé	qu'il	aime
nous	aimons	nous	avons aimé	que nous	aimions
vous	aimez	vous	avez aimé	que vous	aimiez
ils	aiment	ils	ont aimé	qu'ils	aiment
Imparfait *I loved*		**Plus-que-parfait** *I had loved*		**IMPÉRATIF**	
j'	aimais	j'	avais aimé	**Présent** *love*	
tu	aimais	tu	avais aimé		
il	aimait	il	avait aimé	aime	
nous	aimions	nous	avions aimé	aimons	
vous	aimiez	vous	aviez aimé	aimez	
ils	aimaient	ils	avaient aimé		
		PARTICIPE		**CONDITIONNEL**	
Futur *I'll love*		**Participe passé** *loved*		**Présent** *I would love*	
j'	aimerai		aimé	j'	aimerais
tu	aimeras			tu	aimerais
il	aimera	**Participe présent** *loving*		il	aimerait
nous	aimerons			nous	aimerions
vous	aimerez		aimant	vous	aimeriez
ils	aimeront			ils	aimeraient

■ 2nd GROUP - **Finir** *(To finish)*

INDICATIF		SUBJONCTIF
Présent *I finish, I am finishing*	**Passé composé** *I finished, I have finished*	**Présent** *I finish*
je finis	j' ai fini	que je finisse
tu finis	tu as fini	que tu finisses
il finit	il a fini	qu'il finisse
nous finissons	nous avons fini	que nous finissions
vous finissez	vous avez fini	que vous finissiez
ils finissent	ils ont fini	qu'ils finissent
Imparfait *I was finishing*	**Plus-que-parfait** *I had finished*	**IMPÉRATIF**
je finissais	j' avais fini	**Présent** *finish*
tu finissais	tu avais fini	
il finissait	il avait fini	finis
nous finissions	nous avions fini	finissons
vous finissiez	vous aviez fini	finissez
ils finissaient	ils avaient fini	
	PARTICIPE	**CONDITIONNEL**
Futur *I'll finish*	**Participe passé** *finished*	**Présent** *I would finish*
je finirai	fini	je finirais
tu finiras		tu finirais
il finira	**Participe présent** *finishing*	il finirait
nous finirons		nous finirions
vous finirez	finissant	vous finiriez
ils finiront		ils finiraient

■ 3rd GROUP - **Ouvrir** *(To open)*

INDICATIF		SUBJONCTIF
Présent *I open, I am opening*	**Passé composé** *I opened, I have opened*	**Présent** *I open*
j' ouvre	j' ai ouvert	que j' ouvre
tu ouvres	tu as ouvert	que tu ouvres
il ouvre	il a ouvert	qu'il ouvre
nous ouvrons	nous avons ouvert	que nous ouvrions
vous ouvrez	vous avez ouvert	que vous ouvriez
ils ouvrent	ils ont ouvert	qu'ils ouvrent
Imparfait *I was opening*	**Plus-que-parfait** *I had opened*	**IMPÉRATIF**
j' ouvrais	j' avais ouvert	**Présent** *open*
tu ouvrais	tu avais ouvert	
il ouvrait	il avait ouvert	ouvre
nous ouvrions	nous avions ouvert	ouvrons
vous ouvriez	vous aviez ouvert	ouvrez
ils ouvraient	ils avaient ouvert	
	PARTICIPE	**CONDITIONNEL**
Futur *I'll open*	**Participe passé** *opened*	**Présent** *I would open*
j' ouvrirai	ouvert	j' ouvrirais
tu ouvriras		tu ouvrirais
il ouvrira	**Participe présent** *opening*	il ouvrirait
nous ouvrirons		nous ouvririons
vous ouvrirez	ouvrant	vous ouvririez
ils ouvriront		ils ouvriraient

• Être *(To be)*

INDICATIF			SUBJONCTIF
Présent *I am*		**Passé composé** *I was, I have been*	**Présent** *I am*

je	suis		j'	ai	été	que je	sois
tu	es		tu	as	été	que tu	sois
il	est		il	a	été	qu'il	soit
nous	sommes		nous	avons	été	que nous	soyons
vous	êtes		vous	avez	été	que vous	soyez
ils	sont		ils	ont	été	qu'ils	soient

Imparfait *I was*		**Plus-que-parfait** *I had been*		IMPÉRATIF
				Présent *be*
j'	étais	j'	avais	été
tu	étais	tu	avais	été
il	était	il	avait	été	sois
nous	étions	nous	avions	été	soyons
vous	étiez	vous	aviez	été	soyez
ils	étaient	ils	avaient	été

	PARTICIPE	CONDITIONNEL
Futur *I'll be*	**Participe passé** *been*	**Présent** *I would be*

je	serai	été	je	serais
tu	seras		tu	serais
il	sera	**Participe présent** *being*	il	serait
nous	serons		nous	serions
vous	serez	étant	vous	seriez
ils	seront		ils	seraient

• Avoir *(To have)*

INDICATIF			SUBJONCTIF
Présent *I have*		**Passé composé** *I had, I have had*	**Présent** *I have*

j'	ai		j'	ai	eu	que j'	aie
tu	as		tu	as	eu	que tu	aies
il	a		il	a	eu	qu'il	ait
nous	avons		nous	avons	eu	que nous	ayons
vous	avez		vous	avez	eu	que vous	ayez
ils	ont		ils	ont	eu	qu'ils	aient

Imparfait *I had*		**Plus-que-parfait** *I had had*		IMPÉRATIF
				Présent *have*
j'	avais	j'	avais	eu
tu	avais	tu	avais	eu
il	avait	il	avait	eu	aie
nous	avions	nous	avions	eu	ayons
vous	aviez	vous	aviez	eu	ayez
ils	avaient	ils	avaient	eu

	PARTICIPE	CONDITIONNEL
Futur *I'll have*	**Participe passé** *had*	**Présent** *I would have*

j'	aurai	eu	j'	aurais
tu	auras		tu	aurais
il	aura	**Participe présent** *having*	il	aurait
nous	aurons		nous	aurions
vous	aurez	ayant	vous	auriez
ils	auront		ils	auraient

■ IRREGULAR VERBS

• Aller *(To go)*

INDICATIF		SUBJONCTIF
Présent *I go, I am going*	**Passé composé** *I went, I have gone*	**Présent** *I go*

je	vais	je	suis	allé	que j'	aille
tu	vas	tu	es	allé	que tu	ailles
il	va	il	est	allé	qu'il	aille
nous	allons	nous	sommes	allés	que nous	allions
vous	allez	vous	êtes	allés	que vous	alliez
ils	vont	ils	sont	allés	qu'ils	aillent

Imparfait *I was going*	**Plus-que-parfait** *I had gone*	**IMPÉRATIF**

					Présent *go*
j'	allais	j'	étais	allé	
tu	allais	tu	étais	allé	va
il	allait	il	était	allé	allons
nous	allions	nous	étions	allés	allez
vous	alliez	vous	étiez	allés	
ils	allaient	ils	étaient	allés	

	PARTICIPE	**CONDITIONNEL**
Futur *I'll go*	**Participe passé** *gone*	**Présent** *I would go*

		allé		
j'	irai		j'	irais
tu	iras	**Participe présent** *going*	tu	irais
il	ira		il	irait
nous	irons	allant	nous	irions
vous	irez		vous	iriez
ils	iront		ils	iraient

• Boire *(To drink)*

INDICATIF		SUBJONCTIF
Présent *I drink, I am drinking*	**Passé composé** *I drank, I have drunk*	**Présent** *I drink*

je	bois	j'	ai	bu	que je	boive
tu	bois	tu	as	bu	que tu	boives
il	boit	il	a	bu	qu'il	boive
nous	buvons	nous	avons	bu	que nous	buvions
vous	buvez	vous	avez	bu	que vous	buviez
ils	boivent	ils	ont	bu	qu'ils	boivent

Imparfait *I was drinking*	**Plus-que-parfait** *I had drunk*	**IMPÉRATIF**

					Présent *drink*
je	buvais	j'	avais	bu	
tu	buvais	tu	avais	bu	bois
il	buvait	il	avait	bu	buvons
nous	buvions	nous	avions	bu	buvez
vous	buviez	vous	aviez	bu	
ils	buvaient	ils	avaient	bu	

	PARTICIPE	**CONDITIONNEL**
Futur *I'll drink*	**Participe passé** *drunk*	**Présent** *I would drink*

		bu		
je	boirai		je	boirais
tu	boiras	**Participe présent** *drinking*	tu	boirais
il	boira		il	boirait
nous	boirons	buvant	nous	boirions
vous	boirez		vous	boiriez
ils	boiront		ils	boiraient

• Connaître *(To know)*

INDICATIF				SUBJONCTIF
Présent *I know*		**Passé composé** *I knew, I have known*		**Présent** *I know*
je connais	j' ai	connu		que je connaisse
tu connais	tu as	connu		que tu connaisses
il connaît	il a	connu		qu'il connaisse
nous connaissons	nous avons	connu		que nous connaissions
vous connaissez	vous avez	connu		que vous connaissiez
ils connaissent	ils ont	connu		qu'ils connaissent
Imparfait *I knew*		**Plus-que-parfait** *I had known*		**IMPÉRATIF**
je connaissais	j' avais	connu		**Présent** *know*
tu connaissais	tu avais	connu		
il connaissait	il avait	connu		connais
nous connaissions	nous avions	connu		connaissons
vous connaissiez	vous aviez	connu		connaissez
ils connaissaient	ils avaient	connu		
		PARTICIPE		**CONDITIONNEL**
Futur *I'll know*		**Participe passé** *known*		**Présent** *I would know*
je connaîtrai	connu			je connaîtrais
tu connaîtras				tu connaîtrais
il connaîtra	**Participe présent** *knowing*			il connaîtrait
nous connaîtrons				nous connaîtrions
vous connaîtrez	connaissant			vous connaîtriez
ils connaîtront				ils connaîtraient

• Devoir *(Must - Have to)*

INDICATIF				SUBJONCTIF
Présent *I must, I have to*		**Passé composé** *I had to*		**Présent** *I must, I have to*
je dois	j' ai	dû		que je doive
tu dois	tu as	dû		que tu doives
il doit	il a	dû		qu'il doive
nous devons	nous avons	dû		que nous devions
vous devez	vous avez	dû		que vous deviez
ils doivent	ils ont	dû		qu'ils doivent
Imparfait *I had to*		**Plus-que-parfait** *I had had to*		**IMPÉRATIF**
je devais	j' avais	dû		**Présent**
tu devais	tu avais	dû		
il devait	il avait	dû		dois
nous devions	nous avions	dû		devons
vous deviez	vous aviez	dû		devez
ils devaient	ils avaient	dû		hardly used
		PARTICIPE		**CONDITIONNEL**
Futur *I'll have to*		**Participe passé** *had to*		**Présent** *I would have to*
je devrai	dû			je devrais
tu devras				tu devrais
il devra	**Participe présent** *having to*			il devrait
nous devrons				nous devrions
vous devrez	devant			vous devriez
ils devront				ils devraient

• **Dire** (To say - To tell)

INDICATIF		SUBJONCTIF
Présent *I say, I tell* *I am saying, I am telling*	**Passé composé** *I said, I told* *I have said, I have told*	**Présent** *I say, I tell*
je dis tu dis il dit nous disons vous dites ils disent	j' ai dit tu as dit il a dit nous avons dit vous avez dit ils ont dit	que je dise que tu dises qu'il dise que nous disions que vous disiez qu'ils disent
Imparfait *I was saying, I was telling*	**Plus-que-parfait** *I had said, I had told*	**IMPÉRATIF**
je disais tu disais il disait nous disions vous disiez ils disaient	j' avais dit tu avais dit il avait dit nous avions dit vous aviez dit ils avaient dit	**Présent** *say, tell* dis disons dites
	PARTICIPE	**CONDITIONNEL**
Futur *I'll say, I'll tell* je dirai tu diras il dira nous dirons vous direz ils diront	**Participe passé** *said, told* dit **Participe présent** *saying, telling* disant	**Présent** *I would say, I would tell* je dirais tu dirais il dirait nous dirions vous diriez ils diraient

• **Écrire** (To write)

INDICATIF		SUBJONCTIF
Présent *I write, I am writing*	**Passé composé** *I wrote, I have written*	**Présent** *I write*
j' écris tu écris il écrit nous écrivons vous écrivez ils écrivent	j' ai écrit tu as écrit il a écrit nous avons écrit vous avez écrit ils ont écrit	que j' écrive que tu écrives qu'il écrive que nous écrivions que vous écriviez qu'ils écrivent
Imparfait *I was writing*	**Plus-que-parfait** *I had written*	**IMPÉRATIF**
j' écrivais tu écrivais il écrivait nous écrivions vous écriviez ils écrivaient	j' avais écrit tu avais écrit il avait écrit nous avions écrit vous aviez écrit ils avaient écrit	**Présent** *write* écris écrivons écrivez
	PARTICIPE	**CONDITIONNEL**
Futur *I'll write* j' écrirai tu écriras il écrira nous écrirons vous écrirez ils écriront	**Participe passé** *written* écrit **Participe présent** *writing* écrivant	**Présent** *I would write* j' écrirais tu écrirais il écrirait nous écririons vous écririez ils écriraient

271

• Faire *(To do - To make)*

INDICATIF		SUBJONCTIF
Présent *I do, I make* *I am doing, I am making*	**Passé composé** *I did, I made* *I have done, I have made*	**Présent** *I do, I make*
je fais tu fais il fait nous faisons vous faites ils font	j' ai fait tu as fait il a fait nous avons fait vous avez fait ils ont fait	que je fasse que tu fasses qu'il fasse que nous fassions que vous fassiez qu'ils fassent
Imparfait *I was doing, I was making*	**Plus-que-parfait** *I had done, I had made*	**IMPÉRATIF**
je faisais tu faisais il faisait nous faisions vous faisiez ils faisaient	j' avais fait tu avais fait il avait fait nous avions fait vous aviez fait ils avaient fait	**Présent** *do, make* fais faisons faites
	PARTICIPE	**CONDITIONNEL**
Futur *I'll do, I'll make*	**Participe passé** *done, made* fait	**Présent** *I would do, I would make*
je ferai tu feras il fera nous ferons vous ferez ils feront	**Participe présent** *doing, making* faisant	je ferais tu ferais il ferait nous ferions vous feriez ils feraient

• Mettre *(To put)*

INDICATIF		SUBJONCTIF
Présent *I put, I am putting*	**Passé composé** *I put, I have put*	**Présent** *I put*
je mets tu mets il met nous mettons vous mettez ils mettent	j' ai mis tu as mis il a mis nous avons mis vous avez mis ils ont mis	que je mette que tu mettes qu'il mette que nous mettions que vous mettiez qu'ils mettent
Imparfait *I was putting*	**Plus-que-parfait** *I had put*	**IMPÉRATIF**
je mettais tu mettais il mettait nous mettions vous mettiez ils mettaient	j' avais mis tu avais mis il avait mis nous avions mis vous aviez mis ils avaient mis	**Présent** *put* mets mettons mettez
	PARTICIPE	**CONDITIONNEL**
Futur *I'll put*	**Participe passé** *put* mis	**Présent** *I would put*
je mettrai tu mettras il mettra nous mettrons vous mettrez ils mettront	**Participe présent** *putting* mettant	je mettrais tu mettrais il mettrait nous mettrions vous mettriez ils mettraient

• **Pouvoir** *(Can - To be able to)*

INDICATIF		SUBJONCTIF
Présent *I can*	**Passé composé** *I have been able to*	**Présent** *I can*
je peux je puis	j' ai pu	que je puisse
tu peux	tu as pu	que tu puisses
il peut	il a pu	qu'il puisse
nous pouvons	nous avons pu	que nous puissions
vous pouvez	vous avez pu	que vous puissiez
ils peuvent	ils ont pu	qu'ils puissent
Imparfait *I could, I was able to*	**Plus-que-parfait** *I had been able to*	**IMPÉRATIF**
je pouvais	j' avais pu	
tu pouvais	tu avais pu	
il pouvait	il avait pu	pas d'impératif
nous pouvions	nous avions pu	
vous pouviez	vous aviez pu	
ils pouvaient	ils avaient pu	
	PARTICIPE	**CONDITIONNEL**
Futur *I'll be able to*	**Participe passé** *been able to*	**Présent** *I would be able to*
je pourrai	pu	je pourrais
tu pourras		tu pourrais
il pourra	**Participe présent** *being able to*	il pourrait
nous pourrons		nous pourrions
vous pourrez	pouvant	vous pourriez
ils pourront		ils pourraient

• **Prendre** *(To take)*

INDICATIF		SUBJONCTIF
Présent *I take, I am taking*	**Passé composé** *I took, I have taken*	**Présent** *I take*
je prends	j' ai pris	que je prenne
tu prends	tu as pris	que tu prennes
il prend	il a pris	qu'il prenne
nous prenons	nous avons pris	que nous prenions
vous prenez	vous avez pris	que vous preniez
ils prennent	ils ont pris	qu'ils prennent
Imparfait *I was taking*	**Plus-que-parfait** *I had taken*	**IMPÉRATIF**
je prenais	j' avais pris	**Présent** *take*
tu prenais	tu avais pris	
il prenait	il avait pris	prends
nous prenions	nous avions pris	prenons
vous preniez	vous aviez pris	prenez
ils prenaient	ils avaient pris	
	PARTICIPE	**CONDITIONNEL**
Futur *I'll take*	**Participe passé** *taken*	**Présent** *I would take*
je prendrai	pris	je prendrais
tu prendras		tu prendrais
il prendra	**Participe présent** *taking*	il prendrait
nous prendrons		nous prendrions
vous prendrez	prenant	vous prendriez
ils prendront		ils prendraient

• **Savoir** *(To know)*

INDICATIF		SUBJONCTIF
Présent *I know*	**Passé composé** *I knew, I have known*	**Présent** *I know*
je sais	j' ai su	que je sache
tu sais	tu as su	que tu saches
il sait	il a su	qu'il sache
nous savons	nous avons su	que nous sachions
vous savez	vous avez su	que vous sachiez
ils savent	ils ont su	qu'ils sachent

Imparfait *I knew*	**Plus-que-parfait** *I had known*	IMPÉRATIF
		Présent *know*
je savais	j' avais su	
tu savais	tu avais su	
il savait	il avait su	sache
nous savions	nous avions su	sachons
vous saviez	vous aviez su	sachez
ils savaient	ils avaient su	

	PARTICIPE	CONDITIONNEL
Futur *I'll know*	**Participe passé** *known*	**Présent** *I would know*
je saurai	su	je saurais
tu sauras		tu saurais
il saura	**Participe présent** *knowing*	il saurait
nous saurons		nous saurions
vous saurez	sachant	vous sauriez
ils sauront		ils sauraient

• **Tenir** *(To hold)*

INDICATIF		SUBJONCTIF
Présent *I hold, I am holding*	**Passé composé** *I held, I have held*	**Présent** *I hold*
je tiens	j' ai tenu	que je tienne
tu tiens	tu as tenu	que tu tiennes
il tient	il a tenu	qu'il tienne
nous tenons	nous avons tenu	que nous tenions
vous tenez	vous avez tenu	que vous teniez
ils tiennent	ils ont tenu	qu'ils tiennent

Imparfait *I was holding*	**Plus-que-parfait** *I had held*	IMPÉRATIF
		Présent *hold*
je tenais	j' avais tenu	
tu tenais	tu avais tenu	
il tenait	il avait tenu	tiens
nous tenions	nous avions tenu	tenons
vous teniez	vous aviez tenu	tenez
ils tenaient	ils avaient tenu	

	PARTICIPE	CONDITIONNEL
Futur *I'll hold*	**Participe passé** *held*	**Présent** *I would hold*
je tiendrai	tenu	je tiendrais
tu tiendras		tu tiendrais
il tiendra	**Participe présent** *holding*	il tiendrait
nous tiendrons		nous tiendrions
vous tiendrez	tenant	vous tiendriez
ils tiendront		ils tiendraient

All verbs ending in **enir** have the same conjugation.

• Vivre *(To live)*

INDICATIF		SUBJONCTIF
Présent *I live, I am living*	**Passé composé** *I lived, I have lived*	**Présent** *I live*
je vis	j' ai vécu	que je vive
tu vis	tu as vécu	que tu vives
il vit	il a vécu	qu'il vive
nous vivons	nous avons vécu	que nous vivions
vous vivez	vous avez vécu	que vous viviez
ils vivent	ils ont vécu	qu'ils vivent
Imparfait *I was living*	**Plus-que-parfait** *I had lived*	**IMPÉRATIF**
je vivais	j' avais vécu	**Présent** *live*
tu vivais	tu avais vécu	
il vivait	il avait vécu	vis
nous vivions	nous avions vécu	vivons
vous viviez	vous aviez vécu	vivez
ils vivaient	ils avaient vécu	
	PARTICIPE	**CONDITIONNEL**
Futur *I'll live*	**Participe passé** *lived*	**Présent** *I would live*
je vivrai	vécu	je vivrais
tu vivras		tu vivrais
il vivra	**Participe présent** *living*	il vivrait
nous vivrons		nous vivrions
vous vivrez	vivant	vous vivriez
ils vivront		ils vivraient

• Voir *(To see)*

INDICATIF		SUBJONCTIF
Présent *I see*	**Passé composé** *I saw, I have seen*	**Présent** *I see*
je vois	j' ai vu	que je voie
tu vois	tu as vu	que tu voies
il voit	il a vu	qu'il voie
nous voyons	nous avons vu	que nous voyions
vous voyez	vous avez vu	que vous voyiez
ils voient	ils ont vu	qu'ils voient
Imparfait *I saw*	**Plus-que-parfait** *I had seen*	**IMPÉRATIF**
je voyais	j' avais vu	**Présent** *see*
tu voyais	tu avais vu	
il voyait	il avait vu	vois
nous voyions	nous avions vu	voyons
vous voyiez	vous aviez vu	voyez
ils voyaient	ils avaient vu	
	PARTICIPE	**CONDITIONNEL**
Futur *I'll see*	**Participe passé** *seen*	**Présent** *I would see*
je verrai	vu	je verrais
tu verras		tu verrais
il verra	**Participe présent** *seeing*	il verrait
nous verrons		nous verrions
vous verrez	voyant	vous verriez
ils verront		ils verraient

• **Vouloir** *(To want)*

INDICATIF		SUBJONCTIF
Présent *I want*	**Passé composé** *I wanted, I have wanted*	**Présent** *I want*
je veux	j' ai voulu	que je veuille
tu veux	tu as voulu	que tu veuilles
il veut	il a voulu	qu'il veuille
nous voulons	nous avons voulu	que nous voulions
vous voulez	vous avez voulu	que vous vouliez
ils veulent	ils ont voulu	qu'ils veuillent
Imparfait *I wanted*	**Plus-que-parfait** *I had wanted*	**IMPÉRATIF**
		Présent
je voulais	j' avais voulu	
tu voulais	tu avais voulu	veux (veuille)
il voulait	il avait voulu	voulons (veuillons)
nous voulions	nous avions voulu	voulez (veuillez*)
vous vouliez	vous aviez voulu	
ils voulaient	ils avaient voulu	* is the only form used.
	PARTICIPE	**CONDITIONNEL**
Futur *I'll want*	**Participe passé** *wanted*	**Présent** *I would want*
je voudrai	voulu	je voudrais
tu voudras		tu voudrais
il voudra	**Participe présent** *wanting*	il voudrait
nous voudrons		nous voudrions
vous voudrez	voulant	vous voudriez
ils voudront		ils voudraient

■ **IMPERSONAL VERBS**

• **Falloir** (to express necessity or obligation)

INDICATIF		SUBJONCTIF
		Présent
Présent	**Passé composé**	qu'il faille
il faut	il a fallu	
Imparfait	**Plus-que-parfait**	**IMPÉRATIF**
il fallait	il avait fallu	Pas d'impératif
Futur	**Participe passé**	**CONDITIONNEL** **Présent**
il faudra	fallu	il faudrait

• **Pleuvoir** *(To rain)*

INDICATIF		SUBJONCTIF
Présent *it is raining, it rains*	**Passé composé** *it rained, it has rained*	**Présent** *it rain*
il pleut	il a plu	qu'il pleuve
Imparfait *it was raining*	**Plus-que-parfait** *it had rained*	**IMPÉRATIF**
Il pleuvait	il avait plu	Pas d'impératif
Futur *it'll rain*	**Participe passé** *rained / plu*	**CONDITIONNEL** **Présent**
il pleuvra	**Participe présent** *raining / pleuvant*	il pleuvrait

VOCABULARY INDEX

GRAMMAR & TOPIC INDEX

Cet ouvrage a été composé par
TÉLÉ-COMPO – 61290 BIZOU

IMPRIMÉ EN FRANCE PAR BRODARD ET TAUPIN
Usine de La Flèche (Sarthe), le 31-05-1991.
1454E-5 - Dépôt légal : juin 1991.

PRESSES POCKET - 8, rue Garancière - 75006 Paris
Tél. 46.34.12.80